Assembly-Line Auteur

Assembly-Line Auteur
*The Pre-Code Films
of William Wellman*

DAVID MEUEL

McFarland & Company, Inc., Publishers
Jefferson, North Carolina

ALSO BY DAVID MEUEL
AND FROM MCFARLAND

Joan Crawford in Film Noir: The Actress as Auteur (2024)
Silent Film's Last Hurrah: The Remarkable Movies of the Long 1928 (2023)
Women Film Editors: Unseen Artists of American Cinema (2016)
The Noir Western: Darkness on the Range, 1943–1962 (2015)
Women in the Films of John Ford (2014)

Frontispiece: William Augustus Wellman, circa early 1930s (Album/Alamy Stock Photo).

LIBRARY OF CONGRESS CATALOGING-IN-PUBLICATION DATA

Names: Meuel, David, 1950– author
Title: Assembly-line auteur : the pre-code films of William Wellman / David Meuel.
Description: Jefferson, North Carolina : McFarland & Company, Inc., Publishers, 2026. | Includes bibliographical references and index.
Identifiers: LCCN 2025043748 | ISBN 9781476696300 paperback ∞
ISBN 9781476657370 ebook
Subjects: LCSH: Wellman, William A., 1896-1975—Criticism and interpretation | BISAC: PERFORMING ARTS / Film / Direction & Production
Classification: LCC PN1998.3.W454 M48 2025
LC record available at https://lccn.loc.gov/2025043748

ISBN (print) 978-1-4766-9630-0
ISBN (ebook) 978-1-4766-5737-0

© 2026 David Meuel. All rights reserved

No part of this book may be reproduced or transmitted in any form or by any means, electronic or mechanical, including photocopying or recording, or by any information storage and retrieval system, without permission in writing from the publisher.

Front cover images: James Cagney (left) and Lee Phelps in the 1931 film *The Public Enemy* (Warner Bros. Pictures/Photofest); (bottom inset) William Wellman publicity photograph

Printed in the United States of America

McFarland & Company, Inc., Publishers
Box 611, Jefferson, North Carolina 28640
www.mcfarlandpub.com

*Once again,
to Kathryn*

*And this time,
to Mary Scott ("Scotty") Martinson,
a great friend for fifty years
and a wonderful editor,
whose work on six of my books
will always be highly valued
and much appreciated*

Acknowledgments

Although a book may have only one credited author, numerous people help in many ways to move a project from concept to completion, and I would like to thank several people in my life for their cogent insights on film, excellent listening skills, patience, and support as this book has taken shape. Specifically, these are Jimmy Meuel, Bonnie Rattner, Bob and Melanie Ferrando, Jim Daniels, Natalie Varney, Elliot Lavine, and Paul Bendix.

I would also like to acknowledge a great debt to the previous work of the scores of film critics and scholars whose various books, articles, and interviews have been indispensable to this project. Their names are all listed in this book's bibliography. From this list, I would like to express a special appreciation for the contributions of four people. The first is William Wellman, Jr., whose fine, very thorough 2015 biography, *Wild Bill Wellman: Hollywood Rebel*, was an invaluable source of information about the author's father, both as a person and a professional. The second is Frank T. Thompson, whose groundbreaking 1983 biography, *William A. Wellman*, also provides a wealth of pertinent and insightful information about the legendary director and his films. And the third and fourth are Cliff Aliperti and Danny Reid, whose pre–Code-themed websites, *Immortal Ephemera* and *Pre-Code.com*, respectively, offer fresh, intriguing perspectives, not only on Wellman's pre–Code films, but also on many other films and facets of this fascinating era.

Table of Contents

Acknowledgments   vi

Preface   1

Introduction: "Here's what I think of your lousy script!"   5

1. "Give me a big slice of you on toast and some French-fried potatoes on the side": *Maybe It's Love* (1930) and *Other Men's Women* (1931)   21

2. "There's not only beer in that keg—there's beer and blood": *The Public Enemy* (1931)   33

3. "I'll kill the next one that says 'ethics' to me": *Night Nurse* (1931)   48

4. "One move outta' you and I'll smear your guts on your own wallpaper": *The Star Witness* (1931)   62

5. "Sure this ain't the YMCA?" *Safe in Hell* (1931)   71

6. "If you keep your head, you should go far": *The Hatchet Man* and *So Big* (both 1932)   84

7. "[I'm] very well, thank you—just a slight touch of leprosy": *Love Is a Racket* (1932)   98

8. "The tougher the going, the more you love 'em": *The Purchase Price* and *The Conquerors* (both 1932)   109

9. "It may be the wrong way, but it's going to be my way": *Frisco Jenny* (1932) and *Lilly Turner* (1933)   125

10. "Whoever he is, he's flirting with the undertaker": *Central Airport* (1933)   141

Table of Contents

11. "It may be the end of us, but it's not the end of America": *Heroes for Sale* (1932) — 152

12. "Now what do you suppose made me think of sex?" *Midnight Mary* (1933) — 164

13. "What good will it do you to send us home to starve?" *Wild Boys of the Road* (1933) — 178

14. "How'd you like to stick your finger in her coffee?" *Female and College Coach* (1933) and *Looking for Trouble* (1934) — 191

Afterthoughts: "It is, perhaps, the end of the beginning" — 205

Chapter Notes — 209

Bibliography — 217

Index — 221

Preface

Along with film noir, one of the areas of interest and study that most fascinates today's classic film enthusiasts is a brief period in Hollywood, from roughly late 1929–early 1930 until mid-1934, that's come to be called the pre-Code era. The term itself is a bit misleading. By this time, the U.S. film industry's self-censorship arm, best known as the Hays Office, had already issued a Production Code, a set of rules and restrictions intended to hold movies to a "higher moral standard" by curtailing or forbidding what could be shown on screen or sometimes even suggested in a storyline. The problem was that, although the Hays Office had a Production Code, it had little power to enforce it. As a result, until an effective enforcement mechanism was put into place in mid-1934, the studios, emboldened by the more libertine, or "modern," attitudes of the late 1920s and early 1930s, took full advantage of the freedoms they had. Movies depicted or suggested sex, violence, and other provocative human behavior in frank new ways, an approach that was refreshingly new, and enormously appealing, to audiences. The result was an outpouring of films that are startingly candid and honest, that bristle with energy, and that often resonate more deeply with modern viewers than many films made after the Code's enforcement.

In addition to the strict censorship of new movies, one of the great tragedies that occurred because of the Code's enforcement is that many good-to-superb pre-Code films—products of a vibrant, highly creative filmmaking era—were effectively banned for decades. It has only been within the last thirty years or so that many of these films have been rediscovered and appreciation for them has grown. And today, judging by the number of books and articles that have been written, college courses offered, and film festivals held devoted to this subject, interest in pre-Code films continues to be high. For many of today's classic film aficionados, it's as if a huge treasure buried long ago has miraculously been unearthed. As a matter of fact, it has.

Of the many noteworthy behind-the-scenes stories that come from the pre–Code era, I have long believed that one of the most fascinating is also one that has never been given its full due: the striking achievement of director William "Wild Bill" Wellman, especially during his epic three-year run at Warner Brothers. Between late 1930 and late 1933—the height of the pre–Code era—the eighteen feature-length films he directed (as well as one he co-directed) while under contract with the studio were released. By today's standards, when it often takes several years to complete a single feature film, this seems like an incredible achievement in itself. During the early 1930s, however, most studios ran on the assembly-line model and slapped feature films out as fast, it seems, as the Ford Motor Company manufactured new automobiles. During the same three years, several of Wellman's Warner Brothers directing colleagues also kept pace, churning out roughly the same number of films. But what makes Wellman's achievement especially notable is that, while he was cranking out films (most of them low-budget) on a studio assembly line, a remarkable number of them were of very high quality—films that people watch, discuss, and write about today. In fact, more than half of the films Wellman directed are shown and discussed regularly. These include masterpieces such as *The Public Enemy* (1931), *Heroes for Sale* (1933), and *Wild Boys of the Road* (1933) as well as others widely acknowledged as "pre–Code gems" such as *Night Nurse* (1931), *Safe in Hell* (1931), *Frisco Jenny* (1932), *Central Airport* (1933), and *Midnight Mary* (1933). In addition, Wellman made several more films such as *Other Men's Women* (1931), *The Star Witness* (1931), *Love Is a Racket* (1932), and *Lilly Turner* (1933) that, for those who wish to look more closely into the director's pre–Code work, are quite intriguing and well worth the time to watch and think about.

*

Despite the fact that Wellman was unmatched during the pre–Code era for delivering both quantity and quality, it has been surprising to learn that, in the handful of books and documentaries about him and his work, relatively little attention has been paid to his early-1930s output relative to the rest of his long Hollywood career. In Turner Classic Movies' fine ninety-minute documentary about Wellman, *Wild Bill: Hollywood Maverick* (1996), for example, only eight minutes are allotted to his pre–Code work and only two of his pre–Code films, *The Public Enemy* and *Wild Boys of the Road*, are discussed.

Part of the reason for this may be the lack of accessibility, which, until fairly recently, has been the fate of many pre-Code films. Simply put, people can't appreciate films if they don't have the opportunity to see them.

Another part may be the rest of Wellman's overall achievement during a directing career that spanned thirty-five-years: it is quite impressive as well. Outside of his pre-Code work, his film resume includes more than a dozen excellent, memorable films ranging from the silent masterpieces *Wings* (1927) and *Beggars of Life* (1928) to classic-era standouts such as the original *A Star Is Born* (1937), *Nothing Sacred* (1937), *Beau Geste* (1939), *The Light That Failed* (1939), *The Ox-Bow Incident* (1943), *The Story of G.I. Joe* (1945), *Yellow Sky* (1948), and *Battleground* (1949). So, with more than thirty additional years of good filmmaking to account for in books and documentaries (not to mention the relative inaccessibility of pre-Code films for many years), it's easy to see how Wellman's early-1930s films could be given short shrift.

All this duly noted, I embarked on this project believing that a book focusing exclusively on Wellman's pre-Code films would finally put the spotlight on an often overlooked but also extremely productive and impressive period in a major Hollywood director's career. In doing so, it would also fill a significant gap in early Hollywood film history and provide an excellent opportunity to look closely at Wellman as an auteur, a filmmaker who infuses his work with an individual style and worldview that give his films a unique personal stamp.

*

After his departure from Warner Brothers in 1933, Wellman became an independent director and, as such, more the master of his own professional destiny. During pre-Code, however, he was essentially a paradox—an auteur working on what was effectively a manufacturing assembly line, yet what Wellman—the assembly-line auteur—managed to accomplish under these circumstances was remarkable. And my hope is that those who read this book will come away from it with a better understanding of the enormity of the director's pre-Code-era achievement as well as a deeper appreciation for the talent and contributions of a sadly under-appreciated classic-era master.

*

Two final notes:

First, although many film historians will grant that the official end of the pre-Code era was July 1, 1934, the day the Hays Office was officially empowered to strictly enforce the film industry's Production Code, there is far less agreement about a specific date to mark the era's official beginning. While some will say that it was as early as 1929, others will place it at some point in early 1930. In evaluating Wellman's pre–Code contributions, I decided that perhaps the best line of demarcation is March 23, 1930, the day Wellman officially signed with Warner Brothers and began to make films that are clearly "pre–Code" in character. As a result, the films spotlighted in this book are all those released after March 23, 1930, and before July 1, 1934.

Second, I'd like to stress that this book is *not* a biography of Wellman and should not be viewed as such. Although it often includes biographical details drawn from numerous sources to provide context and occasionally to bolster arguments, it was conceived and developed mainly to be a critical evaluation of Wellman's work during the pre–Code era.

Introduction

"Here's what I think of your lousy script!"

Professionally, late 1928 and all of 1929 were not especially happy times for film director William Wellman. He was working steadily at Paramount Pictures, one of Hollywood's leading studios, but he was frustrated with the sub-par scripts he was constantly getting. He had, after all, directed the aviation epic *Wings* (1927), at the time Paramount's biggest all-time moneymaker. He had also directed several other financially successful films, regularly bringing them in on schedule and within budget. So shouldn't he be getting more respect as well as more of the better projects that went with it? Paramount's executives, especially Benjamin Percival ("B.P.") Schulberg, who had personally recruited Wellman to come to work for the studio in 1926, were, however, of a different mind. When making *Wings*, the young director had alienated several of them with his brash, combative attitude, and, as far as they were concerned, he had remained unrepentant, defiant, and an overall pain in the neck to work with.

Wanting very much to get out of a contract that still had five years remaining on it, Wellman discussed the matter with his agent, Myron Selznick. Selznick assured him that he could do something and arranged a meeting that, along with the two of them, included the head of production at Warner Brothers, Darryl F. Zanuck.

Just twenty-seven years old, and every bit as much the wunderkind as his counterpart at rival MGM, "boy genius" Irving Thalberg, Zanuck immediately hit it off with the director. What emerged from the process was an offer from Warner Brothers of a two-year contract with periodic salary increases that also included an option to extend for an additional two years with more salary increases. On top of this, Wellman sought and received the promise from Zanuck that he'd especially wanted: the chance to develop his own projects and the studio resources he needed to turn them into distinctively William Wellman films.

Before any of this could happen, of course, Wellman needed to find a way out of his existing contract with Paramount. Very soon afterward, he came up with what seemed to him to be an eminently appropriate course of action.

In the pre-dawn hours one night, Wellman and assistant director and long-time friend Charlie Barton drove up to a deserted Paramount studios in a rented pickup truck filled with manure the two had just shoveled from a horse ranch in the nearby San Fernando Valley. At this point, Wellman produced a key he had stolen from the studio that enabled them to get into B.P. Schulberg's first-floor office, and, within fifteen minutes, a small mountain of horse manure rested on top of the producer's desk. Like the icing on the cake, Wellman then placed the script Paramount had given him for his latest assignment on top of the noxious pile. Attached to it was a note that read, "Here's what I think of your lousy script!"[1]

It's not known exactly how effective this exit strategy was, but Wellman and Paramount quickly parted ways. And on March 23, 1930, Wellman signed that two-year deal with Warner Brothers, one that would lead to what is arguably the most productive and creative three-year period of his storied, thirty-five-year directing career.

*

While most of us might consider this course of action to be an unusually bold—if not needlessly defiant and/or extremely immature—way to achieve his desired result, people who knew William Wellman at the time would see it as very much in keeping with his character.

Born on February 29, 1896, William Augustus Wellman had just turned thirty-four as he prepared to leave Paramount for Warner Brothers, and, in those years, had already led a life filled with more drama, adventures, and shenanigans than the vast majority of centenarians have.

Wellman was born into quite a distinguished family. His father, Arthur Gouverneur Wellman, was a Boston "Brahmin," a respected member of that city's historic upper class as well a descendent of Thomas Wellman, a Puritan who had joined the Massachusetts Bay Colony in 1640, and Francis Lewis, a signer of the U.S. Declaration of Independence. His mother, an Irish immigrant named Celia McCarthy, was a highly respected probation officer who once addressed the U.S. Congress on the subject of juvenile delinquency.

Young William, however, wasn't one to follow his parents' good examples. Despite his mother's commitment to helping juvenile delinquents, he, much to her frustration and dismay, essentially became one. At one point, he was placed on probation for car theft. At another, he was expelled from high school for dropping a stink bomb on the principal's head.

Then, after brief stints as a salesman, lumber yard worker, and minor-league hockey player, Wellman went to fight in World War I, first for the French and, after the United States entered the war, for the Americans. Beginning as an ambulance driver, he became an air fighter pilot and distinguished himself for both his skill and bravery under fire, receiving credit for shooting down several enemy planes and recognitions such as the *Croix de Guerre*, a coveted French military honor for valor, and, in the process, earning the nickname "Wild Bill." During this time, he also made an invaluable personal connection. When sitting in the reception area of a Paris brothel, he spied General John J. ("Black Jack") Pershing, the commander of all U.S. forces in Europe, heading toward a bedroom with a prostitute. In one of his puckish moods, Wellman quietly snuck into the darkened room as the general and the woman were in the midst of a vigorous, rather noisy frolic, skillfully stole the general's pants, and left. Afterward, when Wellman heard the general yelling about the theft of his pants, he approached him, introduced himself, saluted, and—in a very snappy, formal, military manner—returned the pants. Appreciating the daring practical joke, the general laughed and replied, "You crazy son-of-a-bitch airman!"[2]

During the final months of the war and afterward, Wellman taught air combat tactics to young pilots in San Diego, California. On weekends, he often flew his Spad fighter to the Los Angeles area, and, as his landing field, he used the Bel Air polo field of actor and producer Douglas Fairbanks, Sr., the legendary "First King of Hollywood."[3] Fairbanks, who was fascinated by both Wellman's war adventures and personal swagger, promised to give Wellman, if the idea ever appealed to him, a job in the film business. Intrigued, Wellman accepted, and, once out of uniform, he went to work as an actor in Fairbanks' latest film, a romantic comedy/western called *The Knickerbocker Buckaroo* (1919).

Although *The Knickerbocker Buckaroo* was a success, Wellman learned from the experience that he hated acting and told Fairbanks that he wanted to work behind the camera, preferably as a director. While understanding, Fairbanks also made it clear that the job of director was one that people worked up to and placed the young man into his Hollywood apprenticeship. Over the next few years, the aspiring director would work first as an office messenger, then a property man, then an assistant director.

During this time, Wellman never lost his talent for making, and benefiting from, valuable connections. When he was a lowly office messenger, for example, he met the celebrated humorist, writer, and actor Will Rogers, who helped him become a property man. Then, when General Pershing, newly returned to the United States, visited one studio where Wellman, the prop man, was working, the general recognized the young man who had played such a memorable trick on him in Paris. Seizing the opportunity, Wellman asked the general to take him aside and speak to him in a manner that suggested he thought highly of him. Pershing happily obliged, word got around the studio, and the following day Wellman was summoned to the office of the distinguished producer Samuel Goldwyn, who, declaring that the young prop man was exactly the kind of person he wanted working for him, immediately made him an assistant director.[4]

After working as an assistant director on more than twenty films over the next two and a half years, Wellman, in 1923, received his first directing credit. It was for a low-budget Fox Films western called *The Man Who Won*, the first of seven successful westerns Wellman directed for the studio until he—as the result of a heated exchange with studio head William Fox—was both fired and blackballed industrywide for more than a year.

Finally, Wellman began to pick up short-term projects at Columbia Pictures and MGM, which again included some assignments working as an assistant director. One project, however, paid off in a big way. A film Wellman had directed at Columbia, a comedy called *When Husbands Flirt* (1926), was a box-office success. And, after a pre-release screening, Wellman was contacted by someone who had been impressed both by this film and the director's work at Fox, an enterprising young producer at Paramount named B.P. Schulberg.

Once at Paramount, the now-thirty-year-old director's fortunes changed dramatically. After Wellman directed his first Paramount film, a complete flop called *The Cat's Pajamas* (1926), the pressure was now on him and Schulberg to come up with a winner. And they responded with what is arguably one of the director's three best silent films, a melodrama involving a love triangle called *You Never Know Women* (1926). A success both at the box office and with critics, the film trade journal *Variety* even went as far as to say that Wellman's work on this film lifts him "into the ranks of the select directors."[5]

The success of *You Never Know Women* led to the biggest break Wellman had yet received in his eight years in the film business. Despite his lack of experience relative to most of his directing colleagues, he was chosen to direct Paramount's flagship film for 1927, a lavish epic about World War I aviators titled *Wings*. A main reason why Wellman was selected, of course, was his first-hand experience as a combat pilot. More than anyone else who was available, studio executives felt, he could give the film the high level of authenticity the story required. The finished film, as nearly every fan of classic Hollywood films knows, is a masterpiece of action-adventure cinema filled with brilliant aerial photography interspersed with a very moving love story, another triangle, this time starring the enormously popular Clara Bow and actors Richard Arlen and Charles ("Buddy")

On location during the filming of the 1927 aviation epic *Wings*: (from left) producer Lucien Hubbard, director William Wellman, and John Monk Saunders, who wrote the story (Paramount. Masheter Movie Archive/Alamy Stock Photo).

Rogers. The production, however, was filled with numerous delays and other problems. Wellman, known for his efficient, low-cost shoots, ran well over the film's already lavish budget. Various Paramount executives found this very concerning. And their constant questioning of Wellman's judgement and decisions irritated the already-thin-skinned director to no end. As a result, relations between Wellman and Schulberg and others at Paramount became quite strained. The film, of course, received all kinds of critical praise and industry recognition, including the very first Academy Award for Best Picture, an honor that its producer, Lucien Hubbard, accepted at the Academy's first award ceremonies. Despite his herculean efforts, however, Wellman was not nominated for that year's Best Director Academy Award. And, because he was also on the outs at Paramount, he wasn't even invited to the presentation. Instead, he went home that evening and got very drunk.

After completing *Wings*, and as Hollywood was experiencing the turbulent transition from silent films to "the talkies," Wellman directed eight more films for Paramount. One of them, *Beggars of Life*, is a very moving and beautifully acted story about two downtrodden people on the road. It stars the incomparable Louise Brooks in one of her finest roles, and, in this author's humble opinion, it is second only to *Wings* when ranking the best of Wellman's silent films. A second effort, another World War I aviation film called The *Legion of the Condemned*, was a major commercial hit and received considerable critical acclaim. Unfortunately, though, it is currently considered a lost film. The rest, as previously noted, were usually inferior projects that Wellman disliked and resented doing.

Despite all he had done for Paramount by playing the critical role in making *Wings* such an enormous success, the studio was, from Wellman's point of view, clearly giving him the bum's rush. The time, he realized, was fast approaching when he would need to make a change. And, as part of that process, he would also want to express his feelings toward Paramount in the clearest, most emphatic way he could think of.

*

The tumult that seemed to accompany Wild Bill Wellman wherever he went during the 1920s took place within the much larger and, in its own way, much more tumultuous context of the film industry itself. In 1905, Hollywood was little more than a sleepy, nondescript community just to the north of Los Angeles, California. Within just two decades, it had become the undisputed film capital of the world, home to a thriving and rapidly expanding industry whose movies were distributed globally and seen by tens of millions of people each week. Just by themselves, for example, the two top-grossing films of 1925, MGM's *The Big Parade* and *Ben-Hur*, eventually accounted for more than eighty million tickets worldwide. The industry's explosive growth led not only to great wealth for many but also to continuous break-neck-speed development. By 1925, for example, films were typically far more sophisticated in terms of storytelling artistry and technological achievement than they had been in 1920 and almost unrecognizable from films made in 1915.

Along with all this growth and development came a variety of new crises and challenges.

Some of these had to do with the public's perception of the nature of the film industry itself. As actors and other film industry figures became global celebrities, scandals and a constant barrage of tabloid stories invariably followed. One of the most notorious occurred in 1921 and involved comedian Roscoe ("Fatty") Arbuckle, a top film comic who was accused of the rape and manslaughter death of actress Virginia Rappe. Although Arbuckle was eventually acquitted of all charges, the tabloid stories, while effectively destroying his career, also led to calls from government officials, religious leaders, and other self-appointed guardians of the public's morals for increased monitoring of the "decadent" film-industry culture and, specifically, increased censorship of films themselves. When this was followed in 1922 by the mysterious (and still unsolved) murder of film director William Desmond Taylor, the industry decided that, rather than waiting for local, state, and perhaps the federal governments to pass film censorship laws, it would be pre-emptive and create its own office of self-censorship. Enlisting the affable Will Hays, a former U.S. postmaster general, to head up the effort, the Motion Picture Producers and Distributors of America (MPPDA), more commonly known as "the Hays Office," was born. During the 1920s, various efforts were made to curtail material depicted or suggested on screen (such as excessive violence, drug use, nudity, illicit sexual behavior, etc.) that may be deemed morally offensive. Finally, after several ineffectual attempts, a formal Production Code was adopted in 1930. Unfortunately for the Hays Office, though, the Code, while in place, lacked a strong enforcement mechanism, so a common strategy for censors was simply to try to reason, or in some cases plead, with studios to change or omit objectionable content. It wasn't until July 1, 1934, that an effective enforcement authority, one that required all films to obtain a certificate of approval from the Hays Office in order to be released, was put into place.

Other challenges for the film industry also emerged from the sound revolution, which was, for all intents and purposes, launched with the premiere of *The Jazz Singer* at the Warner Brothers' Roxie Theater in New York on October 6, 1927. Although people had been experimenting with adding recorded sound to film presentation for years, this extra dimension was generally seen as a gimmick or a novelty, not an element that could completely transform the medium. *The Jazz Singer* quickly changed this perception, and, within a year and a half, Hollywood embraced what in many ways seemed to be an entirely new art form. Silent films, which had been at the height of their achievement and commercial success just two years earlier, rapidly became relics. Sound was in, and, even though there were doubters for a little while, sound was there to stay.

Much has been written about the sound revolution in Hollywood, of course. Usually, the focus has been on the enormously disruptive change it caused, ranging from the use of the first awkward and cumbersome sound technologies to the abrupt ends of the careers of many actors whose voices or thick foreign accents were deemed unsuitable for the new medium. Receiving far less attention has been the impact of the sound revolution on the efforts of censors to control what eventually gets into a finished film that's distributed to a mass market. Since spoken dialogue gave movies an entirely new dimension, the censors were quite anxious about the inherent moral repercussions of this development. In fact, Father Daniel A. Lord, a Jesuit priest intimately involved in the development of the Production Code, was particularly concerned about the impact of sound films on children, whom he considered particularly impressionable and drawn to their allure.[6]

Still other challenges for the film industry centered on the need to stay relevant in a world of fast-changing social attitudes. As censors were ratcheting up their efforts to shield audiences from objectional material and, in doing so, to champion, in the Code's words, "correct standards of life,"[7] others increasingly thought in quite different terms. Among these were people, many of whom coming of age in the free-wheeling 1920s, with more liberal attitudes about sex and sexuality; the discussion of provocative political topics; and the on-screen depictions of violence, crude language, or other unseemly behaviors. In short, this latter group preferred that stories be told in an authentic and forthright, rather than a pious or preachy, manner—that films showed life more as it was rather than what some people thought it ought to be like. And, as one might suspect, a good number of these people were those who also produced, directed, wrote for, performed in, or otherwise contributed to the movies.

It should be noted, too, that this more modern spirit of openness toward suggestions or depictions of sex, violence, or other controversial subjects was not only about freedom of expression. Presenting these experiences, especially in titillating, shocking, or otherwise provocative ways, also attracted larger audiences and buoyed box-office receipts, two facts of business life that studio executives and film financiers especially appreciated during the economically depressed early 1930s.

As the talkies took hold—and much to Father Lord's dismay—many of these creative types (with the tacit approval of studio executives and film financiers) used the new medium more frequently, and in more different ways, to say or suggest many of the things that Father Lord and his likeminded colleagues had feared would be said or suggested. And, beginning about 1930, the conflict began to escalate in a big way. The Production Code was now approved, published, and well-known throughout the industry. The problem for the censors was that it was still mostly ignored.

*

What followed was an intense, exuberant, often chaotic, and unusually creative four-year period after sound films took hold—but before the Code could be enforced—that we now call the pre–Code era. The term, of course, is a bit of a misnomer. A stickler for clarity might prefer to call it the pre–Code-enforcement era. But "pre–Code" has been the term that has stuck.

During this period, filmmakers took advantage of the inclusion of sound, an evolution in social attitudes, and what many of them foresaw as a time of fleeting freedom before an inevitable censorship crackdown to be unusually honest, irreverent, rebellious, and sometimes more than a bit wild. Sexy, scantily clad women were suddenly abundant on screen. Nudity and partial nudity were even shown occasionally. Violence was depicted or suggested more frankly and graphically. Homosexual men and women were sometimes portrayed. In addition, characters often got away with crimes, even murder, without being brought to justice or at least punished in some way. Police officers and government officials were often represented as corrupt and even downright evil. Gangsters were sometimes treated as complex and even sympathetic human beings. Couples had sex before, or outside of, marriage and were often not penalized for doing so. Women's unique struggles in a world where men ruled were often treated with considerable openness and sensitivity. And the list goes on and on.

After the full enforcement of the Code came into effect in mid–1934, of course, many of the films released between 1930 and early 1934 were either partially censored or banned outright, some even banished to studio vaults where they sat unseen, gathering dust for decades. Then, in the late twentieth and early twenty-first centuries, as censorship has waned, interest in film history has grown, and various new technologies have expanded viewing options and opportunities, access to, and interest in, these pre–Code-era films has proliferated. Today, tens of millions of people worldwide experience them through university-level film studies classes, revival theaters, film festivals, broadcast and cable television channels, VHS and DVD viewing formats, or streaming services. And for many, if not most, of these people, the experience is a revelation. As film critic and pre–Code historian Mick LaSalle has noted,

> If you think of old movies as corny, chances are you're thinking of the movies made after censorship took hold in the middle of 1934. Before then, movies were sexy. They were political. They were surprisingly feminist, and they were adult.... Their appeal is that, through them, you get to hear a long-ago era speak with its own voice, unimpeded by censorship. That voice is surprisingly modern.... When you see Pre-Code movies you realize that this is ... how movies should always have been.... This is the past, without lies.[8]

*

For Wellman—who valued integrity perhaps more than any other quality, and who could be about as outspoken, rebellious, and subversive as anyone—the move to Warner Brothers in March of 1930 was a fortuitous convergence of the right person, the right place, and the right time. The sassy, free-spirited attitude that was pervasive in Hollywood would be a great source of creative inspiration for him. And, of all the major studios at the time, Warner Brothers was probably the best place to be to make films that expressed his own very distinctive, and often very cynical, views about human society and many of the people who were part of it.

One of the main reasons why Warner Brothers stood out in this way at this time was its young production head, Darryl Zanuck, a person the director admired for his intelligence, drive, no-nonsense attitude, and character.

Beginning his film career as a scenario writer, the nineteen-year-old Zanuck (1902–1979) sold his first script in 1922 and was soon hired by the fledgling Warner Brothers production unit.

Darryl F. Zanuck, circa early 1930s (Photofest).

There, he wrote scripts (often under different pseudonyms when working on less prestigious endeavors) for a variety of projects, including numerous silent film serials starring Hollywood's most famous German Shepherd, Rin Tin Tin. Very quickly, he rose in the ranks to Warner Brothers' head of production and made history in 1927 by producing *The Jazz Singer*, the film that triggered the industry's sound revolution.

In the spring of 1933, Zanuck would leave Warner Brothers, produce films under his independent Twentieth Century Pictures banner for two years, take over the ailing Fox Film Corporation, and run the merged Twentieth Century–Fox for the vast majority of the next thirty-six years. During his career, he supervised the production of more than one thousand films, including such undisputed classics as John Ford's *The Grapes of Wrath* (1940) and *How Green was My Valley* (1941), Joseph L. Mankiewicz's *All About Eve* (1950), and Robert Wise's *The Sound of Music* (1965). Along the way, he received numerous industry awards and accolades, and, ultimately, he left an indelible personal stamp on the U.S. film industry.

Now, in 1930, Zanuck was putting his personal imprint on Warner Brothers, one that would define the studio's character and presentation style for years to come. At a time when MGM and other studios believed that the source material for the best films was often found in the classic works of literature and theater, Zanuck steered away from such cultural niceties. Instead, his prime source materials for films were tabloid newspapers, sensational magazine stories, and other media that dealt with more contemporary, and often grittier, material more closely connected to the lives of ordinary people and, he believed, therefore more relatable to viewers. In addition, he was drawn to the distinctive stylings of these media, in particular, the frank, bold, and succinct ways in which they routinely presented this content. As Zanuck biographer George F. Custen notes:

> [Zanuck] was the first producer to grasp a difficult, sensitive, but ultimately transformative fact: the producer does not always attain his highest creative success with his audience by emulating gentility. To Zanuck, street life, the daily stuff of urban activity, was itself a form of art. He saw that the novelty and bluntness and fierce economy with which the tabloids were crafted grabbed the public's attention, and the films that arose from this vision significantly reshaped how the American cinema figured in the public sphere.[9]

During the early 1930s, Warner Brothers, largely under Zanuck's guiding hand, was the undisputed leader in these kinds of raw, "ripped-from-the-headlines" films. Some, such as director Archie Mayo's *The Doorway to Hell* (1930), Mervyn LeRoy's *Little Caesar* (1931), and Howard Hawks' *Scarface* (1932), focused on the scourge of organized crime. Others, such as LeRoy's *I Am a Fugitive from a Chain Gang* (1932), dealt with corruption in state prison systems. Others, such as Alfred E. Green's *Baby Face* (1933), centered on the limited choices and bleak prospects for women in a male-dominated world. Still others, such as Roy Del Ruth's *Employees' Entrance* (1933), explored sexual harassment and abuse in the workplace. And still others, such as LeRoy's *Three on a Match* (1932), took on the horrors of drug addiction.

By this time, Warner Brothers, which had had its financial struggles during the 1920s, had become a highly profitable Hollywood producer of tightly budgeted, technically competent mass-market films. And a key ingredient of this financial success was quantity: each year, the studio completed roughly one hundred feature films and then showed them in its more than 750 theaters both throughout the United States and around the world. An operation on this scale required, of course, a fast-moving, well-functioning assembly line made up of hundreds of people working on every phase of production and promotion—people who either got things done (and done well) or were quickly dismissed. Essential to the assembly line's success were its in-house directors, each of whom was expected to complete anywhere from four to seven feature films each year. And, in turn, each film they turned out had to meet with the approval of, among others, two very demanding taskmasters, Zanuck and studio head Jack L. Warner.

By today's standards, when it often takes several years to complete a single feature film, this seems like an incredible achievement in itself. Yet, during the three years 1931, 1932, and 1933—the height of the pre–Code era—many of Warner Brothers directors kept pace with the studio's relentless demands. During this time, for example, twelve of Mayo's feature-length films were released, thirteen of Green's, fourteen of Del Ruth's, sixteen of Curtiz's, seventeen of staff director Lloyd Bacon's, and eighteen of LeRoy's. In addition, staff directors would often be summoned to work "uncredited" on a film to reshoot scenes or perform other short-term duties. And, considering that they usually worked under such low-budget, fast-turnaround conditions, it is amazing that a good number of these films—such as Green's *Baby Face*, Curtiz's *20,000 Years in Sing-Sing*, LeRoy's *I Am a Fugitive from a Chain Gang* and *Golddiggers of 1933*, and Bacon's *42nd Street* and *Footlight Parade* (both 1933)—are now considered pre–Code classics.

It was into this manic, but still highly regimented, assembly-line environment that Wild Bill Wellman, aspiring auteur and incurable curmudgeon, entered when he signed with Warner Brothers on March 23, 1930. And it was here, where, in three short years, he worked on the films that would make up roughly one-fourth of his total directorial output during a career that stretched between 1923 to 1958—films that were often of very high quality and that people watch, discuss, study, and write about today.

*

Between October 4, 1930, and November 4, 1933, the eighteen feature-length films Wellman directed while under contract with Warner Brothers were released. In 1933, he also made a significant but uncredited contribution to a fascinating pre–Code comedy, *Female*, for which Curtiz ultimately received sole directing credit. So, with eighteen feature films to his credit during this time, he essentially tied LeRoy for the title of studio workhorse.

What makes Wellman's contribution so remarkable is the high quality of not just one, two, or even three of his films during this three-year span, but the high quality of so many, if not most, of them.

Among these, of course, are acknowledged masterpieces such as *The Public Enemy* (1931), *Heroes for Sale* (1933), and *Wild Boys of the Road* (1933). Each of these is, in its own way, an eloquent expression both of Wellman the person, with his bitingly cynical yet intensely compassionate take on humanity, and of Wellman the artist, with his bold, spare, in-your-face style and extraordinary economy as a storyteller. It is little wonder then that, when film writers put together their lists of the top-ten Wellman films, two or three of these films are routinely included.

Wellman also directed several films that we often refer to as "pre-Code gems," films that, despite their age, both engage and resonate deeply with twenty-first-century viewers. Among these are *Night Nurse* and *Safe in Hell* (both 1931), *Frisco Jenny* (1932), and *Central Airport*, *Lilly Turner*, and *Midnight Mary* (all 1933). Common themes among most of these films are the extremely limited opportunities and often grim prospects for women in a male-dominated society. And wonderful features of all of these films are standout performances from such actresses as Barbara Stanwyck, Joan Blondell, Dorothy Mackaill, Ruth Chatterton, Sally Eilers, and Loretta Young. Although Wellman is thought of mainly as a "man's director," he could portray complex and fully fleshed-out female characters with great sensitivity and empathy as well as extract outstanding performances from the actresses playing those characters—two talents for which he is rarely credited.

In addition, Wellman made several more films, which, while sometimes uneven, are still quite intriguing for those who wish to look more closely into the director's pre-Code work. These efforts include *Other Men's Women* (1931), *The Star Witness* (1931), *The Purchase Price* (1932), and *Love Is a Racket* (1932). Among the standout features are the director's abilities to orchestrate highly effective action scenes in *Other Men's Women*; portray violence in a startling, visceral pre-Code way in *The Star Witness*; and splash pre-Code-style cynicism all over the place in *Love Is a Racket*.

Finally, there are a handful of films, which, for various reasons, haven't aged as well as Wellman's other pre-Code efforts, but are still peppered with intriguing elements. Among these are *The Hatchet Man*, *So Big*, and *The Conquerors* (all 1932) and *College Coach* (1933).

In addition to being of good-to-excellent quality or, at the very least, interesting, nearly all the films mentioned above help to bolster the argument that, as well as being the fine craftsman he is often praised for being, Wellman was an "auteur," an artist who infuses his work with an individual worldview that gives his films a unique personal stamp. Largely because he made films in a variety of genres, the "auteur" designation is not usually applied to him, yet it is absolutely deserved. Working within the studio system, he did, of course, make films simply to fulfill contractual obligations and keep the studio's assembly line humming. At the same time, though, he also made numerous films that are highly distinctive both in terms of his filmmaking style and the subjects he explores—films that reflect his unique personality and express his perspectives on the human experience. Again and again, for example, we see his lean, sharp, succinct presentation style at work. And, again and again, his films tackle important and timeless subjects such as the meaning of justice, the perva-

Charlie Barton (left) and Wellman review a script (Photofest).

siveness of corruption, the plight of the downtrodden, and the fragility of love.

How could Wellman deliver these kinds of results in such a short period of time and within this manic, assembly-line system? The question is a compelling one. And the answer might have to do—perhaps more than the Warner Brothers environment at the time, the support of Zanuck, or any other contributing factor—with the exceptional nature of William Wellman, the man. As his colleague and good friend Charlie Barton—yes, the same Charlie Barton who'd helped Wellman shovel horse manure on to producer B.P. Schulberg's desk—shared in an interview many years later:

> I don't think Wellman ever made very many bad films. I really mean this.... He was real. He was honest. When the films were shaky in premise, underdeveloped, poorly motivated, the films still work. It's as if they are propelled forward on the strength of Wellman's convictions. When the scripts provided no originality, when the actors brought no life to their roles, Wellman infused his own into the films until they whirred along with pace, energy, and enthusiasm.[10]

*

After he left Warner Brothers in late 1933, Wellman became an independent director and focused more on developing personal projects that he then brought to independent producers or studios. During pre–Code, however, he was essentially a paradox—an auteur working on what was effectively a manufacturing assembly line. And, while he had the support of Zanuck, who green-lighted several of his pet projects during this time, the young director was constantly under pressure to deliver product to accommodate the seemingly insatiable demands of the studio's theatrical distributors and, of course, early-1930s movie audiences.

What Wellman—the assembly-line auteur—managed to accomplish under these conditions was nothing less than astonishing.

1

"Give me a big slice of you on toast and some French-fried potatoes on the side"
Maybe It's Love (1930) and *Other Men's Women* (1931)

As William Wellman left Paramount for the greener pastures of Warner Brothers, he undoubtedly had high hopes. As a storyteller who loved to dirty his hands with the muck of real life, Wellman must have seen in his new boss Darryl Zanuck a true kindred soul. In addition to connecting closely with the producer's artistic preferences, the director, who by this time had had his fill of duplicitous film industry executives, saw in Zanuck two personal qualities he liked very much: fearlessness and integrity. "I admired him for his guts," Wellman wrote many years later. "[And] there was one thing you could count on. When you wanted an answer, you got it right then and there; if we shook hands on a deal, it was a deal, period."[1]

Wellman would soon learn, though, that Zanuck was a kindred soul in some negative respects as well. Like the director, he could also be stubborn, short-tempered, and, if the spirit moved him, not above resorting to fisticuffs to express his anger or frustration. He could also be quite arrogant and domineering. Their working relationship would have its share of stops and starts and ups and downs, but it also lasted both throughout the time they shared at Warner Brothers and for many years afterward. And it would result in other excellent films, such as 1943's *The Ox-Bow Incident*, the very dark, sure-money-loser western Zanuck agreed to finance for Wellman after numerous other producers had turned him down cold. As both Zanuck and Wellman expected, the film lost money, but, in 1944, it was also nominated for the Academy Award for Best Picture, and today many critics consider it one of the finest westerns ever made.

Now, in the spring of 1930, at a new studio and with a new boss, Wellman was eager to tackle the kinds of projects he craved. It would, however, be several months before this promise was fulfilled. At Warner Brothers, Wellman was to begin slowly—a warm-up period, if you will—with two modest efforts, a college football comedy called *Maybe It's Love* (and later renamed *Eleven Men and a Girl*[2]) and a small-scale domestic drama called *Other Men's Women*.

*

Wellman couldn't have begun his stint with Warner Brothers more modestly than with *Maybe It's Love*, which was made in the spring and summer of 1930 and released in theaters the following October 4. As Wellman biographer Frank T. Thompson has astutely noted, while "not exactly bad, [the film] could be the most trivial and inconsequential movie Wellman ever directed."[3]

Loosely based on the 1904 theatrical comedy *The College Widow* by George Ade, *Maybe It's Love* is the third of four film adaptations of the story. Ade, an Indiana native who worked as a newspaper columnist and fiction writer as well as a playwright, was a key figure of what is now referred to as the Golden Age of Indiana Literature. This was a period from about 1880 to about 1920 when he and other Indiana-based writers such as Booth Tarkington, Theodore Dreiser, and Lew Wallace achieved international acclaim for works such as Tarkington's *The Magnificent Ambersons*, Dreiser's *An American Tragedy*, and Wallace's *Ben-Hur*. *The College Widow*—the title inspired by a slang term used around the year 1900 for a young, unmarried woman who lived near a campus and dated male college students—is one of Ade's most popular plays. After its initial, and very successful, Broadway run, three different touring companies performed the play throughout the United States. Eventually, Ade made more than two million dollars, an enormous sum at the time, from the effort.

It's curious that, in the opening credits to the film *Maybe It's Love*, neither Ade nor the play are mentioned. Instead, we are told that the film is based on a story by Mark Canfield, which, along with Gregory Rogers and Melville Crossman, was one of the three pseudonyms the young Darryl Zanuck often used on projects to which he contributed writing but for which he didn't necessarily want to receive credit.[4] Once we watch a few minutes of the actual film, we can better understand why he felt this way.

*

The story revolves around fictional Upton College and its sputtering football program. For twelve years in a row now, the school has lost its annual big game with arch-rival Parsons College, and Upton's trustees

1. Maybe It's Love *(1930) and* Other Men's Women *(1931)*

Yates (Joe E. Brown) and Nan (Joan Bennett) plot strategies to lure top-ranked college football players to Upton College in hopes of beating the school's arch-rival, Parsons College, in *Maybe It's Love* (Warner Bros./Photofest).

give its president an ultimatum: if Upton doesn't win next year's game with Parsons, the president must resign.

After overhearing this conversation, the president's daughter Nan (Joan Bennett) shares the disturbing information with friend and football player Yates (Joe E. Brown). Knowing that Upton can never beat Parsons with the team it has, Yates makes a suggestion. If Nan glams up, flirts with several excellent football players from other colleges, and gets each of them to think she is interested in him romantically, she could get them to transfer to Upton and play for next year's team. Suggesting that she start by taking off her glasses, he adds, "[If] you could just look at them with your eyes naked, you could recruit a squad of All-Americans."

Nan likes the idea, puts it into motion, and efficiently lures eleven top football players to Upton. Although all these young men are smitten with her, she becomes interested in only one, Tommy Nelson (James Hall). Unfortunately, Tommy's grades aren't up to Upton's academic standards, and Nan schemes to get him admitted. Then, of course, all of the other new Upton recruits learn that Nan has used them to help improve the school's football team. At first, they are quite unhappy about this and confront her. But, after she apologizes and tells him that the reason she lured them all to Upton was to help save her father's job, they forgive her and then go out to win the big game against Parsons.

*

As he routinely did when directing films with dubious scripts, Wellman gamely went about trying to make the tired story material in *Maybe It's Love* more palatable for audiences (as well as, perhaps, himself). The film's pacing is brisk, the dialogue is sometimes clever and quirky, and the shot selection is occasionally inventive and quite interesting. There are also playfully risqué pre–Code moments such as when the lovely Nan emerges from a lake after her canoe has capsized with her wet dress clinging tightly to her slim figure, leaving—as the expression goes—little to the imagination. And the film employs the interesting gimmick of casting actual college All-Americans from football powerhouses such as Notre Dame, Michigan, Purdue, and USC as the eleven players Nan lures to Upton. As actors, these young men aren't very good, but their presence in the film is unusual and fun. Yes, as Frank Thompson noted, the film's "not exactly bad."

That said, the film isn't exactly good, either. The story was old and tired, even for 1930 audiences. And the comedy, frequently supplied by the hammy rubber-faced comedian Joe E. Brown, is often overly exaggerated and tedious. One scene he shares with a bear in a forest is especially annoying. Running a close second is another scene in which he gets into a fight with Tommy Nelson's millionaire father during the big game.

One plus the film has going for it, though, is the chance to see the wonderful Joan Bennett in a relatively early (though not exceptional) film role. Bennett (1910–1990), whose film and television career extended from the 1920s to the 1970s, delivered consistently fine performances in a variety of roles from wide-eyed ingenues to noir femmes fatales, to protective mothers. Among the noted directors who sought her out for various lead and supporting assignments during her career were George Cukor, Otto Preminger, Fritz Lang, Jean Renoir, Max Ophüls, Vincente Minnelli, and Douglas Sirk. And among the roles for which she routinely receives high praise from modern audiences are her performances in Lang's *A Woman in the Window* (1944) and *Scarlet Street* (1945), Ophüls' *The Reckless Moment* (1949), and Sirk's *There's Always Tomorrow* (1956).

It's puzzling to understand why *Maybe It's Love* was the first film that Zanuck and Wellman completed together. Perhaps the producer wanted to try the director out on a relatively mundane project before offering him more ambitious and challenging material. Perhaps the director, eager to please his producer and other new superiors at Warner Brothers, agreed in order to prove he could handle *any* kind of assignment. In any case, for a director who was quickly establishing his own distinctive filmmaking vision and style, *Maybe It's Love* is a very un–Wellman-like effort. Nevertheless, the director took on and completed the assignment in his usual, highly efficient fashion, and the film performed well at the box office.

*

In many respects, Wellman's next project was much closer both to material he had previously handled and to his personal comfort zone. The story focuses on the two-men-in-love-with-the-same-woman theme, harkening back to his silent film hits *You Never Know Women* and *Wings*. The film also allows the director to continue to explore his fascination with the technology of motion, a subject central to *Wings*, *The Legion of the Condemned*, and *Young Eagles*. This time, though, the technology isn't airplanes, but trains, and the film's male leads aren't dashing flyers but ordinary railroad engineers.

The film, *Other Men's Women*, was originally set for release in late 1930 as *The Steel Highway*, a title that clearly emphasized the railroad aspects of the story. In December 1930, the title was changed, perhaps in true pre–Code fashion, to give the film a more risqué marketing hook. Then, on January 17, 1931, the film, in its current form and with its new title, premiered.

The original story and film adaptation are both credited to Maude Fulton (1881–1950), a playwright, actress, and dancer as well as screenwriter whose stage works include the hit Broadway plays *The Brat* (1917) and *The Hummingbird* (1923). In the 1920s, she began to work in films, writing intertitles for such silents as the Ernst Lubitsch's superb adaptation of *Lady Windermere's Fan* (1925) with Ronald Colman and Alan

Crosland's milestone silent/sound hybrid *Don Juan* (1926) with John Barrymore. She continued to work in Hollywood throughout the 1930s, receiving, all totaled, writing credits for twenty-two films and acting credits for five. In addition to *Other Men's Women*, other significant credits include the screenplay and dialogue for the first film version of *The Maltese Falcon* (1931) directed by Roy Del Ruth and the adaptation and dialogue for Wellman's *Safe in Hell*.

*

Other Men's Women begins in a diner beside the train tracks. Bill, a quirky, immature railroad engineer (Grant Withers) jumps off as his freight train continues to thump along car by car, orders a quick breakfast, flirts with the waitress, and counts the passing train cars, knowing he will soon have to hop back on. Like clockwork, he wolfs down his breakfast, hops on the train's departing caboose, climbs to the top, and makes his way to the train's engine by walking on top of all the box cars in between.

While friendly and likable, Bill is also a hard-drinking womanizer who keeps promising, but postponing, marriage to his on-again-off-again girlfriend, another waitress named Marie (Joan Blondell). Soon, Bill is evicted from his boarding house for both his drinking and late rent payments. To help Bill out, his long-time friend and fellow train engineer Jack (Regis Toomey) offers to let him live with him and his wife Lily (Mary Astor).

As the months go by, Bill stops drinking and his friendship with Lily, at first innocent, evolves into passionate love. The two believe that they must confront Jack with the truth, but neither can bear to hurt him. So, without any explanation, Bill leaves. Soon, Jack, thinking that Bill and Lily have simply had a spat, confronts Bill as the two work together in the cab of a train. After trying to evade the issue, Bill confesses the truth, and Jack, outraged at the news, starts a fistfight. In the fight, Jack falls, hits his head, and is blinded.

As Jack struggles with both his blindness and what he considers to be Lily and Bill's betrayal, he tells Lily that she needs time to himself and that she should leave town to visit her parents. Sadly, she complies. In the meantime, Bill starts drinking again. He also reconnects with Marie, and, although she is as eager as ever to get married, he can't go through with it. He, too, becomes increasingly despondent.

Soon, torrential rains come and threaten a key bridge near town. In what could effectively be a suicide mission, Bill tries to convince his superiors at the railroad that—to help bolster the bridge and keep it from being swept away by the flood waters—he should be allowed to drive a train of flatcars loaded with bags of cement over it. His superiors tell him that this

1. Maybe It's Love *(1930) and* Other Men's Women *(1931)* 27

idea is simply too risky, but Bill is adamant about going through with the scheme.

While visiting with other railroad workers one night as the rain pours down, Jack hears about what Bill plans to do. Figuring out that Bill is probably going through with what seems to be a suicide mission for his sake, Jack leaves the gathering, stumbles through the rainy railway yard remembering which engine to go to from memory, climbs aboard, starts the engine, and begins to take the train out of the yard. Seeing this, Bill jumps on board to talk Jack out of putting himself at risk. The two talk, both lamenting the sad situation and

In *Other Men's Women*, Bill (Grant Withers) unexpectedly falls in love with his best friend's wife, Lily (Mary Astor), and she with him, but neither quite knows how to resolve their dilemma (Warner Bros./Photofest).

each believing that he should be the one to take the train over the bridge and clear the path for the other one to be with Lily. Then Jack distracts Bill, knocks him out, gently eases him out of the train, and continues on. As he expects, rather than solidifying the bridge, the weight of the train is too much. The bridge collapses, and Jack goes with the train into the river and to his death.

Months later, we see a scene reminiscent of the very beginning of the film. Bill jumps off a freight train to grab a bite to eat at the same trackside diner. This time, though, he sees Lily, who has just returned to town on a passenger train. She tells him that she wants to return to the house she once shared with Jack and begin again and that, if he would like to, he is welcome to visit. Very soon, though, Bill must leave to return to his train. He does and climbs on top. Thrilled that Lily has returned and is willing to accept him back in her life, he walks excitedly along the top of the boxcars and toward the engine.

*

While *Maybe It's Love* may have been a helpful ramp-up exercise, *Other Men's Women* is the project where Wellman first hits his stride at Warner Brothers. From first shot to last, the director is in full command of his material and how he wants to present it. The result is a film that oozes with the energy of life in scene after scene, a film that in many ways retains its freshness and vitality roughly a century after its making.

The main reason for this, of course, is Wellman's ability to improve seemingly ordinary scenes with fluid, intriguing camerawork; sharp, clever dialogue; fast pacing; and other distinctive creative touches to enhance the feeling or reinforce the meaning of the screen moment.

One of the film's great strengths is its camerawork, the result of a successful collaboration between Wellman and veteran in-house cinematographer Barney McGill (1890–1942). In late 1930, when *Other Men's Women* was in production, most filmmakers still felt bound by the cumbersome new sound technology and their films usually had a static and stage-bound look. Wellman, with his natural affinity for, and attraction to, other technologies of motion such as airplanes and trains, saw the movie camera in a similar way, and throughout *Other Men's Women*, we see vivid examples of this. Among the most striking is the sequence when the blind Jack stumbles through the railway yard on the cold, rainy night to get to the train that Bill has planned to take over the bridge. It's an amazing bit of filmmaking filled with arresting, unexpected shots of dark ominous trains and other railroad yard equipment, one that subtly captures the inner horror and desperation that Jack feels. The long tracking shots of the trains in motion in other scenes are quite captivating, too. Rather than simply depicting the great, brutish machines, the camera also seems to be celebrating them, standing in awe of their power and their potential to help human beings go about the business of daily life.

Other distinctive Wellman-esque touches are bits of memorable dialogue: snappy, cynical lines and retorts that fit the risqué pre–Code-era sensibility like a glove. One that's often quoted is an exchange between Joan Blondell's waitress Marie and a couple of diner patrons:

> MARIE: Anything else you guys want?
> FIRST MAN: Yeah. Give me a big slice of you on toast and some French-fried potatoes on the side.
> MARIE: Listen, baby, I'm A-P-O.
> FIRST MAN: (to man sitting beside him) What does she mean—A-P-O?
> MARIE: Ain't puttin' out…
> SECOND MAN: That's a hot one, Marie.
> MARIE: What do you mean—that's a hot one?
> FIRST MAN: Didn't I see you … with Elmer Brown last night?

1. Maybe It's Love *(1930) and* Other Men's Women *(1931)*　　29

MARIE: (caught off-guard) Er, yes, Elmer's a kind of a cousin of mine.
FIRST MAN: Some cousins are SURE affectionate!

In addition, Wellman constantly tries to make other aspects of the presentation fresh and interesting by doing them differently. For example, to accompany the opening credits, which, in the early 1930s, almost always meant using snappy music and a bland static visual background, he simply uses the sights and sounds of railroad trains and railroad yards. As well as intriguing viewers by its novelty, this also sets up a realistic documentary-like style that is present in other scenes throughout the film. As much as he can, the director also infuses appropriate moments with humor and verve. One such moment is the scene when the character of Ed (James Cagney in a very small early role) enters to meet his date in the lobby of a dance hall wearing his railroad engineer's work clothes. With great gusto, he takes off the work clothes in front of both his date and the hat check woman, revealing a tuxedo underneath; gives the work clothes to the hat check woman; and then executes a sparkling seven-second soft shoe as he leads his date to the dance floor.

Offsetting the creative camerawork and exuberance of *Other Men's Women*, of course, is the film's poignant emotional core. This is, after all, a story about a seemingly innocent betrayal and how it can lead to the destruction of a genuinely good person's life. Noting the film's "broken characters" and their "crisscrossing emotions of pain," pre–Code historian Danny Reid has even gone as far as to say that *Other Men's Women* may actually have more in common "spiritually" with the more somber and brooding poetic realism[5] of the late 1930s French cinema of directors such as Marcel Carné and Jean Renoir than with the ethos of early–1930s Hollywood.[6] We may or may not agree with this point, but at the very least it is a fascinating one to make, and for us to consider.

*

To mine the potentially rich, emotionally fraught roles of Bill, Jack, and Lily, Wellman and Warner Brothers settled on, respectively, actors Grant Withers, Regis Toomey, and Mary Astor. And here is where we begin to see some of the major shortcomings of *Other Men's Women*.

Of the three actors, Astor (1906–1987) is the one best known to classic film audiences today. Just twenty-four when she made *Other Men's Women*, she was already a ten-year veteran in films, mostly silents at this early point in her career. She continued to work in films until the mid-1960s, mostly as a female lead or in featured character roles. Along the way, she won a Best Supporting Actress Oscar for her work in the Bette Davis melodrama, *The Great Lie* (1941). And today, her work in such films as *Dodsworth* (1936), *The Maltese Falcon* (1941), and *Act of Violence* (1948) is also highly regarded.

In *Other Men's Woman*, Astor has the smallest of the three lead roles and manages quite well, ably conveying Lily's kind and gentle nature, youthful naivete, and the enormous sense of guilt she feels about the great pain her love for Bill has caused Jack. She is quite effective in her scenes with Bill, when the two are light-hearted and flirtatious, not fully realizing what's actually happening, and then in her later scenes as she struggles to salvage her deteriorating relationship with Jack.

For modern audiences, however, the two leads, Grant Withers as Bill and Regis Toomey as Jack, are not nearly as well-known as Mary Astor, and there's a reason for this: neither is an especially good actor. Withers (1905–1959) was at the height of his career when he made *Other Men's Women*, and, while he would continue to act in films and then for television up until the late 1950s, his roles were almost always small and undistinguished. For many film and television viewers, Toomey (1898–1991) is one of those actors who, when seen, often inspires the remark, "Hey, I know him—that's what's-his-name!" In a career that spanned from the 1920s to the late 1970s, he amassed hundreds of film and television credits, usually in small roles and almost always turning in adequate, but routine, performances. *Other Men's Women* was a rare opportunity for him to play a lead role.

While both Withers and Toomey gamely tackle their prime roles in *Other Men's Women*, the results are far from compelling. In fact, as film writer Dan Callahan once noted of Toomey, he was an actor "who was always hovering close to ineptitude."[7] Of the two, Withers fares a bit better, especially during his early scenes when Bill seems to revel in being a lovable ne'er-do-well. Toomey is also more credible at first, playing a bland but solid, good-hearted, and respectable person. Neither, however, is effective in the critical scenes when they confront each other over what Jack considers to be Lily's betrayal of their wedding vows and Bill's betrayal of their long-standing and very close friendship.

With the stable of fine actors at Warner Brothers at the time, it's a pity that the lead roles were not cast differently. Just imagine Richard Barthelmess as Jack, Wallace Ford as Bill, or James Cagney in either role.

Speaking of Cagney, his and Joan Blondell's bit parts in *Other Men's Women*—often singled out as highlights of the film—occasionally upstage the performances of the actors in the lead roles. Cagney has a very small part, one that hardly has any relationship to the film's main subject matter, yet he makes the most of his few moments, and, yes, he absolutely shines both as a hoofer and as an actor adept at comedy in the short scene when he meets his date in the lobby of the dance hall. Blondell's role as Marie,

1. Maybe It's Love *(1930)* and Other Men's Women *(1931)*   31

Bill's frustrated on-again-off-again girlfriend, gives the gifted actress a chance to show her talent both in comedy during the diner scene when she announces she's a girl that's "A-P-O" and in real drama later on when, totally drunk at the dance hall, she reacts to Bill's final rejection of her.

Fortunately for both Cagney and Blondell, bigger and better roles were just around the corner. Within months after *Other Men's Women* was released, the two would be major stars at Warner Brothers as well as favorites of William Wellman. We will, of course, return to them later in this book.

*

It would probably come as quite a shock to the critics who first reviewed *Other Men's Women* in 1931 that this modest film is still seen and discussed today. For example, in a short *New York Times* review unenthusiastically titled "Another Triangle," the writer called the film "an unimportant little drama of the railroad yards," and added, "If nothing else, the picture represents a triumph for the Warner rain machines."[8] Most other reviews at the time, while not quite as disparaging, weren't exactly bowled over by the film, either. The best the reviewer at *Variety* could muster, for example, was to call it "a good program picture."[9]

Other Men's Woman is not Wellman's best pre–Code film, but, especially after multiple viewings, it's easier to understand why it still has an allure with classic film aficionados, especially those with a special interest in Wellman, pre–Code, or both. The story is a bit rough around the edges, and the two leading men were not as effective in their roles as better actors would have been, but the film still has much going for it. Certainly, one of its greatest assets is Wellman's ability to infuse well-worn material with real, and occasionally heart-wrenching, emotion. The director treats the tragic love triangle and the well-meaning human beings affected by it seriously and respectfully, and, as viewers, it's difficult not to be moved as the story plays out on the screen. Another of the film's great assets is Wellman's ability to enliven scenes with fascinating creative touches, many of which also serve to intensify mood and/or reinforce meaning. His staging of the blind Jack's stumbling walk through the railroad yard as the rain pours down, for example, is a brilliant piece of filmmaking. Yes, *Other Men's Women* might not be quite at the level of the great Wellman pre–Code films that would soon follow, but it's a major step forward in the director's efforts to master cinematic storytelling in the nascent sound era.

*

With the completion of *Other Men's Women*, Wellman's warm-up at Warner Brothers was also complete. Other, and quite promising, projects were now on the horizon, and the ambitious young director was chomping at the bit for the chance to take on as many of them on as he could.

Over the course of 1931, he pretty much got his wish. Four more Wellman films would be released, all of which were, in one way or another, exceptional. In fact, biographer Frank Thompson has even declared Wellman's next two efforts to be "among the best films he ever directed."[10]

2

"There's not only beer in that keg—there's beer and blood"

The Public Enemy (1931)

One of the intriguing aspects associated with Wellman's next film for Warner Brothers, *The Public Enemy*, is the assortment of conflicting accounts about who actually came up with the inspired ideas that helped make the final product such a memorable piece of work. It sometimes seems as if everyone involved has a different story, and often it's a version that puts the storyteller in quite a favorable light.

Among these inspirations, two are especially noteworthy. The first was the decision to replace actor Edward Woods in the role of the story's lead character, Tom Powers, with film newcomer James Cagney. According to one of the two writers of the film's story, John Bright, he and his writing partner Kubec Glasmon, quickly saw that Cagney, who had originally been cast in a smaller role as Tom's friend Matt Doyle, was the obvious choice to play Tom. They made their case to Wellman, who agreed, and then Wellman made the case to Zanuck, who authorized the change. Zanuck recalled it differently, however, claiming that the inspiration was all his. Years later, Cagney remembered it in still another way, crediting Wellman as being solely responsible because he could immediately see the actor's ability to, as Cagney himself put it, "project that gutter quality"[1] essential to the character. The second inspiration was the decision to call for Cagney, as the incorrigible Tom, to smash half a grapefruit into the face of his girlfriend Kitty (played by Mae Clarke) in one scene as the two are having breakfast. The source of the idea for what has long been known as the film's shocking "grapefruit scene" is another point of contention. Wellman claimed that it had come from a fantasy he'd had one morning while having breakfast with is fourth wife, Marjorie Crawford.

He'd thought about doing it, he recalled, to "break the monotony" in their unhappy marriage, but, after listening to his better angels, had restrained himself, later putting the idea into the film's script.[2] Another version is that the idea was based on an actual incident in which, Hymie Weiss, a notoriously ill-tempered Chicago gangster, shoved an omelet into his girlfriend's face. Then, when the filmmakers considered an omelet too messy, a grapefruit half was substituted. Still another version came from Zanuck, who again asserted that the idea was all his, something he'd come up with during a script conference.

Regardless of the origins of these inspirations, it's understandable why different people wanted credit for them. Simply put, the decisions to act on these ideas changed film history. Cagney's stunning performance as the psychopathic Tom Powers catapulted the actor into instant superstardom. For the next thirty years, he would be one of Hollywood's most popular and respected performers, both as an actor and a dancer. And years after his retirement, his body of work would stir another larger-than-life film figure, director and actor Orson Welles, to call him "maybe the greatest actor who ever appeared in front of a camera."[3] In addition, the grapefruit scene—so sudden, unexpected, and viciously misogynistic—has become as iconic for its time as the unforgettable "shower scene" in Alfred Hitchcock's *Psycho* became for the 1960s and 1970s. Not only did both scenes shock and appall audiences seeing them for the first time, but they broke barriers about what could and could not be shown on screen and, for years afterward, enormously influenced other filmmakers.

Wellman made other uncompromising films during the pre-Code era, but none as fearless, unsparing, jolting, or influential as *The Public Enemy*. It's a testament to the film's enduring power that the American Film Institute, when it compiled its list of the top ten gangster films of all time in 2008—a list that contains *The Godfather, The Godfather Part II, Goodfellas, Bonnie and Clyde,* and *Pulp Fiction*—also included *The Public Enemy*.[4]

*

The story of *The Public Enemy* begins with an unpublished novel colorfully titled *Beer and Blood* and written by the two men mentioned earlier: John Bright, a Chicago-based newspaper reporter, and Kubec Glasmon, a pharmacist and aspiring writer. Perhaps more accurately, their book was a series of crime stories that were thinly disguised accounts based on the real-life escapades of Weiss, Al Capone, and other Chicago gangland figures of the era. Their manuscript found its way to Zanuck, who read it and thought that, if the two writers concentrated on one of their stories and developed it more fully, the material could be turned into

2. The Public Enemy *(1931)*   35

a film. They complied, developing a treatment that centered on two young delinquents, Tom Powers and Matt Doyle, who grow into full-fledged Prohibition-era hoodlums.

At some point, however, Bright and Glasmon became frustrated with project's lack of progress at the studio and approached Wellman, asking him to read their treatment. The director took a shine to the intriguing title, *Beer and Blood*, and agreed. Then, after sailing through the treatment in one sitting, he was so excited about it that he went to Zanuck's office and convinced him to read it as well. The next morning, Zanuck was equally excited, suggesting that the title be changed to *The Public Enemy*. But then he asked Wellman why—so soon after the studio had made several other gangster films—he should make yet another, and, if so, why he should let a studio newcomer like Wellman direct. Without hesitating, Wellman famously responded, "Because I'll make it the roughest, toughest goddam one of them all!"[5]

After *The Public Enemy*, both Bright (1908–1989) and Glasmon (1897–1938) remained in Hollywood and collaborated on treatments and screenplays during the 1930s. Several other Warner Brothers pre–Code hits they worked on include *Smart Money* and *Blonde Crazy* (both 1931) and *The Crowd Roars*, *Three on a Match*, and *Taxi!* (all 1932). Sadly, Glasmon died at age forty of a heart attack. In 1933, Bright became one of the co-founders of the Screen Writers Guild. Then, in the early 1950s, he was targeted by the U.S. House of Representatives' Un-American Activities Committee for his leftist political beliefs and later blacklisted. With his wife, immigrant activist Josefina Fierro, he went to Mexico, where he wrote scripts for at least two Mexican films and a memoir intriguingly titled *Worms in the Winecup*.

Once both Zanuck and Wellman were on board with the project, now officially re-christened *The Public Enemy*, in-house screenwriter Harvey Thew was assigned to develop the screenplay. Well established in the business, Thew (1883–1946) had worked on both story development and screenplays for films since 1916 and would eventually tally more than ninety credits, nearly always as part of a writing team.

During this pre-production phase, the film's casting choices were also made. In addition to Woods and Cagney as the two leads, Wellman selected the very able stage actor Donald Cook to play Tom's straight-arrow brother Mike. Newly arrived in Hollywood to try his hand at talking pictures, Cook would soon have featured roles in three other Wellman pre–Code films, *Safe in Hell*, *The Conquerors*, and *Frisco Jenny*. Joan Blondel, who had received praise for her memorable supporting turn in Wellman's most recent film, *Other Men's Women*, was cast as Matt's girlfriend, Mamie. Another actress Wellman apparently pursued, albeit unsuccessfully, was Louise Brooks, who had delivered a brilliant performance in the director's silent film, *Beggars of Life*. Although Brooks admired Wellman, she'd had more than her share of conflicts with big film studios and turned down the role Wellman had envisioned her playing, possibly Tom's second girlfriend Gwen Allen. This small but key part eventually went to a nineteen-year-old Hollywood newcomer named Jean Harlow, then under contract with eccentric multi-millionaire and, at the time, independent film producer Howard Hughes.

The actual filming of *The Public Enemy* took place during a five-week period between mid–January and mid–February 1931. Another efficiently made, low-budget Wellman effort, it cost $151,000, which, considering the complexity of many of its scenes, was quite impressive from a budgeting perspective, even for the time.

*

The film begins with a montage of Chicago scenes from what we are told is 1909. In the midst of the hustle and bustle, we meet two boys, Tom Powers (Frank Coghlan, Jr.) and Matt Doyle (Frankie Darro), friends who also work together as petty thieves who fence their ill-gotten gains through a Fagin-like character called Putty Nose (Murray Kinnell). After several years, Putty Nose offers Tom (now played by Cagney) and Matt (now played by Woods) a promotion, the chance to join the rest of his gang and go big time, robbing a warehouse filled with expensive animal furs. When Tom and Matt seem a little uneasy about this, Putty Nose assures them that, if anything goes wrong, he will be there for them. To seal their deal, he gives the young men handguns. During the robbery, however, Tom is startled by a stuffed bear and instinctively shoots it. His shots alert the police, who raid the warehouse, killing another gang member. When Tom and Matt then go to Putty Nose for help, however, they learn he has left town.

At home, Tom keeps his criminal activities a secret from his naïve and trusting mother (Beryl Mercer), but his law-abiding, by-the-book older brother Mike (Cook) sees what is occurring and fruitlessly tries to convince Tom to change his ways. In the meantime, the United States enters World War I, Mike joins the Marines, and goes overseas to fight.

By 1920, the Nineteenth Amendment to the U.S. Constitution, which ushered in the Prohibition Era (a time when the sale of alcohol was banned nationwide) has gone into effect. And local gang figure Paddy Ryan (Robert Emmett O'Connor), eyeing unprecedented business opportunities in bootlegging (the illegal sale of alcohol) enlists Tom and Matt to work for him as beer "salesmen," or enforcers. To expand the business further, Paddy also joins forces with well-known gangster Samuel "Nails" Nathan

2. The Public Enemy (1931) 37

(Leslie Fenton). As the bootlegging business becomes increasingly lucrative, Tom and Matt flaunt their new-found wealth.

Just returned from the war, Mike is outraged when he learns that Tom's money is coming from bootlegging. Tom brings a keg of beer home to celebrate Mike's return, but Mike refuses to drink a drop from it, declaring, "There's not only beer in that keg—there's beer and blood, the blood of men."

About this time, Tom and Matt start seeing two young women, Kitty and Mamie, respectively. Matt and Mamie hit it off, but Tom eventually tires of Kitty, and one morning at breakfast he cruelly smashes half a grapefruit into her face. Soon, he takes up with another young woman, Gwen Allen (Harlow). Eventually, Matt and Mamie are married and, at a restaurant the evening of their wedding, Tom and Matt spot Putty Nose, who had deserted them long ago. They follow him home, and, after Putty Nose begs for his life, Tom coldly shoots him as Matt, clearly distressed, looks on.

Later, Tom and Matt hear that Nails Nathan has been killed in a horse-riding accident. Almost instinctively, the two go to the stable that houses Rajah, the horse Nathan had been riding. Tom buys Rajah and promptly marches into the horse's stall and shoots it. Nathan's death has also created a power vacuum among the rival gangs locally, and another gang leader, "Schemer" Burns, seeing an opening for himself, starts a gang war.

One victim in this war is Matt, who is gunned down in the street, and Tom, obsessed with revenge, ambushes Burns and several of his henchmen one rainy night, killing several of them but not Burns. Tom, however, is seriously wounded in the shootout and staggers out into the rain. Shocked at the thought of his own vulnerability, he mutters "I ain't so tough" and falls to the pavement.

Tom doesn't die, however. He is brought to the hospital, where he is treated, makes peace with Mike, and agrees both to move back to the family home and to reform.

Soon, though, Paddy tells Mike that the Burns mob has kidnapped Tom from the hospital; that he, Paddy, has directed all of his men to find Tom; and that he has pledged to Burns that, if Tom is returned to his home, he will quit the rackets for good, allowing his rival to take over his operations. Before leaving, Paddy also tells Mike to stay by the phone and that one of his men will be calling. Later, the phone rings and Mike hears that Tom will be coming home right away. Hearing the good news, Ma Powers joyously begins to prepare Tom's bedroom. A record of the gentle, dreamy song "I'm Forever Blowing Bubbles" is put on the family's victrola as part of the welcome. Mike hears a knock at the door, opens it, and Tom, who is dead and whose body has been propped up against the door, falls stiffly to the floor. The film cuts to Ma Powers happily continuing to prepare Tom's bedroom. It then cuts back to the front door scene as a stunned and shaken Mike walks slowly away from Tom's body as "I'm Forever Blowing Bubbles" continues to play.

*

When *The Public Enemy* opened on April 23, 1931, audiences were both enthusiastic and large. In fact, to satisfy customers eager to see the new film, one theater in New York's Times Square ran it twenty-four hours a day for part of its initial run. The film eventually became one of Warner Brothers' biggest commercial hits of the year, bringing in $557,000 at the box office, more than three and a half times its $151,000 total production cost.

Although audiences flocked to the film, the critics in 1931 were generally mixed in their appraisals. Writing for the *New York Times*, for example, Andre David Sennwald characterized *The Public Enemy* as "just another gangster film ... weaker than most in its story, stronger than most in its acting, and, like most, maintaining a certain level of interest through the last burst of machine-gun fire."[6] Sennwald went on to praise the work of Cagney and Woods for their "remarkably lifelike portraits of young hoodlums" and added that several of the supporting players, including Donald Cook as Mike, Beryl Mercer as Ma Powers, and Robert Emmett O'Connor as Paddy "do splendidly."[7] In its write-up, *Variety* also attempted to present a balanced assessment, noting. "There is no lace on this picture. It's raw and brutal. It's low-brow material given such workmanship as to make it high-brow."[8]

*

With the passing of many decades, however, Sennwald's claim that *The Public Enemy* is "just another gangster film" has lost most, if not all, of the credibility it might have ever had. While often acknowledging certain flaws and shortcomings, the vast majority of film historians and writers have roundly praised the film's brutally honest realism and high level of craftmanship as well as Cagney's electrifying portrayal of Tom Powers.

Among them is director Martin Scorsese, himself no stranger to gangster movies. "[*The Public Enemy*] was the first gangster picture I ever saw," he has noted. "I come from a neighborhood where ... people were like that. It was the most prized of the [gangster] films because of its authenticity to the behavior of the characters. It's a very special picture. It's a film that I cannot stop watching."[9]

Calling *The Public Enemy* "one of the most realistic gangster films

2. The Public Enemy (1931)

ever produced," *TV Guide Magazine* has noted, "Wellman's direction is a frontal attack on the subject. Other than handling a number of violent deaths offscreen, he spares no brutality of emotion, action, or thought in his grim portrayal of a lethal criminal. Cagney is the gangster of his day, cocky, tough as nails, and utterly without conscience, a character molded into evil by his environment.... Tom's casual brutality scars the memory in shot after shot."[10]

Adding to the general acclaim, veteran film writer Glenn Erickson both dubbed *The Public Enemy* "one of the best films of the 1930s" and gave much of the credit to the film's magnetic star, adding that, although he is "given excellent support on both sides of the camera, James Cagney is sensational all on his own. Every scene shows him arrogantly demonstrating his street-smart style, making sly faces at people, doing little punching motions (even at his own clueless mother) and the occasional dance-like pirouette when entering cars or jumping out of trucks."[11]

*

As these last three comments suggest, contemporary viewers tend to give most of the credit for *The Public Enemy*'s success and enduring appeal to the one-two punch of Wellman and Cagney. They are also largely correct. With the exception of *Other Men's Women*, in which Cagney played a very minor role, this film marked the only time that these two major talents ever worked together, and here they complement each other magnificently. In his films, Wellman often strove to achieve a level of stark, unvarnished realism that, even during the pre–Code era, was not all that common for Hollywood, and Cagney, who oozed intensity and conviction no matter what role he was playing, could more than accommodate him. Without either of these highly gifted and distinctive contributors on board, the film would probably not have been nearly as good as it is.

We see Wellman's contributions from *The Public Enemy*'s very first moments to its brutal ending.

One of the most fascinating of these is a musical selection: the decision to use an instrumental version of the popular 1919 song "I'm Forever Blowing Bubbles" over the film's opening credits, from time to time during the story, and again to full effect just before and during Tom's final homecoming. At first listen, this song simply seems an odd choice: a gentle, graceful, waltz-like tune to accompany a violent story about the rise and fall of a notorious hoodlum. But, if we look at the lyrics, as familiar to 1931's viewers as they are to today's, we can see an intriguing tension. Consider, for example, the song's chorus and most famous lines:

> I'm forever blowing bubbles,
> Pretty bubbles in the air,

> They fly so high, nearly reach the sky,
> Then like my dreams they fade and die.
> Fortune's always hiding,
> I've looked everywhere,
> I'm forever blowing bubbles,
> Pretty bubbles in the air.[12]

Although the tune has a very light, dreamy quality about it, the lyrics focus on the fragility of dreams (that "fade and die") and the futility ("Fortune's always hiding") of pursuing them—human experience akin to what we see in the film. Ma Powers, for example, dreams that her two diametrically opposed sons, one of whom is a murderous psychopath, can get along and live with her in the family home. Tom dreams that, by putting his all into being a thug, he can somehow move up in the world, perhaps someday becoming a bigshot of some kind. In turn, this song, with its all-too-familiar, and discordant, music and lyrics, creates—when blended into the film's brutal melodrama—a complicated, jarring, ironic, darkly humorous, and deeply disturbing counterpoint for viewers. Especially in the film's final scenes, the impact of this particular piece of music is nothing short of devastating. Choosing it to be the main musical theme for this story was a masterstroke.

In addition to this musical selection—and, of course, *The Public Enemy*'s iconic and much discussed "grapefruit scene"—Wellman serves up quite a number of other unexpected jolts during the film. Just a few other examples include the scenes when:

- Tom spits a robust stream of beer into the face of a bar owner who is no longer buying Paddy's brew
- Tom shoots Rajah, Nails Nathan's horse
- Tom shoots Putty Nose as the frightened older man plays a familiar tune on his piano
- Tom single-handedly shoots it out with Schemer Burns and his gang on a dark, rainy night
- Tom's body falls in the doorway of the Powers' home as Ma Powers prepares his bedroom for him and "I'm Forever Blowing Bubbles" plays on the family's victrola

What's similar about all these scenes is that they are realistic and, at the same time, outrageous. We might, for example, expect Tom to spit the beer onto the barroom's floor to express his disapproval that this beer is not his product, but instead he spits it directly into the face of the man he is trying (and quite successfully) to intimidate. In addition to being startling, this action also underscores Tom's characteristic unbridled crudeness: there are no limits to what he is willing to do to appear tough.

2. The Public Enemy (1931)

Another interesting example is when Tom shoots Nails Nathan's horse, Rajah. Nails has died as the result of a riding accident, yet Tom treats the incident as if his death was a deliberate gangland hit that deserves "payback." It's as if he knows of no way to respond to the death other than to proceed with an execution of his own. Another interesting aspect of this scene is its very dark humor, which is capped when Tom and Matt leave the horse's stall after the shooting with Tom holding, much like a trophy, a horse blanket with Rajah's name embroidered on it. Again, this is true to Tom's character: absolutely credible and absolutely outrageous.

What's also similar in the scenes in which killings take place is a distinctively Wellman touch. Rather than showing a killing on screen, the director often arranges for it to take place in real time but off-camera. This offers him couple of significant benefits. The first, especially in tightly budgeted productions, is time and cost savings. Simply put, it's much faster, easier, and cheaper to imply the act rather than going through the trouble of staging it. The second—and more pertinent to the quality of the storytelling—lies in the power of suggestion: in this case, the suggestion of a murder rather than the actual staging of one before the camera. This, of course, leaves more to the viewers' imaginations to fill in the horrors taking place, engages them more fully, and ultimately affects them more deeply. In *The Public Enemy*, this artistic choice works repeatedly. In the scene when Putty Nose is killed, for example, all we see at the moment we hear Tom shoot his gun is the shock and revulsion in Matt's face as he witnesses the act. In the scene when Tom kills Rajah, all we hear is a gunshot and all we see is a stable filled with horses, all startled by the sound of the shot. And in the scene when Tom attempts to gun down Schemer Burns and others in his gang, all we hear are a barrage of gunshots and then one long, agonizing, unnerving scream, and all we see is the exterior of the building where the violence is taking place. Over and over again, the effect is chilling.

As well as jolting us in scene after scene throughout *The Public Enemy*, Wellman, as he does in nearly all his films, tells the story in quite creative, and effective, ways visually.

One intriguing bit of foreshadowing, for example, is a juxtaposition during the montage that begins the film. After we've seen shot after shot showing us aspects of Chicago's booming beer business in 1909, we hear, then see, a pro-temperance Salvation Army band energetically marching past a beer pub. Without using any words, the scene is set for the chain of events that will soon drive much of the story's action:

- There's a robust market for beer.
- Temperance groups such as the Salvation Army work to make the sale of alcohol illegal.

- Laws are passed banning alcohol sales.
- Criminal bootleggers step in to distribute illegal alcohol and, in the process, make enormous profits.
- The thuggish behavior of these bootleggers to intimate customers into buying alcohol from them increases.
- The growing conflicts and violence between criminal groups competing with each other for the lucrative business also increase.

Still another visual touch—one that's quite inspired but for some reason rarely mentioned in critiques of *The Public Enemy*—occurs in the scene when the Powers family and the Doyles have dinner to celebrate Mike's homecoming from World War I. Before everyone sits down for the meal, Tom and Matt place a large keg of beer squarely in the middle of the table, as if it were a centerpiece. The effect is more than a bit unsettling, bizarre, and darkly humorous. The keg essentially becomes the eight-hundred-pound gorilla in the room. It dominates several of the shots, often making the people around the table seem small and less

(From left) Rita Flynn, Donald Cook, Edward Woods, and James Cagney all appear quite tense as upright Mike Powers (Cook) confronts his hoodlum brother Tom (Cagney) in *The Public Enemy*'s fascinating keg-on-the-dinner-table scene (Photographer: Scotty Welbourne. Warner Bros. Pictures/Photofest).

significant by comparison. It also obstructs the views characters have of one other. For example, Mike and his mother, who sit at opposite ends of the table, can hardly see each other. Yet, no one, not even the very upright and self-righteous Mike, insists on removing it. The symbolism is clear and pointed: the bootlegging business is both supporting the Powers family and coming between its members. As well as keeping them going (at least for the moment), it threatens to tear them apart.

Overall, Wellman's contributions to *The Public Enemy* are both highly distinctive and quite significant. In many respects, the story of a crude hoodlum's rise and fall was all too familiar and potentially tiresome to many 1931 moviegoers, who, with the growing popularity of the gangster genre in the preceding couple of years, had likely seen many such films. Fortunately, however, the director made good on his promise to Zanuck, coming up with a wide and varied assortment of creative flourishes to make this film, among all the other recent gangster films, "the roughest, toughest goddam one of them all."

It's clear, too, that, if *The Public Enemy* had been made after mid–1934, many of the elements that make it so distinctive, shocking, and real—such as the beer spitting, grapefruit smashing, and suggestions of illicit sex— would have been toned down or even eliminated to appease the industry's censors. Most likely, this would still have been a good film, but not the great one that it is.

*

The other half of the one-two punch that makes *The Public Enemy* truly special is, of course, James Cagney, a vaudeville trouper and stage actor who, along with Joan Blondell, had been brought to Hollywood only a few months before to re-create stage roles they had played for a film called *Sinner's Holiday* (1930).

Wellman was all about authenticity, and, in *The Public Enemy*, Cagney superbly realizes the director's vision. Specifically, the actor immerses himself so fully and uncompromisingly into his character—conveying Tom's seething small-minded cruelty so intensely, convincingly, and charismatically—that he literally compels us to accept Tom as a kind of undeniable truth. "We can't take our eyes off [Cagney]," Glenn Erickson notes, "as he's just so much more 'real' than anyone else."[13] Adds film writer Chris Barsanti, "It's a performance so perfect in its intensity that any other quibbles about the film ultimately recede into insignificance."[14] And, as film writer Matt Zoller Seitz observes:

> Is Cagney wearing eyeliner, or is his Rasputin stare so challenging that it's burning holes in the screen? You get why audiences went mad for Cagney as Tom: he doesn't seem to be pretending to be dangerous, but to actually be

dangerous, like an ex-convict who got out of the joint, took a couple of acting lessons, and became a movie star because he wasn't faking anything. But he was. Cagney grew up a poor Irish kid on New York's Lower East Side.... He had a talent for street fighting.... But he wasn't a criminal and certainly never killed anybody.... So, this was acting, pure and simple: a performer finding a core of rage and need, and projecting it outward.... He was a killer talent.[15]

The other element that Cagney brings to his portrayal is his ability to imbue Tom, a character with few redeeming personal qualities, with a certain, and very relatable, humanity. Although we find Tom abhorrent in many ways, we can also appreciate his no-nonsense transparency, his no-holds-barred fearlessness, his sense of dark humor, and other traits. Tom is by no means a nice guy, but Cagney is so good at giving him complexity and nuance, at making him so lifelike, so real, that Tom thoroughly engages us in every scene he is in. Yes, Cagney absolutely was a "killer talent."

One other—and quite significant—aspect of Cagney's contribution to *The Public Enemy* is the impact and lasting influence it has had on the evolution of film storytelling. In a fascinating 1951 essay called "Cagney and the Mob," the fine British film and theater critic Kenneth Tynan contends that, in *The Public Enemy*, the actor actually "invented a new kind of screen character."[16] To substantiate his claim, Tynan compares the cinema to other popular narrative arts such as theater and the novel, showing how, in their infancies, each of these arts "clings to a broad and exaggerated ethical system, based on pure blacks and whites,"[17] and, as each of the arts evolves, this period of oversimplification ends. He continues:

> [In the films of the 1920s], there was not only a rigid distinction between the good characters and the bad; they were also evenly balanced in numbers and fame. Vice and virtue proclaimed themselves irrevocably within the first hundred feet [of film].... Cagney changed all this. In *The Public Enemy* he presented, for the first time, a hero who was callous and evil, while being simultaneously equipped with charm, courage and a sense of fun. Even more significantly, he was co-starred not with the grave young district attorney who would finally ensnare him, but with a bright, callow moll for him to slap. The result was that in one stroke Cagney abolished both the convention of the pure hero and that of approximately numerical equipoise between vice and virtue.[18]

Tynan's points are well taken. In his essay, he goes on to discuss how other actors who often played nuanced villains or anti-heroes of the late 1930s and 1940s such as Humphrey Bogart, Dan Duryea, and Richard Widmark were influenced by Cagney's work in *The Public Enemy* and other 1930s efforts. Today, we can also add literally hundreds of film and television portrayals to this list from the work of actors such as Joe Pesci in *Goodfellas* (1990) and other Martin Scorsese films to James Gandolfini in the landmark HBO television series *The Sopranos* (1999–2007).

2. The Public Enemy *(1931)*

Cagney's portrayal of Tom Powers catapulted him into to the top-tiers of Hollywood stardom, where he remained until his retirement thirty years later. During his career, which included about sixty films in all, Cagney (1899–1986) played a variety of characters from comic roles to romantic leads, but he is perhaps best known for playing tough guys of various kinds, often hoodlums and gangland figures. After Tom Powers, some of best known of these roles were his Rocky Sullivan in Michael Curtiz's *Angels with Dirty Faces* (1938), Eddie Bartlett in Raoul Walsh's *The Roaring Twenties* (1939), Cody Jarrett in Walsh's *White Heat* (1949), and Martin Snyder Charles Vidor's *Love Me or Leave Me* (1955). He shined in all these roles, receiving Best Actor Academy Award nominations for *Angels with Dirty Faces* and *Love Me or Leave Me*. Today, however, many film aficionados reserve their highest praise for his riveting portrayal of Cody Jarrett, a murderous psychopath with an Oedipal complex, in *White Heat*.

Yet, among all of Cagney's film roles, his favorite was his turn as the multi-faceted entertainer George M. Cohan in Curtiz's musical extravaganza *Yankee Doodle Dandy* (1942). A brilliant dancer with a highly distinctive style who could also talk-sing his way through songs quite skillfully and gracefully, his bravura performance in this film led to both another Best Actor Academy Award nomination and his only competitive Oscar win.

One of the great ironies associated with Cagney's career, however, is that his genius for infusing humanity into villainous or other kinds of tough guy roles quickly typecast him, limiting him from opportunities, such as he had in *Yankee Doodle Dandy*, to dance and show other facets of his talent. He often wished he had had more such opportunities, and, over the decades, many fans of this immensely gifted entertainer have shared this sentiment.

A very private man, Cagney retired to his farm on Martha's Vineyard in Massachusetts to spend more time with his beloved wife, Frances (whom he called "Billie"), and family, and rarely appeared publicly after that. He was, however, coaxed out of retirement to play a key role in Milos Forman's film *Ragtime* (1981) and then, just two years before his death, to star in Joseph Sargent's made-for-TV movie *Terrible Joe Moran* (1984), receiving excellent reviews for both performances.

Throughout his career, Cagney was never one to intellectualize about what made his acting so special, preferring to leave that task to others. Once in the early 1960s, though, he did give some advice to Pamela Tiffin, a young actress working with him on the Billy Wilder film *One, Two, Three* (1961). When she asked him to share the secret of his success, he—in his no-nonsense way—said, "You walk in, plant yourself squarely on both feet, look the other fella in the eye, and tell the truth."[19]

*

With Cagney delivering such a commanding and ground-breaking performance in *The Public Enemy*, some observers have tended to be dismissive of the other actors in the film. While understandable, this isn't quite fair to them, or at least, several of them. For example, Donald Cook, who plays Tom's law-abiding brother Mike, makes the most of a largely thankless role, conveying both Mike's indignation at Tom and the frustration and pain he feels at not being able to get through to him. Beryl Mercer, while pretty much one note as Ma Powers, still plays her one note convincingly and, at times, movingly. As Paddy, Robert Emmett O'Connor is quite good at balancing his character's sleazy aspects with an under-layer of decency, especially near the end of the film when he admits to offering to leave the rackets if Schemer Burns will let Tom live. In smaller roles, Joan Blondell and Mae Clarke both work well as Matt and Tom's girlfriends. Blondell is excellent, for instance, when, in the wedding reception scene, she talks about how much marriage means to a woman.

The film's big acting disappointment, however, is the young Jean Harlow as Gwen. Although Harlow (1911–1937) would soon move on to bigger and better roles and top-tier stardom at MGM, she is beyond dreadful here: forced, affected, and totally unbelievable. The scene when she breaks up with Tom isn't only the worst in the film, but it is so much worse than any other scene that it seems to have been taken from a genuinely bad film from the period and spliced into *The Public Enemy* by mistake. Seeing Cagney, who is so good throughout the film, playing off Harlow, who is so bad in this scene, is beyond painful.

*

As the above appraisal of Harlow's performance suggests, *The Public Enemy* is by no means a perfect film. While Wellman's staging of many scenes, several of the acting performances, and the artful camera work of cinematographer Devereaux ("Dev") Jennings are excellent, the story and script—the combined work of Bright, Glasmon, and Thew—has its share of shortcomings.

One is the story's episodic nature. The plot often seems to be a series of events strung together rather than a natural progression of events with one leading logically to the next. This results in a certain choppiness at times.

Sometimes, too, situations are introduced and then simply dropped. A good example is when Paddy's girlfriend Jane (Mia Marvin) seduces Tom when Paddy insists that his gang members hide out at her place. The episode simply occurs and then leads nowhere. Paddy doesn't find out. Tom doesn't change. We never see or even hear about Jane again. Nada.

Finally, certain key points in the story are not sufficiently developed. One is the contrast between Tom and Matt's love lives. The writers seem to be suggesting that Tom's problems relating to Kitty and Gwen are manifestations of his psychopathic nature and, as a counterpoint, show Matt and Mamie's relationship as much happier and healthier, yet they don't sharpen the contrast enough to effectively make the point, and, as viewers, we are simply left with a vague suggestion.

To Bright and Glasmon's credit, however, the film benefits greatly because they based their original story on real-life events rather than resorting to stock ideas of what hoodlums are like and how they behave. Several of the film's most interesting scenes, such as the payback shooting of Nails Nathan's horse and the machine gun execution of Matt in the street in broad daylight, were based on real-life events that occurred in Chicago in the 1920s.[20] While outlandish, both have a definite ring of truth about them and work quite effectively on screen.

For their efforts, Bright and Glasmon received an Academy Award nomination in the Best Original Story category at the fourth awards ceremony held on November 10, 1931. It was *The Public Enemy*'s only Academy recognition.

*

With *The Public Enemy*, Wellman clearly hit his stride at Warner Brothers. This was his kind of gritty, uncompromising, darkly humorous film made his way, and it featured the star-making performance of James Cagney, an actor closely aligned with his worldview and approach to conveying it.

Although the two never worked together again, Cagney never forgot Wellman or the good fortune that came his way when they collaborated on the film. As Cagney said when he and Wellman appeared together on a television show in the 1950s, "Bill is not only imaginative, but he is also unorthodox." Then, after crediting Wellman as the key person in making the casting change that allowed him to play Tom Powers, he added, "And that was [my] first break. And, Bill, I will always be grateful."[21]

*

Cagney, we might add, was by no means the only major acting talent that Wellman helped launch to stardom. In fact, the director accomplished a similar feat in his very next film, one that starred another Hollywood newcomer recently arrived from Broadway, a twenty-three-year-old actress named Barbara Stanwyck.

3

"I'll kill the next one that says 'ethics' to me"
Night Nurse (1931)

After completing *The Public Enemy*, Wellman immediately plunged into another meaty project, an adaptation of a lurid 1930 novel called *Night Nurse*.

The result—a sassy, cynical, and sometimes disturbing screen version of the book—could very well be one of the most subversive films the director ever made, pre-Code or otherwise. It depicts a largely uncaring world in which the law, medical ethics, and other protocols designed to protect individuals and keep society from going off the rails are ineffective and often abused: a world in which corruption reigns, exploitation is pervasive, and—if they want to survive—people must pretty much fend for themselves.

The implications of this premise are quite intriguing. In a world such as this, where, for example, laws and codes are routinely disregarded and conventional enforcement is ineffective, is it right to break the law or disregard other widely held strictures in order to achieve a more just and/or humane result? If so, who decides what this result should be? And who decides what the best approach to achieving this result actually is?

In addition, *Night Nurse* is an amazingly well-crafted film. As was his habit by now, Wellman threw himself wholeheartedly into the effort, tightening, refining, and bringing greater cohesion to the script; arranging shots and scenes so that the film's visual design reinforces the narrative in striking, creative ways; and casting the best available actors for the film's key roles. Although it might seem rough and ragged around the edges on a first viewing, *Night Nurse* is one of those films that gets better each time we see it and notice more of the wonderful and sometimes very subtle touches Wellman has added to the experience.

Not incidentally, one of these "best available" actors was the twenty-

3. Night Nurse *(1931)*

three-year-old Barbara Stanwyck, who had earlier impressed the up-and-coming director Frank Capra at rival studio Columbia Pictures with her work in his films *Ladies of Leisure* (1930) and *The Miracle Woman* (1931). *Night Nurse* provides her with one of her earliest starring roles and is the first of five films she would make with Wellman during the 1930s and 1940s. The two got along famously, both noting throughout their lives the high regard they had for each other both professionally and personally. "He loved his work, and gave every bit of vitality and knowledge to it," Stanwyck said about Wellman more than a half-century after they made *Night Nurse* together. "I never saw him in a temper, [but] I imagine it would have been hell."[1]

Also in the cast were two other relative newcomers to featured film roles. One was the excellent Joan Blondell, who had only been making movies for about a year, but was already appearing in her tenth feature and her third for Wellman. The other was a bit player under contract with MGM on loan to Warner Brothers to play a small role in this film. His name was Clark Gable, and, before the end of 1931, his strong performances opposite MGM megastars Norma Shearer, Greta Garbo, and Joan Crawford in a succession of hit films would transform him into a megastar as well.

*

The story of *Night Nurse* begins with the original source material, the 1930 novel of the same title by actress, screenwriter, and novelist Grace Perkins (1900–1955), who wrote it, as she wrote much of her fiction, under the pen name of Dora Macy. Upon publication, the *New York Times* called the book "sordidly realistic," the *Times* reviewer adding that "such cheap and unpleasant stuff ... should never have been put forth at all."[2]

One reason Perkins was willing to put forth "such cheap and unpleasant stuff" was that it sold well. In the 1920s and 1930s, her work—which included stories and novels with such titillating titles as *Ex-Mistress*, *Promiscuous*, and *Public Sweetheart No. 1*—was in great demand. In addition to *Night Nurse*, several of her stories and novels were turned into films such as the comedy *No More Orchids* (1932) starring Carole Lombard and the drama *Torch Singer* (1933) starring Claudette Colbert.

Warner Brothers, which, at the time, also thrived on turning sordidly realistic subject matter into mass entertainment, quickly snatched up the rights to the novel and assigned screenwriters Charles Kenyon and Oliver H.P. Garrett to develop an adaptation. After this, Wellman took over, making numerous changes and putting his personal stamp on the narrative.

Both studio staff writers at the time, Kenyon and Garrett brought different experiences and perspectives to this assignment. Beginning in the silent era, Kenyon (1880–1961) was by now a long-time film industry veteran and would eventually contribute scripts to more than one hundred films, including such classics as *A Midsummer Night's Dream* (1935) and *Petrified Forest* (1936). A relative newcomer to screenwriting, Garrett (1894–1952) also worked at various times as a newspaper reporter and a film director. As a reporter, he also had the unusual distinction of conducting interviews with both Al Capone and Adolf Hitler.

The production was tightly budgeted at an estimated $260,000, and filming took place entirely at the Warner Brothers studios in Burbank in mid-1931. One of the very few hitches involved a casting change. Originally, James Cagney had been assigned to a supporting role. William Wellman, Jr., contends that he had been slated to play one of the hospital interns.[3] Film writer Wheeler Winston Dixon has said, however, that Cagney was to portray the villainous chauffeur, the role that was eventually assigned to Gable.[4] Whichever is the case, the change was made in light of the huge success of Cagney's breakout role in *The Public Enemy*. By this point, Warner Brothers executives saw him as the studio's hottest new star, an actor much too valuable to play small supporting roles any longer.

*

The film version of *Night Nurse* begins with a series of slice-of-life scenes set in a hospital. An ambulance races in with a new patient. An expectant father is anxious as his wife is wheeled into the delivery room. A patient is given privacy because he is dying. In the midst of all this, young Lora Hart (Stanwyck) is applying to enter the hospital's training program for nurses. At first, she is rejected because she hasn't earned her high school diploma. Soon, however, she accidentally encounters Dr. Bell (Charles Winninger), the hospital's chief administrator, who puts in a good word for her. Bowing to the doctor, the head nurse waives the high school requirement, admits Lora, and introduces her to another trainee and her new roommate, Maloney (Blondell). The two are quite opposite in nature, Lora world-wise but also idealistic and inspired by what she sees as a calling to help the sick, Maloney more self-involved and cynical. The pair, nevertheless, become fast friends.

Immediately, Lora assumes many of a nurse's duties: working in the maternity ward, the emergency room, and elsewhere in the hospital. While in emergency, she encounters an extremely likable bootlegger named Mortie (Ben Lyon), and treats him for a gunshot wound. He's clearly smitten with her and quite charming, asking if she could simply not report this incident, a legal requirement. She is sympathetic but hesitant, saying:

> LORA: Why, we have professional ethics.
> MORTIE: Yea, that goes for my line, too.

3. Night Nurse (1931)

Bootlegger Mortie (Ben Lyon) tries to sweet-talk his nurse, Lora Hart (Barbara Stanwyck, right), out of reporting his gunshot wound as Lora's colleague and friend, Maloney (Joan Blondell), skeptically looks on in *Night Nurse* (Warner Bros. Album/Alamy Stock Photo).

> LORA: The things my profession keeps quiet about are what we believe is for the public's own good.
> MORTIE: Yea, ditto!

Ultimately, and at great risk to herself, however, she agrees not to report the wound, and he is very appreciative, shaking her hand and calling her "my pal."

Soon, it's graduation day, and, along with the other newly certified nurses, both Lora and Maloney recite the "Florence Nightingale Pledge," their commitment to adhere to the high ideals and strict standards of conduct required of all nurses. Lora takes this pledge quite seriously. Maloney chews gum throughout.

Lora gets her first assignment as a fully certified nurse: work on the night shift caring for the two young Ritchie girls, Nanny and Desney, in their home. Almost immediately, she realizes that a great deal is not right there. The family is wealthy, yet the two girls are both suffering from malnutrition and anemia. The deeper Lora digs into the situation, the more horrifying it becomes to her. The children's father and other sister are dead. Their mother, a hopeless alcoholic, spends her time drinking and partying. The physician in charge of the case, Dr. Ranger (Ralf Harolde), is ordering that the two girls receive as little nourishment as possible. And a brute of a chauffeur named Nick (Gable) is there to enforce the doctor's orders. Eventually, Lora goes to Dr. Ranger and realizes that he is both behind some dark scheme and, by his body language, also seems to be a serious drug (perhaps cocaine) user. Soon, some extra money unexpectedly comes her way. She immediately suspects that it's to provide incentive to keep her mouth shut and shows the money to Maloney:

LORA: It's funny what people think money will do, isn't it?
MALONEY: Yea, keeping our noses out of patients' private affairs is part of our professional ethics.
LORA: I'll kill the next one that says "ethics" to me.
MALONEY: Says you.
LORA: Yea, says me in a big way, sister.

Out of desperation, Lora then sees Dr. Bell, who had previously treated the girls but now tells her that, for ethical reasons, he can't interfere in another doctor's case. She doesn't understand, saying that if the patients are the victims here, someone has to do something. Eventually, Dr. Bell relents, advising Lora to go back and watch the girls and suggesting, that, between the two of them, they will find a way to protect them.

Lora takes Bell's advice, but, despite her help, Nanny becomes very weak and Lora fears that she will die. Serendipitously, Mortie drops by the house with some liquor for Mrs. Ritchie's perpetual party, reconnects with Lora, and begins to help her out. Soon, Lora also learns the reason behind the plot to harm the two girls. When their father died, he'd left them a trust fund, and, with Dr. Ranger's help, Nick is deliberately starving them to death (and may have also had a hand in the third sister's death) so the trust fund can go to Mrs. Ritchey, whom Nick would then marry.

After trying to reach Dr. Ranger, Lora asks Mortie to get Dr. Bell to come to look at Nanny. Bell arrives, sees that Nanny is near death, and tries to take her to the hospital. Learning about this, Nick knocks him out. Mortie, however, threatens Nick with what might be a gun in his pocket, and Nick backs off. Then, in a last-ditch effort to save Nanny, Dr. Bell—with Lora, who has the same blood type, volunteering—gives Nanny a blood transfusion at the house. Happily, it is successful.

The next day, in the thick of city traffic, Mortie and Lora chat in his car. As Lora mentions that she worries about the impact the scandal resulting from Nick's imminent arrest will have on the Ritchey girls, they see an ambulance, with siren blaring, passing them. Coyly, Mortie suggests that Nick might not be arrested. When Lora asks why, Mortie adds that he was talking to a couple of guys last night and just happened to mention that he didn't like Nick.

The film immediately cuts to the inside of the ambulance, the camera placed right behind the front seat in a way reminiscent to the first shots at the beginning of the film. Again, the ambulance stops at the same hospital. This time, though, the ambulance attendant tells the hospital attendant that this delivery is for the hospital's morgue, that it seems that the man inside had been the victim of a gangland hit. The hospital attendant asks if this man could have been a bootlegger. The ambulance attendant doubts it, saying that the man was wearing a chauffeur's uniform.

*

Opening in theaters on August 8, 1931, *Night Nurse* was accompanied by quite a provocative promotional campaign. One ad appearing in a newspaper from Schenectady, New York, led with the headline, "Tells the Naked Truth About Happenings in the Dead of Night!"[5] Another ad, one that ran in an East Lansing, Michigan, newspaper read, "Hot from the diary of a night nurse who 'has seen everything!' She risks all to blast the veil of mystery from the night watch!"[6] The campaign certainly helped to lure viewers into theaters, and the film eventually became, along with *The Public Enemy*, one of Warner Brothers' top-grossing films for 1931.

Night Nurse wasn't quite as effective at winning over the critics of the time, however, receiving decidedly mixed notices. The reviewer for the *New York Times*, for example, called it "a potpourri of various things,"[7] ending the piece with the very lukewarm observation, "last night's audience seemed to like parts of *Night Nurse*. At times it is exciting."[8] *Variety* took a somewhat dimmer view, calling the film "a conglomeration of exaggerations, often bordering on serial dramatics," and chiding Wellman for not doing much "with this chaotic subject matter."[9] While conceding that Blondell and Charles Winninger gave "legitimate performances," the reviewer also disparaged Stanwyck's work, saying that she played "her dancehall type of girl on one note throughout" and adding that her effort was "shy of [the] shading [needed] to lend her performance some color."[10]

*

From a twenty-first-century vantage point, however, there seems to have been a seismic shift in critical and audience attitudes toward *Night Nurse*. Writing for the Turner Classic Movies website, for example, Jeff Stafford observes:

> Often overlooked as a minor feature in the collective careers of Barbara Stanwyck, Clark Gable, and director William Wellman, *Night Nurse* is actually more engrossing than some of their more highly regarded films. For one thing,

the often-sordid subject matter is directed with considerable verve. Wellman punches up the film's raciness with a steady stream of double entendre wisecracks, mostly delivered by Stanwyck and fellow compatriot Joan Blondell as they parade around in various stages of undress. The violence in the film is rather strong for the period as well.... More controversial was the depiction of the film's villains—so callous they could murder children for profit—and the movie's pro-vengeance ending, which suggested that the police and the courts were completely ineffective in dealing with certain unlawful situations.[11]

Stafford, of course, is by no means alone in his positive assessment. Pre-Code historian Danny Reid notes, "I wholly believe there are few [films] I've seen that are as infectiously fun and crazy as 1931's *Night Nurse*. It's a deceptively tight B-movie, filled to the brim with everything that makes pre–Code fun while toying with social issues and never losing an ounce of momentum.... Director William A. Wellman has concocted a roller coaster for the ages."[12] Film writer Veronica Magdalena adds, "*Night Nurse* could easily be skipped over as an unassuming B-movie upon first glance, but it reveals a refined, compelling storyline with both thrilling and heartfelt tender moments. It is a welcome indulgence and a gratifying, quintessential pre–Code."[13] Finally, among various online posts about *Night Nurse*, one, written by a real-life pediatric night nurse, especially stands out:

> *Night Nurse* is my favorite film—in a big way, sister! It does help to be an actual pediatric night nurse to understand this movie to its full potential. The camp is both intentional and unintentional. The movie has a rebel flair with the nurses mouthing off to authority and even befriending a bootlegger.... I own the video and have passed it along to co-workers who are also pediatric night nurses, and it has become a cult favorite amongst my colleagues.[14]

*

A big reason why appreciation for *Night Nurse* has grown considerably over time has been a growing appreciation for Wellman's many contributions to the film. From the first scenes to the last, we can see his imprint throughout.

One way Wellman significantly improved the material was by bringing more cohesion to the narrative. As originally conceived, *Night Nurse* is effectively two different stories, the first Lora's experiences as a nursing trainee (the film's first twenty-five minutes) and the second her crusade to save the Ritchey girls from being starved to death (the film's last forty-five minutes). To make these seem more like one continuous story, Wellman makes several elements of the hospital sequences integral to the Ritchey home sequences. These include the inclusion of key characters such as Maloney, Dr. Bell, and Mortie to help advance the plot as well as such

3. Night Nurse (1931)

Wellman-esque verbal touches as Mortie's repeated use of the phrase "my pal" to express his appreciation to/affection for Lora and, of course, the frequent use of the word "ethics" to mean its opposite. These also include some interesting plot twists and visual touches. One of the most fascinating of these is the dramatic focus on the ambulance bringing someone to the hospital at both the very beginning and the very end of the story. The first time, the ambulance brings a man who may become a patient for an aspiring nurse such as Lora. The second time, it brings the body of Nick, whom Lora's friend Mortie arranged to have killed. As well as giving the film added cohesion, this juxtaposition provides it with quite a satisfying sense of closure.

Another way Wellman improved on the material was his fluid use of the camera throughout the film. As previously noted, in the first days of the "talkies," when most films were static and stagy because of the cumbersome early sound technology, he kept the camera moving. And, as an early user of the mobile "boom" microphone,[15] he kept the sound recording apparatus moving right along with it.

Still another way is Wellman's infusion of his characteristically cynical, wisecracking dialogue into the script. And, perhaps because Blondell was so good at delivering these kinds of lines, her character gets more than her fair share of them. In one very funny scene just after they first meet, for example, Lora and Maloney are talking when a flirty intern comes up and mentions that he's just come from the delivery room:

> MALONEY: (to intern) What are you doing here, baby frightener?
> INTERN: Sometimes I don't like you, Maloney.
> MALONEY: If only I could make that permanent.

After the intern leaves, Maloney turns to Lora:

> MALONEY: Take my tip and keep away from interns. They're like cancer. The disease is known but not the cure.

In addition, Wellman provides a variety of signature pre-Code eye-openers that give the film an unusually contemporary feel and that even modern viewers sometimes find startling to watch. Among these are a few "cheesecake" scenes with Stanwyck and Blondell wearing only their lingerie, moments of harsh violence, and a moment when Stanwyck's Lora—looking at the drunken Mrs. Ritchey passed out on the floor—mutters in disgust, "You mother...!" We can argue whether or not these touches improve the film artistically, but they certainly give it added immediacy and authenticity, strengths that modern audiences readily appreciate.

Finally, underscoring all of these Wellman contributions is his ability to infuse *Night Nurse* with his very distinctive blend of cynicism and humanity, giving the film a very cohesive and Wellman-esque worldview. Yes, society, especially in the economically depressed, pervasively corrupt early 1930s, is clearly in trouble. And yes, we often cannot count on the people who are employed to act in the best interests of others to do so. But, despite all this, we all still have a moral obligation to do what we can to help right wrongs. But then, for example, does this mean going as far as Mortie does when he puts the wheels in motion for Nick's murder? For Wellman, this might just be an open question that the film's viewers must decide for themselves.

Overall, Wellman brought an enormous amount of his artistry and of himself to *Night Nurse*. The only quibbles we might have are a couple of the scenes with the perpetually drunk Mrs. Ritchey, especially the scene in which she defends the evil Dr. Ranger. They are longer and more repetitious than they need to be, and it's a shame that Wellman and his editor, Edward McDermott, didn't trim them more. But, as noted, these are only quibbles.

*

In addition to Wellman, several other contributors, namely the key actors, made notable contributions to *Night Nurse*.

Heading the list, of course, is Barbara Stanwyck in a very early role in what would eventually be a film and television career that would continue for another fifty-five years. Although *Variety*, in its 1931 review, chided her for the lack of "shading" in her lead turn in *Night Nurse*, the vast majority of contemporary film historians and aficionados view this performance, as well as most of her other pre–Code work, in a much more favorable light. As Mick LaSalle has noted, "If you've never seen Stanwyck in a pre–Code film, you've never seen Stanwyck.... Never in her career, including [Billy Wilder's 1944 film noir] *Double Indemnity*, was she ever as hard-boiled as she was in the early 1930s. She had a wonderful quality of being both incredibly cool and yet blazingly passionate. Her cynicism was profound, and then, without warning, she would explode into shrieking, sobbing."[16]

Today, Stanwyck (1907–1990) is widely regarded as one of the best—if not *the* best—actress of Hollywood's "classic" studio era, a period extending from the 1930s through 1950s.

Orphaned when she was just four years old and partially raised in foster homes, Stanwyck debuted in the chorus of the Ziegfeld Follies revue in 1923 at age sixteen, played the lead role in the hit Broadway play *Burlesque* at twenty, moved to Hollywood, and, at twenty-three, was starring in feature films. *Night Nurse*, made soon afterward, was only her fourth lead role. And, along with other early–1930s Stanwyck efforts such as Capra's

3. Night Nurse (1931)

The Miracle Woman and *The Bitter Tea of General Yen* (1933), and Alfred E. Green's *Baby Face*, her portrayal of Lora Hart stands as one of the best examples of her pre–Code work.

In an era in which many actors gave mannered, self-conscious performances, Stanwyck was known—and widely regarded—for the naturalness, directness, and honesty she brought to each of her roles, and, in *Night Nurse*, this is certainly the case. Rather than playing Lora, she literally becomes Lora, convincingly conveying a complex young woman's many sides. Lora is idealistic, but also practical, especially when it comes to stretching the truth or bending the rules to help others. She is serious, especially about her work and the welfare of others, but also playful and fun-loving with friends such as Maloney and Mortie. She is sensitive and kind, but also tough and quick to express her outrage at wrongdoing and to stand up to intimidating, and perhaps even life-threatening, opposition. She is, ultimately, a very well-rounded character, one who's made all the more real by the genuine and wholehearted emotional investment Stanwyck puts into her.

Stanwyck, who, as noted earlier, got along famously with the sometimes-cantankerous Wellman, would soon work with him in two pre–Code films released in 1932, *So Big* and *The Purchase Price*, and then later on two other films, the western *The Great Man's Lady* (1942) and the comedy-mystery *Lady of Burlesque* (1943). Nominated for the Best Actress Academy Award for four performances—King Vidor's *Stella Dallas* (1937), Howard Hawks' *Ball of Fire* (1941), *Double Indemnity* (1944), and Anatole Litvak's *Sorry, Wrong Number* (1948)—she never won a competitive Oscar. She did, however, receive an Academy Honorary Award for her body of work in 1982. And, in 1987, she was only the third woman (after Bette Davis and Lillian Gish) to receive the American Film Institute's much coveted Lifetime Achievement Award. In 1960, about the time her film career was winding down, she moved to television, where she worked off and on for another twenty-five years and, in the process, won three Emmy Awards for her acting. Among her television projects, she is probably best remembered today for her starring role in the hit western series *The Big Valley* (1965–1969).

As Stanwyck's sidekick Maloney, Joan Blondell excellently provides a cynical counterpoint to Stanwyck's Lora. Maloney is not as complex a character as Lora, but Blondell infuses into her a basic decency to go along with the cynicism. In addition, she gives the character the kind of energy and charm that make her quite appealing. As an acting duo, Stanwyck and Blondell have great chemistry and complement each other extremely well. While they both appeared in Warner Brothers' *Illicit*, a film released earlier in 1931, they never appeared together in a film after *Night Nurse*.

And this is a shame. They excelled as buddies and would have been great, for example, as the title characters in 1991's *Thelma & Louise*. (But then they were both born about fifty years too early to be considered for that opportunity!)

A film actress for less than a year when she made *Night Nurse*, Blondell (1906–1979) had come to Hollywood from New York in 1930, where she had been born into a vaudeville family and then worked as a fashion model, circus hand, and store clerk before turning to stage acting in the late 1920s. There, she soon achieved almost-instant success, co-starring with James Cagney in the Broadway play *Penny Arcade* (1930). The play had a short run, but the enormously popular singer and actor Al Jolson saw it, loved it, bought the film rights, and insisted upon bringing both Cagney and Blondell to Hollywood to act in the film adaptation. Often playing smart, sassy, sexy, and world-wise women, she fit the pre–Code sensibility quite well and would go on to appear in a total of thirty-two films during the pre–Code era, mostly in meaty supporting roles such as Maloney.

Blondell's star began to fade in the 1940s, but she continued to work steadily in character roles in films, occasionally in the theater, and increasingly on television, always delivering strong, vivid portrayals. Just a few of her post–pre–Code highlights include her performances in Edmond Goulding's noir masterpiece *Nightmare Alley* (1947); Curtis Bernhardt's historical drama *The Blue Veil* (1951), for which she received a Best Supporting Actress Oscar nomination; and Norman Jewison's well-received drama *The Cincinnati Kid* (1965), for which she won the National Board of Review's award for Best Supporting Actress and received a Golden Globe nomination for Best Supporting Actress—Motion Picture.

The other fabled Hollywood figure to appear in *Night Nurse* was, of course, Clark Gable as Nick, the evil chauffeur, one of the last small roles he would play before becoming a star in his own right. Unlike Stanwyck and Blondell, who quickly reached stardom once they had started making movies, Gable (1901–1960) had spent a decade training to be an actor, acting on the stage, and working as an extra and bit player in silent films and very early talkies. In 1930, Warner Brothers had tested him for a role in its gangster film *Little Caesar* and quickly rejected him, Darryl Zanuck famously declaring, "His ears are too big and he looks like an ape."[17] Soon afterward, though, Gable was signed by MGM, whose production head, Irving Thalberg, clearly saw greater star potential in him. Before this potential was fully realized, however, he was loaned back to Warner Brothers for the small but key role in *Night Nurse*.

Although Zanuck might not have thought much of Gable, at least at this point in the actor's career, it's hard to imagine while watching *Night Nurse* that Wellman shared his boss' lack of enthusiasm. In the film,

3. Night Nurse *(1931)* 59

As Nick, the villainous chauffeur in *Night Nurse*, the young Clark Gable (left) is an imposing force to be reckoned with for Ben Lyons's Mortie, young Betty Jane Graham's Desney, and Barbara Stanwyck's Lora (Warner Bros. Photo 12/ Alamy Stock Photo).

Gable's on-screen magnetism is riveting and his portrayal of a human being without any redeeming character traits is, at times, frightening.

One fascinating element in the film, in fact, is the way Wellman and veteran cinematographer Barney McGill design Nick's entrance to give it maximum impact. Nick enters just as one of Mrs. Ritchey's suitors tries to put the moves on Lora. He quickly pulls the suitor off Lora, punches him, and orders Lora to give Mrs. Ritchey a "stomach wash," presumably to reduce the amount of alcohol in her system. What's especially interesting here is not what's said or done but how the visuals are planned to spark viewer curiosity about this just-introduced character. For example, we don't see Nick's face until after he pulls the man off Lora and slugs him. In addition, even though Nick tells Lora he is the chauffeur, he is wearing what appears to be an expensive Asian dressing robe. And he has just come from his own room in the house, a room not in the servants' quarters but just down the hall, suggesting that, in addition to performing his chauffeur's duties, he might be providing sexual services for Mrs. Ritchey. (A few moments later, when Mrs. Ritchey begs him to kiss her, this suspicion is confirmed.) Finally, when Nick tells Lora his name, the camera moves quickly to his face in a way reminiscent of John Wayne's star-making entrance in John Ford's classic *Stagecoach* (1939). Could Wellman have sensed that there was something really special about Gable and, therefore, worthy of such a carefully orchestrated entrance? Perhaps. Or perhaps he simply wanted to give the story's villain as much of a build-up as possible. In either case, the succession of shots works wonderfully here. Both Nick and Gable get a great introduction.

Gable, who was soon to supplant Douglas Fairbanks, Sr., as "the King of Hollywood," went on, of course, to be one of the towering figures of the U.S. film industry's classic era, starring or featured in more than sixty films over the next thirty years, receiving three Best Actor Academy Award nominations, and winning an Oscar for his work in Frank Capra's comedy classic *It Happened One Night* (1934). Just a few of his many memorable films include Frank Lloyd's *Mutiny on the Bounty* (1935), W.S. Van Dyke's *San Francisco* (1936), Victor Fleming's *Gone with the Wind* (1939), and John Huston's *The Misfits* (1961).

Two other performances in *Night Nurse* also deserve special mentions. One is Ben Lyon as Mortie, who quite possibly might be the most charming and likeable bootlegger and instigator of a gangland murder ever to appear in a film. What makes Mortie so likeable, of course, is his boyish attraction to Lora and the enthusiasm he brings to helping her out in all the ways that he does, and Lyon pulls the role off quite handily. A moderately successful character player in 1930s films, Lyon (1901–1979) later became an executive at Twentieth Century–Fox, where his great claim to fame came in 1946 when he saw the star potential in a young actress named Norma Jean Dougherty. After arranging a successful screen test for her, he signed her to her first studio contract with the new name of Marilyn Monroe. The other actor deserving of special mention is Charles Winninger as the basically decent but still safe and staid Dr. Bell. At first skeptical of Lora's claims against Dr. Ranger and hesitant to help, Bell is eventually persuaded to take a major risk himself, and Winninger conveys the character's change of heart with great conviction and understated emotion. It is a fine supporting turn. Often cast in comedies and musicals, Winninger (1884–1969), an excellent and versatile character actor, was active in films and then television from 1915 to 1960. In all that time, he played the lead in only one film, the wise and wily Judge William ("Billy") Priest in John Ford's memorable comedy-drama *The Sun Shines Bright* (1953).

*

Today, *Night Nurse* remains a pre-Code staple, one of the Hollywood films made during this short, highly productive, and incredibly vital era that has become essential viewing for classic film aficionados. It is essential, of course, because it speaks across the decades through its darkly humorous point of view; its honesty, especially in regard to human behavior; and, perhaps above all, its innate—and fiercely unsentimental—humanity. We like it, of course, because it constantly reminds us about our own experiences, people we've come across, and the very imperfect twenty-first-century world we inhabit.

4

"One move outta' you and I'll smear your guts on your own wallpaper"
The Star Witness (1931)

Wellman's next release, *The Star Witness*, is a fascinating curiosity. On one hand, it's a serious and all-too-real crime drama about ordinary people who witness a gangland double murder, learn that testifying against the chief mob culprit will involve great risks, and struggle to find the courage to take those risks. On the other, it's a story that betrays its own very promising premise, backing away from the challenging issues it presents and resorting to what we disparagingly call a "Hollywood ending." Reflecting this lack of conviction, the film often vacillates between stark Wellman-esque realism, which at times is quite striking and effective, and one important character's clownish, mugging presence, which greatly diminishes the story's credibility and dramatic impact.

This is all quite unfortunate, because in many respects *The Star Witness* has the ingredients that could have made it a fine addition in the impressive early–1930s Warner Brothers grit-and-realism tradition that includes such electrifying films as *Scarface* and *I Am a Fugitive from a Chain Gang*. Instead, it is now generally considered one of Wellman's lesser pre–Code efforts, perhaps the least notable release of the director's banner year of 1931.

*

Unlike *The Public Enemy* and *Night Nurse*, which are adaptations of existing fictional stories, *The Star Witness* is based on an original scenario by two writer-producers, Lucien Hubbard and Bud Barsky, who often worked on Warner Brothers projects at the time. Their idea was intriguing: a crime story that centered, not so much on criminals or the police, but

4. The Star Witness *(1931)*

on innocent people who essentially become pawns in the power struggle between mobsters and law enforcement. Once the scenario was approved, Hubbard developed the screenplay.

Of the two writer-producers, Hubbard (1888–1971) is far better known today, mainly for producing *Wings* at Paramount in 1927 and subsequently picking up the very first Academy Award for Best Picture in 1929. During the 1930s, he would focus less on writing and more on serving in various production capacities. In those roles, he worked again with Wellman on such pre–Code films as *So Big* (as associate producer) and *Midnight Mary* (as producer). After *The Star Witness*, Barsky (1891–1967) took on various roles ranging from independent producer to general manager at Columbia Pictures.

According to film writer Stephanie Thames, *The Star Witness* had originally been slated to be Wellman's first film at Warner Brothers but soon encountered what she called, "some changes in development."[1] These, in turn, led to significant scheduling delays prior to shooting. So, in the meantime, the studio put Wellman to work on other projects, and, instead of being the director's first Warner Brothers release, *The Star Witness* turned out to be his fifth.

To handle the cinematography on *The Star Witness*, Wellman turned to veteran cameraman James Van Trees, with whom he would again collaborate on three 1933 releases, *Lilly Turner*, *Heroes for Sale*, and *Midnight Mary*, as well as the 1935 drama *Stingaree*. Very much in demand over a long career, Van Trees worked on more than 170 films between 1916 and 1947 and then moved to television, where he filmed hundreds of episodes of numerous shows until the early 1960s. Among his credits are installments of such classic series such as *I Married Joan*, *The George Burns and Gracie Allen Show*, and *The Many Loves of Dobie Gillis*.

Guided by Wellman's highly efficient, no-nonsense approach to shooting, the production phase of *The Star Witness*, which likely took place in the spring and early summer of 1931, proceeded relatively quickly and smoothly. The only complaint Wellman ever voiced was about one of the film's actors, Charles "Chic" Sale, whom he called "tough to handle, late on the set, complaining about everything and everyone."[2] According to the director, he told Sale that, if he didn't change his attitude, he'd knock him about. The warning apparently got through, and, after that, Sale, as Wellman noted, "behaved himself."[3]

*

The Star Witness opens as the Leeds family sits down for dinner in their very ordinary home in a large unnamed U.S. city. They include Pa Leeds (Grant Mitchell), Ma Leeds (Frances Starr), and their four children, a young adult man and woman and two young boys. In the middle of the proceedings, fife-playing Grandpa Summerille (Sale), visiting from the local old soldier's home, joins them. Then, soon afterward, they hear a ruckus outside and rush to the window just in time to see the notorious gangster Maxey Campo (Ralph Ince) shooting two men in the street.

Then, in an almost surreal turn of events, Maxey and his henchmen, in search of an escape route from the crime scene, enter the Leeds' home with guns drawn. "One move outta' you,'" Maxey tells the family members, "and I'll smear your guts on your own wallpaper." Soon, the criminals leave by the back door and are gone.

The next day, the Leeds family and Grandpa Summerill meet with District Attorney Whitlock (Walter Huston). An incensed Whitlock tells the family that the two men Campo killed worked for his office, that he wants to send the gangster to the electric chair, and that he needs the help of the family to convict him. The members agree to cooperate, all seeming quite naïve about the possible consequences of doing so, and Whitlock vows to put the family in protective custody. Before this happens, though,

With no other options, District Attorney Whitlock (Walter Huston, left) must ultimately rely on the testimony of Grandpa Summerill (Chic Sale) to help convict the murderous gangster Maxey Campo in *The Star Witness* (Warner Bros./Photofest).

4. The Star Witness *(1931)*

Pa Leeds is kidnapped and brutally beaten. Immediately, Whitlock confines all the Leeds family members to their home and assigns officers to guard them day and night. Now, however, the family members begin to disagree about whether or not to testify. Most of them, fearing for their safety, are torn about what to do, but Grandpa, seeing it as his patriotic duty, is adamant about telling the truth, regardless of the consequences.

Then, on the day that Campo is to be indicted, one of the young sons, Donny, slips out of the house to play baseball. Campo's henchmen kidnap him and phone the Leeds family, threatening to kill Donny if any of them identifies Campo at the hearing. Whitlock's men have traced the kidnappers' call to a specific area of the city, however, and soon the police are conducting a massive search for Donny. Hearing where the police are focused, Grandpa slips out to conduct his own search. As the hunt continues, the other Leeds family members change their stories about what they saw the night Campo gunned down the two men. Now, the only one who will tell the truth is Grandpa, and Whitlock has no idea where he is.

Meanwhile, Grandpa walks about the search area playing his fife in hopes that Donny will recognize it and somehow signal him. Then, as Donny talks baseball with one of his captors in the room where he is being held, he hears the fife, recognizes who is playing it, and throws his baseball through a window. Grandpa sees the ball, recognizes it as Donny's, and leads the police to the room. After a gun battle, Donny and Grandpa are rushed to the indictment hearing and Grandpa testifies, sealing Campo's eventual conviction and execution.

In the very last scene, Grandpa returns to the old soldier's home and, along the way, passes what appears to be a military cemetery. He looks out at the rows of headstones, all of them, the scene suggests, commemorating proud Americans who, like him, did their duty to their country, sometimes taking great risks to help make the world a better place.

*

On August 3, 1931, *The Star Witness* opened in New York City to both enthusiastic crowds and positive reviews.

The crowds were partially the result of a real-life incident that had occurred in New York's Harlem neighborhood just a few days earlier, on July 28. As a local gangster, Vincent "Mad Dog" Coll, was trying to kidnap a member of a rival gang, a shoot-out occurred. Caught in the crossfire were a number of children; one, just five years old, was killed; and others were wounded. When police tried to get statements from family members who witnessed the shootings, however, those people, fearing for their own lives, refused to cooperate. The event generated enormous press coverage and, within days—as the saying goes—the whole town was talking about it.

Keenly aware of the similarities between *The Star Witness* and this real-life shooting, Warner Brothers decided to generate some press coverage of its own. Immediately, the studio moved up the film's original New York release date and pledged to turn over all the proceeds from the film's first two screenings at the Winter Garden Theater on Broadway to the families of the victims. As Stephanie Thames notes, "This sensational ploy worked like a charm."[4] People flocked to the theater, and soon the film became one of Warner Brothers' biggest hits of the year.

Adding to the public's embrace of *The Star Witness*, the critics were generally quite positive. *Film Daily*, for example, declared the film a "sure-fire box-office smash."[5] And, in his review for the *New York Times*, Mordaunt Hall called it "a well-knit melodrama with an effective vein of sentiment," adding that, "as an entertainment, it is highly successful." He also praised several of the acting performances, calling Chic Sales' Grandpa "a capital characterization" and noting that, as Pa Leeds, Grant Mitchell "gives a splendid interpretation."[6] The following year, the film also received Academy Awards recognition when Lucien Hubbard was nominated for his work on the original story.

*

Unlike *Night Nurse*, which initially received tepid reviews and is now considered a pre–Code classic, *The Star Witness*, which received mostly positive reviews in 1931, has not fared nearly as well in the twenty-first century. As pre–Code historian Danny Reid notes, "Unfortunately, the film shies away from risks to make it a truly shocking or outstanding production.… While Wellman's films usually have a harder edge, driven by Warner's more reality-driven sensibilities, *The Star Witness* feels unusually neutered."[7] And, although film writer Glenn Erickson praises Wellman's "direct style" in the film, he also finds the story's climax, when Sale's Grandpa goes after the gangsters with gun in hand, to be "almost as simplistic as a Popeye cartoon."[8] Numerous online bloggers have also posted rather harsh evaluations. One, for example, finds the film "off-putting" because "its message is both unclear and inconsistent" and because of Grandpa's xenophobic rants about the threat to real Americans posed by "dang dirty foreigner" criminals (most likely references to gangsters of Italian descent).[9] Another blogger notes how the film "suffers from inept writing and the irritating presence of Chic Sales."[10] Still another goes all out, saying, "[T]his early crime drama with a sermonizing Walter Huston as a D.A., is so full of annoying and clichéd moments that it seems far longer than its sixty-eight-minute running time. Everything about it is so dated, it's hard to recommend it as anything but a museum piece."[11]

Many of these points are well taken.

4. The Star Witness *(1931)*

One distinctively pre–Code element of *The Star Witness* that remains shocking even to today's audiences is its uncompromising depiction of violence in scenes such as this, as the villainous Maxey Campo (Ralph Ince) viciously beats up the helpless Pa Leeds (Grant Mitchell) (Warner Bros./Photofest).

Wellman, for example, does handle a number of scenes in *The Star Witness* with great aplomb.

Perhaps the most compelling is the sequence when the naïve Pa Leeds is kidnapped by members of Campo's gang and, after he refuses to take a bribe, brutally beaten. The scene when one thug takes Pa by the legs and repeatedly swings his torso against a wall as the others look on impassively is chilling, an excellent example of the lengths to which filmmakers such as Wellman went during the pre–Code era to depict horrific violence as realistically as decorum would permit.

Of special note in these scenes, too, is actor Grant Mitchell's superb portrayal of the absolutely terrified Pa Leeds. This relatively sheltered and clueless character, a man who smugly prides himself on being a model father and valued company man, has never even imagined being subjected to such brutality. And the stark, overwhelming fear Mitchell conveys here is strikingly real. Especially for film viewers used to seeing this actor, who often played bland characters in small-to-medium-size supporting roles, these scenes are quite shocking.

A familiar face for many fans of classic Hollywood films, Mitchell (1874–1957) was the son of American Civil War general John G. Mitchell and, on his father's side, a great nephew of U.S. president Rutherford B. Hayes. After graduating from Harvard Law School, he initially worked as an attorney but soon gravitated toward a life-long love, the theater, where, in 1902, he began acting professionally. With the coming of sound, he relocated to Hollywood where, during the 1930s and 1940s, he appeared in more than 125 films. Obviously impressed with Mitchell's work in *The Star Witness* (only his second appearance in a talking picture), Wellman recruited him to play supporting roles in four of his later Warner Brothers pre–Code efforts: *Central Airport, Lilly Turner, Heroes for Sale,* and *Wild Boys of the Road.*

Another scene in *The Star Witness* that Wellman handles quite well comes at the very end of the film. As Grandpa passes the military cemetery on his way back to the old soldier's home, he looks at the graves of all those other people, who, like him, risked their lives for their country and what it stands for, and non-verbally communicates a sense of solidarity with them. The sentiment here might seem a bit ham-fisted to some contemporary viewers, but the way it is executed is quite simple and elegant— very much a Wellman touch.

In addition, the director does an exceptional job of staging and shooting *The Star Witness'* city street action scenes and montages. Especially effective is the montage late in the film that depicts the massive search for the kidnapped Donny. Considering the great complexity involved in the filming of many of these scenes, they are quite well orchestrated.

Altogether, there is much about this film that is worth seeing and thinking about.

On the other side of the ledger, however, *The Star Witness* also has more than its share of shortcomings.

Heading the list is the problematic story and script by Hubbard and Barsky. While the premise is intriguing, the overall story lacks focus and depth and can at times come across as both preachy and xenophobic.

First, is this film a serious drama or not? Most of the story is told in a very serious vein. People, after all, have been killed and other people's lives are now being threatened. Yet, in the midst of all of this is Grandpa Summerill, a contrived and unbelievable caricature who embodies just about every "dag-nabbit" geezer cliché there is. Rather than being a pivotal figure in a drama that is purportedly tackling life-and-death issues, he actually is much closer to the Popeye character that Glenn Erickson likens him to.

Second, the story's other pivotal character, District Attorney Whitlock, is also grossly underdeveloped. Portrayed by the usually excellent

Walter Huston (who gets top billing in the film), Whitlock is one note throughout: an obsessed law-and-order man who, curiously, shows surprisingly little empathy for the members of the distraught Leeds family.

Third, largely because Grandpa and Whitlock lack any real depth or complexity, they essentially become sermonizing mouthpieces for specific points of view—Grandpa saying that people have to take risks to help make the world a better place, and Whitlock, in a similar vein, saying that people have a civic duty to help him take the bad guys off the streets. With little more to say, both characters spend much of the film saying the same things over and over again and, in the process, becoming quite tedious.

Incidentally, it's especially frustrating to see an actor of Walter Huston's caliber stuck in the thankless role of Whitlock. During his twenty years in Hollywood, Huston (1883–1950)—the father of legendary director-writer-actor John Huston and grandfather of actors Angelica and Danny Huston—gave many memorable performances, along the way receiving four Academy Award nominations and one Oscar for his work. In *The Star Witness*, he gamely tries to make the most he can out of the role, but he simply does not have much to work with and the character falls flat.

Finally, Grandpa's xenophobia, which is quite blatant throughout the film, is never called into question by any of the other characters. This attitude may have been generally acceptable to, or at least more easily tolerated by, moviegoers in 1931, but today it simply comes across as highly prejudiced immigrant bashing. Interestingly, one online blogger has also pointed out a curious inconsistency related to this story element. "What makes this inherently offensive storyline ... very strange," the blogger notes, "is that not a single one of the mobsters that we hear speak has an accent that suggests a birthplace any different from that of the Leeds's. So, what are we to take from this? Are they criminals and therefore 'foreign' no matter where they were born or what language they speak?"[12]

It's unfortunate that, of all the contributions that went into making *The Star Witness*, one of the weakest, the actual writing, was the only one singled out for Academy Award recognition. Most likely, its Oscar nomination was the result of interest in the story's initial concept and perhaps acknowledgment of the film's popularity rather than appreciation for an intelligent and skillfully plotted and written story and script. But, as film fans have been aware of for a century, such are the inexplicable vagaries of the Academy Awards selection process.

In addition to the script's many flaws, *The Star Witness* suffers from what seems to be a major casting error: the selection of Chic Sale to play Grandpa Summerill. Sale (1885–1936), only in his mid-forties when he played Grandpa, was a veteran vaudevillian who specialized in playing comic rural parts, often caricaturing cantankerous old geezers, and often resorting to mugging and other acting gimmicks for effect. He was more of a clown than an actor, and thus totally inappropriate to play a pivotal role in a serious story, yet he was cast, and Wellman had to work with him.

It's interesting to imagine who, other than Sale, could have done a better job in the role. The first challenge, of course, would have been to rewrite the character to be less of a stereotype and more of a fully formed human being. That, for certain, would have helped create a more interesting drama. This then brings us to the second challenge: casting an older actor with the gravitas to make the role believable. One candidate who comes to mind is Harry Davenport, an actor with considerable talent who played, among many other fine portrayals, Dr. Meade in *Gone with the Wind* (1939). Another is the consistently under-appreciated Charley Grapewin, who, incidentally, later did play a similar role in Warner Brothers' *The Man Who Dared* (1939), a film that was essentially a remake of *The Star Witness*.

*

With the release of *The Star Witness*, Wellman was riding high at Warner Brothers. This was his fourth feature-length film to reach the theaters in only eight months. And, along with *The Public Enemy* and *Night Nurse*, it was also one of studio's top 1931 moneymakers.

Yet, there seemed to be no letting up for the workaholic director. Before the year was out, still another Wellman feature would be released, one with perhaps the most complicated legacy of all his films, pre–Code or otherwise: a legacy that would involve derisive initial reviews, removal from circulation, decades in obscurity, and—roughly three-quarters of a century later—rediscovery, reevaluation, and widespread acclaim.

5

"Sure this ain't the YMCA?"
Safe in Hell (1931)

Although Wellman is often thought of as a "man's director," a filmmaker who prefers stories that focus on men and distinctly male issues, many of his best pre–Code films are about women, frequently women in distress. Already in 1931, he had made *Night Nurse*, approaching the subject with a great understanding of, and sympathy for, the embattled heroine's point of view and challenges. And soon he would tackle the subject several more times in such 1932 and 1933 releases as *The Purchase Price*, *Frisco Jenny*, *Lilly Turner*, and *Midnight Mary*.

In between *Night Nurse* and these releases, he also completed yet another woman-in-distress picture, one that remains among the darkest and most despairing films he ever made (which is saying quite a bit for the director who also brought us *The Ox-Bow Incident*). The film is *Safe in Hell*, a melodrama that shares key similarities with the many classic film noirs of the 1940s and 1950s in which a sympathetic but flawed protagonist follows a fateful path to personal ruin, outright doom, or both. In addition, the film stands as one of Wellman's strongest statements about the devastating impact of patriarchal and misogynistic attitudes and behaviors on women, especially those women viewed as "fallen" or "loose." It's strong stuff, and it is little wonder that the film was first released with the extremely rare-for-the-time warning "Not Recommended for Children," kept locked in a Warner Brothers vault during the entire thirty-four-year period when the Production Code was enforced, then kept off television until the final years of the twentieth century.

All this duly noted, *Safe in Hell* has, in the first decades of the twenty-first century, been re-discovered and widely hailed, not only as one of Wellman's best pre–Code films, but also as essential viewing for anyone with a sincere interest in learning more about what makes pre–Code films special. Working for the only time in his career with actress Dorothy Mackaill, who is remarkable in the lead role, as well as two gifted African

American actors, Nina Mae McKinney and Clarence Muse, who shine in key supporting roles,[1] the director infuses the grim story with great depth and humanity. And working on the first of what would be several partnerships with talented Warner Brothers' cinematographer Sid Hickox, the director and cameraman constantly fill the screen with captivating camera angles and other visual touches to make a basically static story much more vivid and vibrant. Ultimately, this is a film that is riveting when we watch it for the first time, and, with repeated viewings, it only gets better.

*

The lead-up to *Safe in Hell* is filled, it seems, with as many twists and turns as we'd find in an intricately plotted melodrama.

The first version of the story was an unproduced stage play of the same name by writer Houston Branch. In addition to plays, the Minnesota-born Branch (1899–1968) wrote novels and—between 1927 and 1958—contributed story scenarios, adaptations, and additional dialogue to more than fifty, mostly low-budget, films.

Warner Brothers bought the property and assigned two in-house writers to develop the adaptation. One was Maude Fulton, who had written both the story and the screen adaptation for Wellman's *Other Men's Women*. The other was Joseph Jackson (1894–1932), an incredibly prolific screenwriter who worked on more than fifty films between 1927 and his early death in 1932. Just six months earlier, he had received his only Academy Award nomination for his scenario work on the James Cagney–Edward G. Robinson drama *Smart Money* (1931).

Then, in the spring of 1931, the twists and turns really started coming. On April 1, 1931, the trade publication *Film Daily* announced the project with some fanfare, calling it "one of the biggest productions on the Warner program for the year"[2] and noting that Warner workhorse Roy Del Ruth had been slated to direct. Soon, actress Barbara Stanwyck was assigned to star, and Del Ruth was put on another project and replaced by director Michael Curtiz. Then, because of a salary dispute with Harry Cohn of Columbia Pictures (a result of an unusual contract arrangement the actress had with both Warner Brothers and Columbia at the time), Stanwyck was legally forbidden to star in *Safe in Hell*. Other changes also kept coming. In May, the film's working title was changed to *The Lady from New Orleans*. (Another title, *Lost Lady*, was considered at one point as well.) Two different actresses Marilyn Miller and Lilian Bond, were then assigned to play the lead. The first, Miller, quickly dropped out of the project, and Bond was dismissed by Darryl Zanuck, who was unhappy with her work. After Bond's departure, the studio gave the role to actress Dorothy Mackaill. Soon after that, though, there was a possibility of getting

5. Safe in Hell *(1931)*

Stanwyck back, and pre-production came to a sudden halt while everyone waited for clarity. During this time, too, Curtiz was assigned to another project, Wellman was brought in to direct, and the film's title was changed again, this time back to *Safe in Hell*.[3]

Ultimately, though, clarity came. Stanwyck's participation never materialized, Mackaill and Wellman stayed with the project, production began in mid-September, and filming wrapped up on October 18, 1931, about five weeks later.

*

As the film opens, a New Orleans prostitute named Gilda (Mackaill) receives a call from her madam along with an assignment to show a new client "a good time." When Gilda shows up at the client's hotel room, however, she learns that she already knows him. His name is Piet, and earlier he'd been responsible for her losing her job and, with no other immediate employment options, being forced into prostitution. Although she is repulsed by the sight of him, he forces himself on her. She breaks free,

Now an iconic pre–Code image, this opening shot from *Safe in Hell* instantly tells viewers what New Orleans call girl Gilda (Dorothy Mackaill) does for a living (Warner Bros./Photofest).

throws a champagne bottle at his head, knocks him unconscious, and hurriedly leaves. Unknown to her, though, an ashtray has also fallen during the fracas, and the sparks have ignited a curtain. Soon, she learns that the building has burned down, that Piet has died in the blaze, and that she'd been spotted running from his room.

Then, as she tries to absorb these grim developments, her absent boyfriend, a sailor named Carl (Donald Cook), unexpectedly shows up. After hearing her story, he devises a plan to smuggle her aboard the freighter he works on and take her to a small Caribbean island where she can be safe because the island's government has no extradition treaties. Once on the island, he gets her a room at its only hotel. It's an unsavory-looking place, and, as they check in, Gilda gamely cracks, "Sure this ain't the YMCA?" The two also try to get married, but, because the island's only clergyman has recently died and no other person is available, they perform their own "unofficial" marriage ceremony, and Gilda vows to be faithful to Carl. Soon, however, Carl must return to his ship. He gives Gilda money and promises to send her more while she waits for him to return.

Once Carl has left, Gilda finds herself in the midst of an intriguing cast of characters. The hotel's two black employees, Leonie (Nina Mae McKinney), the manager, and Newcastle (Clarence Muse), the porter, are kind and considerate. The establishment's other guests, however, are—to say the least—a disturbing lot, all stuck on the island to avoid extradition for various crimes. As they tell their stories to Gilda, we also learn that these men range from a crooked lawyer and a safecracker to a murderer to a South American general who not only is a murderer but prides himself on having assassinated both a president and a vice-president. The most intriguing of the group, however, is an old sea captain who, without an ounce of guilt or regret, recounts, "I burned my ship. Unfortunately, the passengers and the crew were either drowned or roasted to death. I and the cook, we managed to save ourselves. He met with a little accident afterwards. I collected the insurance for my boat, eighty thousand dollars. And I hope to live happily ever after."

"Amen," Gilda responds, absorbing all of these dark backstories in stride.

Since Gilda is the only white woman on the island, several of these men make attempts to seduce her. All are fairly unthreatening, some even laughable. But another of the island's residents, its main law enforcement officer—its "jailer and executioner," as he puts it—Mr. Bruno (Morgan Wallace), is far more menacing. As well as making frequent overtures toward Gilda, he also intercepts the letters Carl has sent to Gilda and steals the money Carl has enclosed. His plan, of course, is to make Gilda think that Carl won't be coming back, become desperate as Carl's money runs out, seek Bruno's help, and agree have sex with him to obtain it. Adding to his fearsome gravitas, Bruno also has the distinction of uttering one of the film's most-often-quoted bits of dialogue. "My activities are confined to island crime," he tells the other characters. "While we do not believe in the international laws of extradition, our own laws are very strict. As long as you behave yourselves here, you are safe from both jail and the gallows—safe in hell."

Soon, a major development occurs. Piet, who Gilda had thought was dead, arrives on the island. He tells her that he had escaped from the hotel fire, that someone else's charred body was found, and that the authorities had presumed that it was his, so he came up with a plan to fake his death and collude with his wife to collect his $50,000 life-insurance policy. After receiving the money, however, Piet took it and left his wife, who then told the whole story to the authorities. To avoid arrest, he fled New Orleans for, yes, the same Caribbean island with no extradition treaties.

With Piet now on the island, Bruno, pretending to be concerned for Gilda's safety, gives her a revolver to protect herself, saying that, while possession of a gun is illegal on the island, this will be their little secret. Later, however, Piet comes to Gilda's room and tries to rape her. In desperation, she grabs the gun and shoots, killing him. She is tried for Piet's murder and is all but assured of acquittal by a sympathetic jury. Then, as she awaits the jury's verdict, Bruno tells her that, even if she is found innocent, he will arrest her for possessing the "deadly weapon" he had given to her. The sentence will be at least six months in his prison camp, where he promises to set her up very nicely in exchange for sex.

Gilda rushes back to the judge and falsely confesses to killing Piet "in cold blood," preferring to be executed rather than break her vow to Carl. As Gilda sits in her room awaiting execution, she is surprised to learn that Carl has returned. She asks the two policemen guarding her to step away for a few minutes so Carl won't see that she is under house arrest, and the couple chat. He joyously tells her that he will soon have a new and better job and begins making plans for their future life together back in New Orleans. Rather than telling him the truth about her circumstances, Gilda tearfully bids him goodbye and leaves him with the impression that she will soon join him. After he departs on his ship, Gilda asks the lawyer to tell Carl about her death and remarks that Carl, who always loved being at sea, would ultimately be happier there than anywhere else. Then, along with Bruno and the two policemen, she soberly walks to the gallows.

*

Despite the topsy-turvy nature of its pre-production phase and the resulting delays, *Safe in Hell* still managed to open in theaters before year-end—on December 12 or 22, 1931, depending on the source—and, ironically, just in time for Christmas. Although the film did relatively well at the box office, it generally displeased critics. *Variety*, for example, called the story "hardboiled and sordid," derided the film's "sad and unsatisfactory finish," and complained about the "constantly depressing air of evil which prevails throughout the picture."[4] While conceding that the film is "sporadically exciting," *Time Magazine* called it "crude" and "trite."[5] As if to underscore his dismissive attitude toward the film, the *New York Times'* Mordaunt Hall placed his brief write-up last in a laundry list of mini-reviews he attached to the end of his more serious and substantive review of a new film version of Noel Coward's play *Private Lives* just out in theaters. While seeming bored overall with *Safe in Hell*, Hall did, however, compliment actress Nina Mae McKinney's work, calling her "the most entertaining item in the film."[6]

It's curious that several of the 1931 reviewers also felt the need to mention that Warner Brothers had placed the notice mentioned earlier at the beginning of the film: "Not recommended for children." No doubt *Safe in Hell*'s sordid subject matter and—even for pre-Code—unusually downbeat ending contributed to the studio's decision. (Even today, the film might not be the best choice to show impressionable eight- or-nine-year-old youngsters.) No doubt, too, the film's relentlessly dark view of human behavior and truly tragic ending would have been difficult for many adults not to find unsettling if not downright depressing. At any rate, there would have been no way this film could have passed muster with Hollywood's censors after the Code was seriously enforced, and, as noted earlier, it was removed from circulation and remained—with the exception of occasional showings on the Turner Classic Movies cable channel during the 1990s—virtually unseen and forgotten for the next three-quarters of a century.

Since its DVD release in 2011, however, *Safe in Hell* has experienced a renaissance of sorts. And today, it is regularly viewed by classic film buffs, shown at pre-Code film festivals, and studied in university film classes throughout the United States and elsewhere.

Both fueling all this attention—and inspired by it—are numerous positive assessments of *Safe in Hell*. Online reviewer M.G. Conlin, for example, calls it "a great movie, a forgotten gem that deserves to be better known than it is and an example of the Hollywood studio system working on all cylinders and producing something that acknowledged the clichés and yet also defied them quite movingly."[7] Finding the film "a revelation," online reviewer Hilda Crane also observes, "The atmosphere is palpable— you can almost feel the heat and smell the sweat. This movie is uncanny in being both intensely grim and very funny, [incorporating] wonderful

5. Safe in Hell (1931)

camera set-ups, such as the front-on shot of the row of seated disreputable lechers, legs spread and ogling [Gilda] as she climbs the rickety stairs to her hotel room."[8] Pre–Code historian Danny Reid notes that "director Wellman's camera is so energetic and crazy that [the film is] a dizzying experience, ... Wellman takes rather stodgy material, most of it set in one hotel, and imbues it with a lurid sense of anger and dread. [The film is] amazing."[9] In addition, reviewer Betsy Sherman had called the film both a "crackling feature" and "a hugely enjoyable foray into the pre–Code fallen-woman genre."[10]

Perhaps one key reason for *Safe in Hell*'s relatively new-found acceptance and unexpected popularity is our twenty-first-century viewing perspective. With its mix of gritty realism, cynicism, poignant tragedy, and dark humor, this is clearly a film that was well ahead of its time. And maybe it simply needed to age a few decades for audiences—now consciously or unconsciously conditioned by a second world war, film noir, the Italian neo-realism and French New Wave film movements, the harsh realism of many post–1970s films, and numerous other developments—to understand and appreciate it more fully. It's difficult to know for sure if this is an accurate assessment, but, in any case, the film clearly resonates with viewers today in ways it simply didn't back in 1931.

*

Once again, Wellman's ability to elevate the storytelling by fortifying dubious material with intelligent alterations, inventive visual touches, and enormous vitality is very much in evidence.

As usual, Wellman's staging and shot selection for specific scenes are outstanding. Several contemporary writers (including two quoted above), for example, have commented quite insightfully on the excellent job the director does in handling the often-static scenes in the lobby of the island's hotel. One of the most challenging experiences to depict in an interesting way is bored people sitting around and waiting for something—anything—to happen. So, to enliven these scenes, Wellman takes a darkly humorous stance, shooting the hotel's unsavory male guests as an audience of comical but eternally hopeful lechers, each slouched in his chair, each with his legs wide open, waiting for a glimpse of—and with luck maybe even more from—Gilda. While funny, these scenes also underscore the ever-present threat of rape that Gilda, as the island's only white woman, must live with.

Some of the film's early scenes are also especially well conceived and orchestrated. One of these is when a joyous Carl comes to Gilda's room in New Orleans. At first, Gilda doesn't know whether or not to tell Carl that she is in serious trouble, and Wellman often shoots her looking away from him, revealing a range of conflicting emotions only to the audience. Soon, when Carl shows Gilda a shawl he has brought her, he spreads it across her face, covering it just below her eyes to give her face a hint of mystery and perhaps to subtly reinforce her attempts to conceal the truth from him. Then, as she looks away from Carl again and into a mirror, he sees her reflection and realizes that something is wrong. After this, they look straight at each other. She tells him everything, he reacts angrily at first, but, when he hears a police siren, he immediately springs into action to help her escape. In every second of this four-minute scene, the camera is optimally placed to capture both action and reaction. It's all executed quite well. Another impressive early scene is when Carl visits Gilda as she hides in a storage area on the ship taking them to the island. For the entire scene, we see her—from behind a narrow opening on what appears to be a shipping crate—speaking to him. Part of the time he is in front of her, outside the crate and in full view of the audience, and part of the time he is inside with her. Essentially, this is an exposition scene. No major drama occurs. But, wanting to make the exchange more interesting, Wellman

Gilda (Dorothy Mackaill) and her sailor-boyfriend Carl (Donald Cook) reunite in New Orleans as she faces imminent arrest. To help her, he suggests taking her to a small Caribbean island where U.S. authorities can't touch her in *Safe in Hell* (Warner Bros./Photofest).

chose to partially conceal, first, Gilda and then Gilda and Carl together to make the visuals a bit different and more intriguing and to give the scene a greater sense of intimacy. Again, it's quite effective.

Many contemporary articles and blogs on *Safe in Hell* make a point of singling out two African American actors in the film: Nina Mae McKinney and Clarence Muse. At a time when black characters were often stereotyped in Hollywood films, the two actors portray Leonie and Newcastle as quite intelligent, decent, and caring individuals—perhaps the two most upright characters in the story. According to Wellman biographer Frank Thompson, McKinney and Muse's scenes in the original shooting script were filled with a white scriptwriter's patronizing attempts to mimic black dialogue. In the actual film, however, the two speak quite differently, neither in the stereotypical ways black actors often did in films of the 1930s and 1940s.[11] Muse even uses an upper-crust English accent and such expressions as "Right-o," suggesting that Newcastle has had some exposure to the British upper-class. The results are fresh, non-stereotypical performances by both actors. It isn't clear whether McKinney and Muse demanded to change the stereotypical language or whether Wellman—with his preference for fresh, honest portrayals—suggested the different approach. It is clear, however, that he supported the move, and, as a consequence, the portrayals were far more real, lively, and interesting than they otherwise might have been.

*

On the subject of acting, the lead story in *Safe in Hell* is Dorothy Mackaill's magnificent portrayal of Gilda. From beginning to end, Mackaill dominates this film, bringing strength, nuance, and depth to a character that, in a lesser actor's hands, could have simply come across as a hapless victim.

Virtually unknown today, Mackaill (1903–1990) was born in the English county of Yorkshire; began to pursue a career as both an actor and a dancer in her teens; and moved to New York, where, at seventeen, she danced in the Ziegfeld Follies and began to act in films. Her film acting soon led her to Hollywood, where she found regular work, appearing in more than fifty silent and early sound films from the early 1920s to the mid–1930s and, along the way, becoming a naturalized U.S. citizen.

What makes Mackaill's performance as Gilda in *Safe in Hell* so memorable is the actress' ability to dig deep into the character, find a heart-wrenching reality beneath the script's clichés, and then convey it with great effectiveness. Gilda is certainly a victim. Raped by Piet and then fired from her job at his company, she is, while her boyfriend Carl is away at sea, without options and forced into prostitution. Ultimately, too, she is faced with another horrible choice—either break her vow of fidelity to Carl and become Mr. Bruno's kept woman or stay true to Carl and go to the gallows. Throughout these ordeals, Mackaill conveys Gilda's anxiety, anger, and fear with disarming honesty, never resorting to histrionics the way many actresses of the era would have. In addition, Mackaill ably captures Gilda's more subtle characteristics, ones that help to round out her character more fully. An interesting example in the film is the scene in which Gilda, who is truly trying to steer clear of trouble while on the island, is so bored just playing solitaire in her hotel room that she puts on her party dress and joins the motley group of lechers in the hotel's lobby for a party. As soon she sits down with them, one of the men says, "Wine is what you need, senorita." Suggestively, perhaps teasingly, Gilda replies, "Wine is only part of it" and then adds "Oh boy, am I glad to be here!" Yes, Gilda wants to be good for Carl, but she also has a party girl side that likes to have a good time drinking, smoking, and whooping it up while surrounded by male admirers. Finally, Mackaill does a fine job of conveying both Gilda's love and respect for Carl and her understanding of his basic naivete. Carl is all about living happily ever after with, as he puts it, "my girl." Gilda sees life and people in far more complex and perhaps realistic terms. Will she, Gilda may be wondering, eventually tire of a staid life with Carl just as she tires of playing solitaire in her hotel room? And will Carl really find true happiness with her? It's curious that, just after she says goodbye to him for the last time, she mentions that his real first love is not her but the sea. It's a fascinating remark to mull over, as though she's already worked out in her head that perhaps the best thing for Carl in the end is not her but an idealized memory of the woman who sacrificed herself to be true to him.

Although Mackaill was just twenty-eight when she starred in *Safe in Hell*, she made only eight more films, retiring in 1937 at the age of thirty-four, reportedly to take care of her ailing mother. In 1955, she settled in Hawaii where, after three previous marriages that ended in divorce, she remained single, and lived for the rest of her life as a permanent guest at the Royal Hawaiian Hotel on Waikiki Beach. In her seventies, she was coaxed out of retirement by her friend, actor Jack Lord, to guest star in two episodes of his popular television show *Hawaii Five-0*. About this time, she also shared her thoughts with film historian John Gallagher about working on *Safe in Hell* and with its colorful director. "Wellman had an exciting personality besides having the distinguished ability to make you see exactly how he wanted a scene played," she noted. "I've had many clever directors, but must say I put Wild Bill at the top of my list.... [He was] the most exacting.... I wish I could have made more movies with him, as he was a treasure to work for."[12]

5. Safe in Hell (1931)

Relegated to obscurity after her retirement in 1937, Mackaill has achieved a modest level of celebrity in the twenty-first century, especially among fans of pre–Code films. A major reason why, of course, has been the rediscovery and growing popularity of *Safe in Hell*.

Among the other actors, Nina Mae McKinney also deserves praise for bringing so much of her talent and charisma to the supporting role of Leonie and infusing the character with intelligence, charm, concern for others, a wry sense of humor, and a zest for life. Wellman must have been especially impressed with McKinney because, in one scene, he has her sing a song to the hotel's guests as Leonie refills their wine glasses at dinner. The song, incidentally, is "When It's Sleepy Time Down South." It was written in 1931 by the African American songwriting team of Leon and Otis Rene and the multi-talented Clarence Muse, who, of course, plays Newcastle in the film. Soon afterward, jazz great Louis Armstrong made the wonderfully evocative piece his signature song, recording it more than a hundred times during his career.

Born in South Carolina, McKinney (1912–1967) moved to Georgia and then New York, where, in her mid-teens and with virtually no professional experience, she was hired as a chorus girl in the stage show, *Blackbirds Revue*. The show was soon renamed *Blackbirds of 1928* and moved to Broadway, where, with the added star power of legendary dancer Bill "Bojangles" Robinson, it ran for more than 500 performances. This led to an audition that won her a lead role in director King Vidor's 1929 musical drama *Hallelujah!*, a very early talking motion picture that featured an all-black cast. As a result, McKinney became the first African American actress to play a lead role in a mainstream U.S. film. A big gamble for Vidor and MGM, *Hallelujah!* surprisingly turned out to be an enormous box office success. Vidor was nominated for an Academy Award for his direction, and McKinney was widely praised for her work. "Nina was full of life, full of expression, and just a joy to work with," Vidor recounted afterward. "Someone like her inspires a director."[13]

In another era, such fanfare would have meant instant success and perhaps a long career for a performer with McKinney's talent and charisma, but such was not the case. Finding work difficult to get in Hollywood as an African American actor, even one with her abilities, she spent most of the 1930s in Europe, where she worked sporadically in both theater in films. She eventually returned to the United States, where she continued to work intermittently, usually in small, sometimes uncredited roles and often playing maids. She died in New York of a heart attack at the age of fifty-four.

In his smaller role as Newcastle, the hotel's porter, Clarence Muse, does a fine job as well. In addition to the upper-class British accent he mimics, largely for comic relief, he is quite good at subtly showing Newcastle's distain for the lecherous and generally sleazy behavior of many of *Safe in Hell*'s other characters.

A screenwriter, director, and singer as well as an actor and song composer, Muse (1889–1979) fared somewhat better as a performer than McKinney in an era that offered limited opportunities for African Americans. In the 1920s, he acted with two theater companies closely tied to the Harlem Renaissance, the intellectual and cultural revival of African American arts, politics, and scholarship centered in New York's Harlem neighborhood at the time. Moving to Hollywood in 1929, he appeared in more than 150 films and on several television shows over the next fifty years. Although he did win a good number of meaty roles along the way, he was—as was the case with most African American actors—often relegated to small, sometimes uncredited parts. He died on October 13, 1979, one day before his ninetieth birthday and on the same day that his final film, *The Black Stallion*, which also featured actors Mickey Rooney and Teri Garr, was released.

Among the other key performances in *Safe in Hell*, somewhat less effective is Donald Cook's portrayal of Carl. While Cook does have one electric moment—when the earnest, affable Carl unexpectedly slaps Gilda after he learns that she's been working as a prostitute—he generally comes across as quite bland. This might not be all Cook's fault; the character, while far more decent than most of the other characters in the film, is essentially a very ordinary, not-terribly-interesting fellow. But Cook, who was far more engaging in *The Public Enemy*, doesn't give his portrayal in this film anything special to help make Carl more distinctive or memorable. Generally, he just plays it straight, which, with this challenging, underwritten role, is not enough.

*

Working behind the camera with Wellman for the first time on *Safe in Hell* was veteran Warner Brothers cinematographer Sid Hickox, who would collaborate with the director on six more of his pre–Code films. A good fit with Wellman, who liked a constantly moving camera, Hickox was widely respected as an action photographer, who, as film writer I.S. Mowis put it "had the uncanny ability to make productions shot on a modest budget [such as most of Wellman's pre–Code features] look a lot classier."[14]

During the 1940s, Hickox (1895-1982) would become a favorite cinematographer of director Raoul Walsh at Warner Brothers, making major contributions on such Walsh classics as *Gentleman Jim* with Errol Flynn (1942), *Colorado Territory* (1949) with Joel McCrea, and *White Heat*

(1949) with James Cagney. In the 1950s, he moved to television, where he ended his career serving as director of photography for 249 episodes of the classic television series *The Andy Griffith Show* (1960–1968) and then seventy-eight episodes of its sequel, *Mayberry R.F.D.* (1968–1971).

*

Throughout his career, Wellman was always quite clear in expressing that his preference was to direct a variety of films rather than being "type cast" as a specialist in, say, comedies, crime dramas, or westerns. Yet, with his major success in *Night Nurse* and expert handling of challenging material in *Safe in Hell*, his Warner Brothers superiors quickly saw that, among his other talents, he had a real knack for handling woman-in-distress stories—the kind of films that were then popular and that could also be quite profitable for the studio.

As a contract director working on the studio's assembly line, however, Wellman, of course, had limited say about assignments. Whether he preferred it or not, he would have to take the projects he was given, even if that meant script after script focusing on women-in-distress. This was one significant professional challenge he faced during the pre–Code years, a situation that would become increasingly difficult for him to live with and that, as we might suspect, would eventually lead to a reckoning with his studio superiors.

6

"If you keep your head, you should go far"
The Hatchet Man and *So Big* (both 1932)

After a succession of 1931 releases that included *The Public Enemy*, *Night Nurse*, and *Safe in Hell*, Wellman continued to churn out films at a remarkable rate, and, in 1932, six more of his features premiered. But, while the number of assignments he tackled, the range of subjects he explored, and the creativity and energy he brought to each of his projects remained impressive, his 1932 films often don't resonate as well with viewers today as his best 1931 films do. The reasons vary, from problematic scripts to the outmoded practice of casting Caucasian actors to play Chinese Americans, as in Wellman's first 1932 release, *The Hatchet Man*. Yet, despite elements that may not sit well with some contemporary viewers, each of these films—mainly because Wellman is behind the camera—benefits from his unique talents and contributions. None of these efforts may qualify as a flat-out Wellman masterpiece. (We'd have to wait until 1933 to see more of those.) But, especially for people intrigued with this director's work, all have significant strengths and are well worth seeing.

This chapter will focus on the first two of these releases: *The Hatchet Man* and *So Big*.

*

The Hatchet Man, a film about two generations of Chinese Americans set mostly in early-twentieth-century San Francisco, is a fascinating effort to deconstruct. On one hand, it is a well-crafted melodrama featuring fine performances from actors Edward G. Robinson, J. Carrol Naish, and Dudley Digges; excellent atmospheric cinematography from Sid Hickox; and wonderfully evocative sets from Warner Brothers' superb in-house art director Anton Grot. On the other hand, however, the film's racial attitudes and the casting practices associated with them can, and

6. The Hatchet Man *and* So Big *(both 1932)*

often do, make it particularly hard for many of today's film viewers to swallow.

Let's look first at what modern audiences find—and what Asian-American audiences have undoubtedly always found—difficult to accept about *The Hatchet Man*. At the top of the list, of course, is the decision to cast Caucasian actors in the roles of Chinese-American characters. For decades now, of course, viewers have not accepted this practice, many finding it offensive. But, in the early 1930s, well-known stars were what lured fans to the movies, and, since the vast majority of U.S. movie fans were white, so were virtually all of the stars. In filming a story involving nearly all Asian characters, one solution was to cast white stars and character actors in key roles and make them up to look like Asians—or, in today's parlance, put them in "yellowface"—and supplement with Asian actors in small roles or as extras. This, in turn, led to another problem. As film writer Brian Cady notes, "Makeup artists had noticed that audiences were more likely to reject Western actors in Asian disguise if the faces of actual Asians were in near proximity. [So,] rather than cast the film with Asian actors, which would have then meant no star names to attract American audiences, studios simply eliminated most of the Asian actors from the cast."[1] For the film, Wellman and the key actors appear to be making sincere efforts to portray the characters and their distinctly Chinese-American perspectives honestly and respectfully, efforts that were not all that common at a time when racial stereotyping in Hollywood was rampant. Despite these efforts, however, the inherent dishonesty of yellowface makeup seriously undermines their good intentions. Even Robinson, Naish, and Digges, who all work hard to deliver honest, intelligent, and deeply felt performances, don't quite pull it off.

Another fascinating aspect of *The Hatchet Man* is, for its Chinese-oriented subject matter, the abundance of classically American pre–Code elements it contains. Not only is the story's noble main character essentially an assassin for a Chinese gang, but, during the story, he commits two murders to avenge his gang's honor and inadvertently delivers deadly poetic justice to a ne'er-do-well. In addition, provocative subjects such as adultery and the use of narcotics are treated with some sympathy and understanding. In fact, the film's happy ending centers on the joyous reunion between the assassin and his adulterous wife. Needless to say, such a film would not have had a prayer of being made in Hollywood after mid–1934.

*

The source material for *The Hatchet Man* is an unproduced play called *The Honorable Mr. Wong* by Afghanistan-born writer Achmed Abdullah and famed Broadway impresario David Belasco. Best known for his pulp stories and novels in the crime, mystery, and adventure genres, Abdullah (1881–1945) also wrote for films, co-authoring, among other efforts, the screenplays for the great Douglas Fairbanks–Raoul Walsh silent film *The Thief of Bagdad* (1924) and the Gary Cooper action-adventure hit *The Lives of a Bengal Lancer* (1935). Belasco (1853–1931) wrote, directed, and/or produced more than a hundred stage plays over nearly half a century, scores of which were later made into films. In addition, he was quite a champion of promising young actors, helping to launch the careers of such future stage and film stars as James O'Neill (the father of playwright Eugene O'Neill), Mary Pickford, and Barbara Stanwyck.

To develop the screenplay for *The Honorable Mr. Wong*, Warner Brothers assigned J. Grubb Alexander (1887–1932), who wrote for more than ninety films, mostly in the silent era. Sadly, Alexander died of pneumonia at age forty-four just three weeks before *The Hatchet Man*, his second-to-last film project, was released.

Among the actors selected for *The Hatchet Man*, the two best known today are its star, Edward G. Robinson, and, in a supporting role, Loretta Young. Robinson (1893–1973) is perhaps most familiar to modern audiences for his various gangster roles in such Warner Brothers classics as *Little Caesar* (1930) and *Key Largo* (1948) as well as for his role as a cagy insurance investigator in the seminal film noir *Double Indemnity* (1944). Highly respected by colleagues for his acting talent, Robinson, in a film career that spanned half a century, was, oddly, never even once nominated for an Academy Award and is often cited as one of the best actors never to have received this recognition. We'll discuss Young, who also had a long and successful Hollywood career, in a later chapter.

As noted earlier, two other actors who made significant contributions to the film were J. Carrol Naish and Dudley Digges. Naish (1896–1973), whose film and later television career earned him hundreds of credits, developed a special talent for effectively playing characters of various nationalities, so many that he earned the nickname "Hollywood's one-man U.N."[2] Born in Ireland, Digges (1879–1947) spent most of his career in the United States, where he performed in hundreds of stage plays and more than fifty films over a span of forty-three years.

In addition to Sid Hickox, who had worked with Wellman on *Safe in Hell*, another major behind-the-scenes contributor to *The Hatchet Man* was art director Anton Grot, who designed the film's lavish, exotic sets. Born and raised in Poland, Grot (1884–1974) came to Hollywood to work on Douglas Fairbanks' films in 1922 and eventually signed with Warner Brothers where he contributed to more than eighty films before his retirement in the late 1940s. Often praised for his talent to visually reinforce the

6. The Hatchet Man *and* So Big *(both 1932)*

The Hatchet Man's title character, Wong Low Get (Edward G. Robinson), stands in his opulent, well-appointed home. This set is the creation of Warner Brothers' brilliant art director Anton Grot, whose eclectic designs ranged from the low-down and gritty to the sumptuous and exotic, depending on what a film's story required (Warner Bros./Photofest).

mood of a film and for his versatility at creating environments ranging from harsh realism to ornate romanticism, he is perhaps best known for his long partnership with director Michael Curtiz, with whom he collaborated on fifteen films.

The Hatchet Man was shot in late 1931 at the Warner Brothers lot in Burbank. As was Wellman's habit by this time, production was well organized, efficiently run, and completed in about a month.

*

The story of *The Hatchet Man* begins in San Francisco's Chinatown in the 1910s. This was during the time of the "Tong Wars," a series of violent disputes that periodically erupted between rival Chinese-American gangs, or Tongs, that were based in several major U.S. cities. A powerful member of one Tong is murdered, and its council president Nog Hong Fah (Digges) summons the group's "honorable hatchet man," or assassin, Wong Low Get (Robinson) to avenge the killing. Wong soon learns that the man he must kill is Sun Yat Ming (Naish), a close friend he's known since childhood. With great sadness, Wong accepts the assignment.

When he comes to Sun's home, Wong learns that his old friend has already prepared for his own death, making out his will and leaving all his worldly possessions to Wong. He also asks Wong both to raise his young daughter, Toya, and to marry her when she comes of age. Wong agrees and then reveals that he is the one who must carry out the assassination. Calmly accepting the grim irony of the situation, Sun kneels and forgives Wong's "innocent hand its stroke of justice."

The story then skips ahead to San Francisco's Chinatown in the early 1930s. The warring Tongs are largely a thing of the past, and many of the Chinese have adopted modern American ways. Wong has become a successful businessman, and Toya (now played by Young) has become a beautiful young woman. It is her birthday and, by Chinese tradition, the day when she should be betrothed. Wong, who loves her deeply, is also concerned about the considerable age difference between them, and says he would never want to stand in the way of her happiness. Breaking with tradition, he offers her the choice to marry or not. "My father's wish is also mine," she replies. Hearing this, Wong is overjoyed, and they are married.

On the day of their wedding, however, an outlaw Tong based in Sacramento declares war on its counterparts in San Francisco. For protection, Nog hires bodyguards, including a handsome young gangster Harry En Hai (Leslie Fenton), who is assigned to guard Wong and Toya. After the Sacramento Tong creates additional problems for Nog, Wong, and others, Wong travels to Sacramento to negotiate with its leaders and allies. For the trip, Wong takes along the tools of his trade, two very sharp hatchets that he hasn't used in years. In Sacramento, Wong is mostly successful in his negotiations. Only Big Jim Malone, a white gangster who'd started the war, refuses to cooperate. Wong finds Malone arrogant, but coyly compliments him on his capabilities, adding, "If you keep your head, you should go far." Malone falls for the flattery. Then Wong quickly kills him, effectively ending the war.

While Wong is in Sacramento, however, the amoral and opportunistic Harry seduces the impressionable Toya. Upon his return, Wong finds the two embracing, and, when Toya proclaims her love for Harry, Wong—because he had once promised that he would never stand in the way of her happiness—sadly gives Toya and her happiness to Harry. Before they leave, however, he also tells Harry that, if he ever considers mistreating Toya in any way, "The great Lord Buddha will find you no matter where you are on the face of the Earth."

Because of this break with tradition—this "unworthy act," as he is told—Wong is now shunned by his Tong and driven into poverty.

After some time, Wong receives a note from Toya and learns that the U.S. government had caught Harry selling opium and deported both Harry and Toya to China, where they are in a miserable state. Toya also declares that she had made an enormous mistake and now realizes that she loves only Wong. Hearing this news, Wong redeems his hatchets from a pawn shop and, working as a ship's stoker, heads to China.

Once in China, Wong learns that Toya and Harry are at an opium den and brothel where he is now an addict and she, we assume, works as a prostitute. Wong rescues her, and, when confronted by the brothel's madam, he claims his right to take Toya back according to ancient Chinese law and the honor of the hatchet man. When the madam scoffs at the idea that he is a hatchet man, he takes his hatchet out and proves his prowess by hitting the eye of a dragon in a painting hanging on a nearby wall. He promises to come back for Harry, and he and Toya leave. On the other side of the wall on which the painting hangs, however, we see that the hatchet has not only gone through the dragon's eye in the painting but also through the wall and partially through the skull of Harry, who apparently had been eavesdropping on the conversation. As a person tries to remove the hatchet from Harry's head, his body twitches eerily, as though he were still alive.

The film then cuts to a statue of Buddha, and we hear Wong repeat his warning to Harry, "The great Lord Buddha will find you no matter where you are on the face of the Earth."

*

The Hatchet Man opened in theaters on February 6, 1932. It was a major hit with audiences, with box office receipts coming to roughly $742,000, almost three times the film's budget of $263,000. Critics, though, were mixed. Noting that Robinson [referring to the actor's previous roles] "is a better barber, gambler, gangster, and tabloid editor than he is a Chinese hatchet man," Mordaunt Hall nevertheless called the film "a fast-moving tale" and praised the performances of Naish, Digges, Young, and Fenton as well as their Asian make-up. What's curious here, of course, is how complimentary Hall, very much a man of his time, was of what he saw as the competent implementation of a practice that many modern viewers find offensive.

As we might expect, most contemporary film writers see *The Hatchet Man* very differently from Hall. "The story is racist at its base, yet creates some strong characters," notes Glenn Erickson, who goes on to credit Robinson for showing "no stage affectations as Wong" and coming off "well."[3] He also praises the art direction of Anton Grot, credits the film's "mature screenplay," and ends his review saying, "Under William A. Wellman's assured direction, the movie's exciting ending is worthy of Edgar Allan

Poe."[4] And, while pointing out the film's racism, the "absolutely atrocious" makeup applied to Young and Fenton, and the questionable morality of a hitman hero, pre–Code historian Danny Reid praises the film's set design and, in certain scenes, Wellman's visual wit. "While it's a well-made movie," Reid, on a very mixed note, concludes, "it's a purely vicarious thrill machine that just leaves something hollow and sad behind."[5]

*

Setting aside the film's use of white actors to play Chinese-American characters, some stereotyping, and other racially insensitive practices of the period, *The Hatchet Man* actually works on many levels as a well-crafted melodrama.

As usual, Wellman exhibits his great command of craft throughout, from the superbly orchestrated funeral procession/crowd scenes at the very beginning of the film to the macabre (and quite surprising) accidental killing at the end. And, collaborating with cinematographer Hickox, art director Grot, and others at Warner Brothers, he helped both to envision and then portray scenes of various parts of Wong's home that are simultaneously sumptuous and exotic, sometimes even breathtaking. Finally, in a few scenes, such as when Sacramento gangster Big Jim Malone treats Wong and other Chinese-Americans with condescension, the director does something unusual for Hollywood films of the time—he comments on the prejudices and disdainful attitudes of white Americans toward Asians. In many respects, we can fairly say that Wellman ably carried out a tricky assignment.

Several of the actors also perform with real conviction and empathy for their characters. Foremost among them are Robinson, Naish, and Digges. Although Robinson neither looks like nor is able to talk like a credible Chinese American, he more than ably conveys Wong's integrity; sensitivity; deep affection for Sun, the old friend he must kill; love for Toya; and stoicism as he endures suffering. Naish is particularly good in his small role as Sun, showing great sensitivity for the old friend who has now come to kill him while also appreciating the great irony of the situation. Of all the white actors portraying Chinese characters in the film, he actually comes the closest to being somewhat credible. And, as Nog, Digges (although he still looks more Irish than Chinese, even under all his makeup) is quite effective conveying his character's respect for tradition, commitment to duty, and disdain for "new ways" along with his affection for Wong.

Among the film's main characters, though, the big disappointment is Loretta Young's Toya. Not only is Young made up in a garish, totally unbelievable way, but there just doesn't seem to be any real center to Toya. In

6. The Hatchet Man *and* So Big *(both 1932)*

Young's defense, however, Toya is not nearly as well-developed as Wong, Sun, or other key characters in the film. And watching Young stumble through the role, also makes one wonder how much better the young and talented Chinese-American actress, Anna May Wong, might have been in it instead. But then, if Wong had been cast and then brought something truly authentic to the thinly written character, her contribution would, of course, have only made Robinson and the other white actors in yellowface look less credible, and perhaps even sillier.

*

Overall, *The Hatchet Man* certainly has more than its share of flaws, but it's also hard not to admire the amount of effort and artistry that Wellman, Hickox, Grot, Robinson, Naish, Digges, and others put into it. If nothing else, their work is a testament to the high level of professionalism that existed at Warner Brothers at the time. All involved seemed particularly committed to doing the best they could with what they had to work with.

*

Shortly after completing *The Hatchet Man*, Wellman went to work adapting another completely different kind of story to the screen. This new film was based on Edna Ferber's best-selling and Pulitzer-Prize-winning 1924 novel *So Big*, an epic saga that follows the life of heroine Selina Peake from girlhood to mature middle age during the late nineteenth and early twentieth centuries. And for the director, one great attraction associated with this project was the opportunity to work again with Barbara Stanwyck, the fast-rising star who had delivered such a fine performance in *Night Nurse* and had, during the making of that film, been such a pleasure for him to work with.

The result, though, is a film that, in both subject and tone, is one of the "least pre–Code" among Wellman's 1931-to-1933 films. *So Big*, of course, was made with the director's usual attention to craft, and Stanwyck is always enjoyable to watch in whatever role she plays. But, with its episodic storyline, often-cloying tone, leisurely pacing, occasional preaching, and tedious comedy scenes, it lacks the tight plotting, fast pacing, visceral charge, sense of urgency, and biting dark humor that characterize Wellman's best pre–Code efforts. In addition, it seems wildly at odds with Warner Brothers' early–1930s emphasis on gritty, hard-hitting, tightly edited, and often lurid contemporary stories.

Why did Zanuck and Warner Brothers choose to produce a film based on *So Big* at this time? The answer is—as it almost always has been in Hollywood—money. Edna Ferber, long an enormously popular brand name in her own right, had also written the best-selling 1930 novel *Cimarron*, which was quickly turned into a hugely successful 1931 film for RKO that went on to win the Academy Award for Best Picture. From a business perspective, making a film of *So Big* to capitalize both on the Ferber name and on the recent success of *Cimarron*, the movie, clearly made sense.

*

The story of the Wellman-Stanwyck film version of *So Big*, of course, begins with the 1924 novel by Ferber. Based very loosely on the life of Antje Paarlberg Waagmeester, a resilient widow who lived in the Dutch farming community of South Holland, Illinois, in the mid to late 1800s, *So Big* is a sprawling story that unfolds over many decades. When delivering the manuscript to her publisher, Doubleday, Ferber was anxious about its prospects for success, feeling that the public would not embrace a novel without a traditional plot that told the story of a middle-age woman farmer with bad teeth. To her surprise, the editors at Doubleday loved it. So did readers, and, during its first year of publication, hundreds of thousands of copies were sold. Before the year was out, Hollywood had also gotten into the act, making the first feature film version of the story, a silent starring actress Colleen Moore in her first important dramatic role. This was followed, of course, by the Wellman-Stanwyck version. And, in 1953, a third version, directed by Robert Wise and starring Jane Wyman, was made.

For those unfamiliar with her, Ferber (1885–1968) was an especially popular and highly respected early and mid-twentieth-century novelist, short story writer, and playwright, whose work was often adapted for films. In addition to *So Big* and *Cimarron*, examples of these adaptations include novels such as *Show Boat* (1926) and *Giant* (1952) and plays (co-authored with George S. Kaufman) such as *The Royal Family* (1927), *Dinner at Eight* (1932), and *Stage Door* (1936).

Already in possession of the screen rights to *So Big*, Warner Brothers assigned staffer J. Grubb Alexander, who had worked with Wellman on *The Hatchet Man*, to work on the adaptation for the 1932 version. And, likely due to Alexander's ill health and early–1932 death, the studio added writer Robert Lord to complete the screenplay. Lord (1900–1976), a producer as well as a writer, worked mainly in films from the mid–1920s to the 1950s. By far the majority of his most notable credits are from the pre-Code era, during which he contributed to such highly respected films as *One Way Passage* (1932) and *Footlight Parade* (1933) as well as Wellman's *The Purchase Price* and *Heroes for Sale*. For his work on *One Way Passage* Lord also received an Oscar for Best Story at the Sixth Academy Awards in 1934.

In addition to Stanwyck, actors cast in the film included several

6. The Hatchet Man *and* So Big *(both 1932)*

familiar faces from the Warner Brothers stock company at the time. These ranged from the versatile Alan Hale to George Brent (whom we'll discuss in a later chapter), to a young Bette Davis in a relatively small role.

For film trivia buffs, *So Big* is also the only film in which Stanwyck and Davis, two of the most celebrated actresses of Hollywood's classic era, ever appeared together on screen.[6] Apparently, one major reason for this was an intense dislike they had for each other. According to Wellman, Davis "was jealous because a contemporary [she and Stanwyck were virtually the same age] had achieved stardom quickly while she had to grind through small roles and bad pictures."[7] He also noted that Stanwyck believed that, while making *So Big*, Davis had used her mannerisms and fidgeting to draw attention to herself and away from the other actors, adding that, perhaps as retribution, Stanwyck had sometimes scolded Davis her in front of others when she muffed lines.[8] In an interview years later, Stanwyck—who was usually extremely tactful when speaking publicly—was quite blunt in her assessment of Davis, saying, "She was always so ambitious, you knew she'd make it. She had a kind of creative ruthlessness that made her success inevitable."[9]

Again, Wellman turned to cinematographer Sid Hickox, who had done an excellent job with the camera work on both *Safe in Hell* and *The Hatchet Man*.

Shooting for *So Big* went quickly, beginning on January 11, 1932, and wrapping up less than four weeks later on February 3.

*

The film version of *So Big* begins in the 1880s. Selina Peake (Anne Shirley), a precocious young girl, and her father Simeon (Robert Warwick), a gentleman gambler, live in Chicago where she attends a finishing school. After several years, though, Simeon is killed, murdered during a dispute in a poker game. Finding herself penniless, Selina (now played by Stanwyck) obtains a job working as a schoolteacher in a small Dutch farming community and boards with a family of Dutch immigrants, the Pools. At one point she remarks how beautiful she finds the rows of cabbages on the farms, and the Pool family patriarch, Klaas (Alan Hale), doubles over with laughter that someone should find rows of cabbages beautiful. He shares this remark with others, who also find Selina to be a little strange. One person who does value Selina's appreciation for beauty, though, is the family's twelve-year-old son, Roelf (Dick Winslow). And one day, Roelf draws her a sketch of rows of cabbages and gives it to Selina, who offers to give him books to read, a gesture that greatly excites him.

Young Roelf develops a crush for Selina, but she eventually meets and marries a sensitive but still rough and awkward farmer, Pervus De Jong

(Earle Foxe). Now a farmer's wife, Selina finds the life tedious and hard but takes it all in stride. The two soon have a son, Dirk, and Selina, enthralled with the baby, introduces him to a ritual that the two will share over the years. She stretches out her arms and asks him, "How big is my baby? How big is my man?" Then she, and eventually he, answers "So big." She also gives him "So Big" as a nickname.

Meanwhile, Roelf Pool, dissatisfied with life on the farm, leaves home for bigger and better things. A while after this, Pervus dies, and Selina is left a widow who struggles to turn a profit from farming so that she—with hopes that young Dirk (now played by Dickie Moore) will someday become an architect—can send her son to college. She learns that asparagus, while it takes time to develop, can be a highly lucrative crop, changes the farm's emphasis to producing it, and makes enough to build a fine new home and pay for Dirk's education.

The story then skips ahead many years. Now, Selina is older and careworn, and, Dirk, now working as an architect, is unhappy and longs to

Young Dirk (Dickie Moore) and his mother, Selina (Barbara Stanwyck), share a tender moment in Wellman's *So Big*, the second of three films that have been based on Edna Ferber's best-selling and Pulitzer-Prize-winning novel (Warner Bros./Photofest).

make a lot of money while he is still young so he can spend it on a lavish life. Selina counsels him, saying that a life of focusing on beauty and creativity is more important and fulfilling, and mentions how Roelf Pool has now become one of the world's most respected sculpturers, contributing so much more to the world than someone who concentrates only on accumulating and spending money. Her words, though, have no effect on him.

We quickly learn that Dirk is involved with a married woman who encourages him to make money and fixes it for him to be hired by her husband's bond firm. At the firm, he meets and falls for an unconventional artist, Dallas O'Mara (Bette Davis), but she repeatedly turns down his proposals of marriage. Soon, Dirk meets Roelf (now played by George Brent), who learns that Selina is Dirk's mother. Along with Dallas, the two men go to Selina's farm, where Roelf and Selina have a warm, loving reunion. Watching them, Dallas remarks that Selina radiates with a kind of great human spirit that she would like to capture in a painting. Dirk looks on, only vaguely understanding what she is talking about.

*

Opening in U.S. theaters on April 30, 1932, *So Big*—just as Zanuck and Warner Brothers had calculated—was a big hit with audiences, tallying up box office receipts that far exceeded its estimated production budget of $228,000. Critics, however, were largely mixed. *The New Yorker* called Stanwyck's performance "the best work she has yet shown us,"[10] and the *New York Daily Mirror* enthusiastically seconded the motion, saying, "Her great talent as an actress never has been demonstrated more brilliantly."[11] At the same time, though, *Variety*, in criticizing the film's "choppy continuity," viewed it as both "a disjointed affair" and "overly long."[12] Andre David Sennwald, the recently hired film critic for the *New York Times*, went considerably further, calling the film "a faithful and methodical treatment of Miss Ferber's novel, but without fire or drama or the vitality of the original." Continuing, Sennwald noted that, although Stanwyck is "a fine actress," she "seems ill-suited to a role that hustles her in jerky steps from girlhood to old age, a role in which she is asked to express rugged grandeur and the beauty of a life well lived from behind a mask of grease paint." Finally, he assessed the supporting cast, with the two notable exceptions of Dickie Moore and Bette Davis, as "generally capable but uninspired."[13]

Although twenty-first-century film writers often are at odds with their early–1930s counterparts in their assessments of Wellman's pre–Code efforts, they are, in this case, generally in synch with the negative ones. Film writer Patrick Nash, for example, notes that *So Big* is "unevenly paced" and concludes, saying that, while the it "features a memorable cast," it is ultimately "but a minor entry in the careers of all its stars and its director."[14] Similarly, Melanie Novak, a fan of the original Ferber novel, observes that "watching *So Big* is like drinking flat champagne—all the elements are there but there's just no fizz." Later, she adds that, of the more-than-one-hundred films she's written about, "*So Big* is the one I'd most like to see remade.... Hollywood's taken three swings at it and never hit the ball out of the infield. I think there's a great film in the pages of Ferber's masterpiece.... But no one's made it yet."[15]

*

Perhaps the best bottom-line assessment of *So Big* is that it is a well-intended misfire. The story—largely a rumination about how we choose to live our lives; what we want to find, learn, or achieve on in the process; and, when all is said and done, what constitutes personal fulfillment—is thoughtfully conceived and has universal appeal. It's easy to see why the novel was so popular and why it still has fervent fans such as Novak today. Yet, despite the contributions of Wellman, Stanwyck, and many other able people, this film version ultimately doesn't succeed as compelling cinema. Wellman, of course, loved to direct various kinds of films and often succeeded admirably in genres ranging from comedy to drama, action-adventure, and the western. But this was clearly not the kind of story that excited him, and, although he works hard here at the craft of telling a story well through film, his lack of passion for the subject matter betrays him. We see this, for example, in the many scenes in which he portrays the Dutch farmers as oafs and otherwise strains to find comedy. We also see this in the scenes when Selina preaches her philosophy of life. A good example of this is the film's saccharine last scene when the older Selina reunites with the now-world-famous Roelf and they exchange lines that are about as subtle as a subtitle that reads "AUTHOR'S MESSAGE":

> RAOLF: "There are only two kinds of people in the world that really matter. One kind is wheat, and the other kind is emeralds. You're the wheat, Selina."
> SELINA (SMILING): "And you're the emeralds."
> RAOLF: "And you're the reason for it all."

Stanwyck, too, seems out of place in *So Big*. Especially at this point in her career, she was especially good at playing tough, no-nonsense women who took no guff but could also be quite sensitive and vulnerable. Here, though, she comes across as so sweet and saintly that, later in the story, one almost wishes that her Selina would lose it and blast her son Dirk for being the shallow, self-centered, and materialistic guy that he is. Like

6. The Hatchet Man *and* So Big *(both 1932)*

Wellman, she tried hard to make this film work, and like him, she came up a bit short this time.

Some film historians have suggested that Stanwyck's work portraying the self-sacrificing, almost saintly Selina in *So Big* provided her with a foundation that later helped her achieve success in a similar role: the endlessly self-sacrificing title character in King Vidor's *Stella Dallas* (1937). This may be true. Her work in *Stella Dallas* resulted in her first Best Actress Oscar nomination and is, even among today's more sentiment-adverse film viewers, still widely respected. Yes, the seeds for this triumph may very well have been sown in *So Big*. But, like the asparagus Selina sets out to grow in the Illinois soil, the seed is one thing and the fruit of the harvest is quite another.

*

After completing *So Big*, Wellman turned to filming his next project, a story much more in keeping with the fast-paced, urban, and irreverent Warner Brothers pre–Code style—an experience that inspired its young star, Douglas Fairbanks, Jr., to call Wellman "reckless and wild," yet also "one of the three or four best" directors in the business.[16]

7

"[I'm] very well, thank you—just a slight touch of leprosy"
Love Is a Racket (1932)

Although fans of Wellman's films will sometimes quibble about his directorial strengths and shortcomings, nearly all agree on one of his great talents: his magician-like ability to take a slight or flawed story and turn it into a compelling—or, at the very least, interesting—film. And, among his 1932 releases, one of the more intriguing examples of this talent is his next fast-turnaround programmer, a romantic comedy/drama (with a murder thrown in for good measure) called *Love Is a Racket*. While the plot is filled with twists and turns, and the script nicely peppered with witty lines, at heart there isn't much to it—no vivid, well-rounded characters; no gut-wrenching emotion; no hilariously comic scenes; no profound insights into the human condition. For a viewer, it's a little like having a light meal of cotton candy and popcorn: depending on your tastes, it might be quite pleasant as you consume it, but it doesn't quite deliver that filling, stick-to-the-ribs result that a meal of steak and potatoes usually does. Sometimes, though, insubstantial but quite pleasant can more than do the trick, and that's pretty much what this directorial magician offers us in this film.

What makes *Love Is a Racket* special, then, is its implementation rather than its initial concept or story. The film abounds with signature Wellman touches to give scenes added texture and vibrancy. The acting is also quite good, the players all working hard to give their mostly flatly written characters greater complexity and humanity. And the result is a well-steeped blend of creative energy, cynicism, and dark humor that's reflective of, and deeply embedded in, both Wellman's own sensibilities and pre–Code era attitudes and style. Watching this brisk, breezy outing, it's easy to see why Wellman and pre–Code era moviemaking were such a good fit for each other.

7. Love Is a Racket *(1932)*

*

The initial version of *Love Is a Racket* is a 1931 novel written by a young journalist named Rian James, who worked in the late 1920s and early 1930s as an arts and entertainment columnist for the newspaper, *The Brooklyn Eagle*. Soon after the novel's publication, Warner Brothers purchased the screen rights and brought in James to help develop the film treatment.

James (1899–1953), who clearly drew upon his newspaper experiences (and last name) to create the main character in *Love Is a Racket, New York,* newspaper gossip columnist Jimmy Russell, is an intriguing figure. Sharing Wellman's interest in trying his hand at a curious range of professions, he also worked—at various points in his life—as a parachute jumper, stunt man, airmail pilot, Air Force lieutenant, vaudeville actor, and film director and producer. After coming to Hollywood to help develop the screen version of *Love Is a Racket*, he settled there, and for the next fifteen years worked on scripts for more than forty films for various studios. The vast majority of these are forgettable budget pictures, but he did contribute to several "prestige" efforts such as Warner's *42nd Street* (1933) with Warner Baxter, RKO's *Swing Time* (1936) with Fred Astaire and Ginger Rogers, and Twentieth Century–Fox's *Down Argentine Way* (1940) with Don Ameche and Betty Grable. Wellman must have appreciated his contributions as well because, several months later, he was brought in to write the screenplay for the director's adventure-romance *Central Airport* (1933).

To develop the screenplay for *Love Is a Racket*, Warner Brothers assigned writer Courtney (also known as Courtenay) Terrett (1903–1950), who worked on more than a dozen films for various Hollywood studios during the 1930s. Among these efforts, perhaps the best-known today is Michael Curtiz's drama *20,000 Years in Sing Sing* (1932).

In addition to working with the writers on developing and refining the script for *Love Is a Racket*, another challenge for Wellman was selecting the kinds of actors who could bring additional nuance and depth to the film's main roles. And, in this process, he had some good fortune. To play the lead role of newspaper columnist Jimmy Russell, he was able to obtain Douglas Fairbanks, Jr. Just twenty-two years old at the time, Fairbanks was already an able leading man who could deftly handle both drama and comedy. As Russell's colleague and sidekick Stanley Fiske, he cast Broadway veteran Lee Tracy, who would soon establish himself as a memorable character actor. And, as Sally Condon, the woman who not-so-secretly pines for Russell, he cast the nineteen-year-old—and remarkably poised, polished, and mature—Ann Dvorak. Another interesting casting choice was Frances Dee, an actress with a talent for playing sincere characters, to play the especially insincere and manipulative Mary Wodehouse, the object of Jimmy Russell's affections.

Once again, Wellman recruited Sid Hickox, with whom he had worked on his three previous films, to handle the cinematography.

Yet another low-budget assignment for Wellman, *Love Is a Racket* was shot on the Warner Brothers lot in the spring of 1932 and completed in about a month's time.

*

This film opens with shots of short, sassy items from a gossip column that appears in the newspaper the *New York Globe*. The column is called *Up and Down Broadway*, and it's written by a Jimmy Russell. These items range from current theatrical chatter to a fashion update concerning New York's high-living mayor Jimmy Walker, to a few lines noting that the "lovely ingenue," Mary Wodehouse, is just back from Paris and accompanied, as always, by her very protective and always hovering Aunt Hattie.

Immediately, the scene cuts to a nicely appointed hotel room where we see Mary (Frances Dee), putting on hosiery in slightly risqué pre–Code fashion, as Aunt Hattie (Cecil Cunningham) lectures her about not getting involved with Russell or, for that matter, any newspaperman. Aunt Hattie's main objection: newspapermen never have "any dough."

Meanwhile, at Jimmy Russell's place, it is 5:00 p.m. and Jimmy (Fairbanks) is just waking up to a ringing phone. An operator at the *Globe* tells Jimmy that the editor-in-chief wants to see him right away. Just then, Sally Condon (Dvorak), a friend of Jimmy's, comes in. The phone rings again. This time it's Mary, who apologizes for standing Jimmy up for dinner the previous night and offers to make it right by meeting him for dinner later that evening. Sally also finds Stanley Fiske (Tracy), another reporter at the *Globe*, sleeping off a hangover on Jimmy's couch and, at Jimmy's request, wakes him up. Jimmy then draws a very cold bath for Stanley to wake him up more fully, and Stanley gets in, pajamas and all, bristling at the brutality of this kind of remedy.

Jimmy meets with the managing editor of the *Globe*, who wants him to work on a story tying gangland figure Eddie Shaw to a scheme to unfairly raise the price of milk and make it more difficult for parents to buy the much-needed food staple for their children. Although the editor believes the story will be dynamite, Jimmy, realizing that crossing Shaw would be dangerous, turns down the assignment and leaves it for another reporter to take on.

That night Jimmy meets Mary at Sardi's, the New York restaurant famous as a meeting place for show business people and other celebrities. At another table, Sally and Stanley are also having dinner. We learn that,

7. Love Is a Racket *(1932)*

A late sleeper, New York gossip columnist Jimmy Russell (Douglas Fairbanks, Jr.) takes a call from his bed as his friend Sally Condon (Ann Dvorak) looks on in *Love Is a Racket* (Warner Bros./Photofest).

just as Jimmy is smitten with Mary, Sally is gaga over Jimmy. Although she admits it, Sally also sensibly declares, "But I'm not jumping off any bridges on his account." A moment later, gangster Eddie Shaw (Lyle Talbot) walks in and over to Jimmy and Mary's table, where he invites himself to a seat. When Mary leaves for a few moments to ingratiate herself with the noted Broadway producer Max Boncour (Andre Lugent), Shaw indicates to Jimmy that he has a thing for Mary as well.

Later, at Jimmy's place, Mary confesses to him that she's been passing bad checks and is seriously in debt. To help her, Jimmy suggests she get a job as soon as possible to pay off her debts and offers to try to talk her creditors into waiting until she can. Then, he takes her home.

Still later, as Jimmy is working on his next column, he receives a visit from Burney Olds (Warren Hymer), an enforcer for Shaw. Burney tells him that Shaw knows about the story implicating him in the scheme to raise the price of milk; doesn't like it one bit; and, if the story runs, there will be consequences for Jimmy and anyone else behind it. Jimmy immediately denies involvement, learns that the story will soon run, phones the newspaper, and has it killed. That's enough to satisfy Burney, and Shaw, for the moment.

The next evening, as Jimmy and Mary again dine at Sardi's, he tells her that he has gone to her creditors and that someone else has already been to them and paid off the checks. The next day, Mary shares a telegram with Jimmy that she has just received. It's from Shaw, who reveals that he has serious designs on her, saying that, if she is "the smart little girl I think you are," she will join him for a tryst in Atlantic City and, by the way, not to worry any more about the bad checks. Again, Jimmy figures that the best thing he can do is to talk Shaw out of this idea.

Arriving in Atlantic City, however, Jimmy doesn't run into Shaw. Instead, Burney is there to meet him, and forcibly detain him. By drawing Jimmy out of town, Shaw is pulling a fast one, sending flowers and an extravagant bracelet to Mary as an inducement to rendezvous with him at his New York penthouse that night. Mary is horrified, can't contact Jimmy, and asks Stanley for help finding him. Looking on, Aunt Hattie comments that the only real solution here is for Shaw to get "a belly full of lead." Meanwhile, Jimmy escapes from Burney, returns to New York, and phones his home, where Sally answers and updates him.

That night, Jimmy goes to Shaw's penthouse and, just as he arrives, spots Aunt Hattie leaving with a gun in her hand. First, he makes sure that she doesn't see him. Then, entering the penthouse, he spots Shaw's body sprawled out on the floor. He pulls Shaw's wallet out of his pocket, takes the bad checks from it, and returns the wallet to the pocket. After this, he covers up all evidence of a shooting, spreads liquor around to make it look like Shaw has been drinking heavily, and carries the body out to the penthouse patio and tosses it over the side of the building. All signs now point to a dead-drunk Shaw walking to the edge of his patio and falling to his death, the victim of either an accident or suicide.

Later, Jimmy and Stanley are assigned to cover Shaw's demise for the *Globe*. The police declare that the death was accidental, and word is that there won't even be an autopsy, so Jimmy's ruse has worked: Aunt Hattie is in the clear, and Jimmy won't be charged with tampering with evidence.

That night, Jimmy, Sally, and Stanley also learn that Mary, who has always prioritized money and her career over Jimmy's love, has just agreed to a package deal with producer Max Boncour: the lead in his new play and marriage. In fact, the pair have already tied the nuptial knot.

Jimmy takes the news in stride, realizing that this is probably how things would have ended up between Mary and him anyway. Ever the cool-headed one, his first act is to send the bad checks and the evidence proving that Shaw's death was a murder to Aunt Hattie via courier.

Then, when Stanley asks Jimmy how he feels, he says that he's all right because his experience with Mary has taught him something very important, namely that:

7. Love Is a Racket *(1932)*

Love's just a mental disorder. Sure, it is. Love is spending all your dough for fifteen-dollar stockings and twenty-dollars-an-ounce perfume. It's lying awake nights worrying about whether she's kidding you or not. It's eating your heart out every time she has a cold sore in her lovely little lip. It's laughing at the oldest jokes in the world and dancing with your arches caved in.... It's waiting for two hours for dinner when you're as hungry as a toothless timber wolf. Oh, love is give, give, give your time and your money and your patience. And when you've shot the works, what have you got? Love....? Love's just a racket.

Stanley suggests they all toast to these sentiments. As they do, Jimmy declares, "So, help me—I'll never fall in love with a girl as long as I live." Then, he glances at Sally, who looks back at him with a twinkle of affection. He responds with a knowing, and what may also be affectionate, smile and says "Oh, you racketeers!"

*

Premiering in theaters on June 10, 1932, *Love Is a Racket* drew both good-sized audiences and generally positive reviews. The *Motion Picture Herald* noted that "the film is possessed of enough lightness, speed, and general activity to safeguard your promise of an entertaining picture."[17] And *Variety* declared that the "picture has persuasive comedy, capital melodramatic moments, engaging romance, and a cast of players that handle it neatly."[18]

Now, more than ninety years after its opening, *Love Is a Racket* continues to receive mostly complimentary comments. Film writer Dennis Schwartz, for example, calls it "enjoyable," "snappy," "effective," and "unpredictable"; praises the "winning performances" of the cast members; and notes how Wellman "does a nice job of highlighting the amoral Broadway scene, where gangsters mingle with celebs, theater people, and socialites in swank restaurants like Sardi's."[19] Film writer Erich Kuersten goes so far as to praise elements of the film as "pre–Code gold."[20] Various online bloggers have shared positive words as well. One notes that the film "holds up amazingly well due in large part to the skilled acting of the leads, a witty script that keeps everything lighthearted, and the masterful direction of William Wellman."[21] Another observes, "It's brilliantly put together.... It plays with your emotions with menace, excitement, and hope, and you will enjoy watching this."[22]

Yet, one of the curious aspects of many of these online commentaries is a hesitation to declare *Love Is a Racket* as a first-rate pre–Code effort. While calling the film "highly entertaining," for example, one blogger writes that it "just misses being a pre–Code classic." A little later, the same blogger adds that, while "the wise-cracks are plentiful and fun, ... they don't quite jump up off the paper."[23] "Maybe because it's so well made," another blogger notes about the film, "you don't notice how lightweight the story actually is."[24]

These last couple of comments are fascinating to consider. They certainly reinforce the contention that, as a film craftsman with magician-like powers, Wellman could—and, in this case, clearly did—make a film that rises above its superficial source material, so *Love Is a Racket* might not quite be a silk purse. But, if it did start out as a sow's ear, it was completely transformed by Wellman, Hickox, and the actors—interpretive artists all—who together injected enormous energy and many clever creative contributions into the storytelling. While not deathless art, the film is an enjoyable, exceedingly watchable entertainment that engaged audiences in 1932 and continues to interest viewers today.

*

As the case nearly always is in Wellman films, the director's signature touches are scattered throughout *Love Is a Racket*.

One that's quite compelling is the director's decision to set climatic scenes—much as he did in films such as *Other Men's Women* and *The Public Enemy*—in the midst of a rain storm in order to enhance dramatic impact. Here, a storm accompanies Jimmy on his wasted trip to Atlantic City, follows him back to New York, and is still in full force as he spies Aunt Hattie fleeing the murder scene, cleans up the scene, and throws Shaw's body over the penthouse patio fence. The result, of course, is to create an environment that reinforces the story's action: just as the weather is gloomy and thoroughly unpleasant, Wellman suggests, so too is the dark, distasteful business of cleaning up the murder scene and dumping the body.

Another very distinctive Wellman touch is to make enforcer Burney Olds into a prankster (much like Wellman himself was) who can't resist playing practical jokes on Jimmy. This gives Burney some added texture: now he is not just a thick-headed thug but a thug with an odd sense of humor and an underlying layer of fondness for Jimmy.

Still another is the deliberately odd blocking at the end of the film when Jimmy gives his "Love's just a mental disorder" soliloquy. For much of the speech, Jimmy's back is to the camera, and the impact is to nudge viewers into feeling a little more detached from, and less emotionally caught up with, the obvious pontificating. It's a curious decision but also an effective one that makes us a little more skeptical about whether Jimmy actually means what he is saying.

Finally, the director is unsparing in his depiction of the milieu of this film—an intersection of the early–1930s newspaper, entertainment, criminal, and law enforcement worlds—which he sees as largely corrupt and filled with jaded people who see principles as luxuries and are just trying to survive. Similar to *Night Nurse*, he even resolves the film in cynical, darkly humorous pre–Code fashion by having a reasonably good character murder the bad guy (because no one else will do it) and then get away with the deed.

*

In addition to Wellman, the actors also do more than their share to elevate the slight material.

Although quite young when he made *Love Is a Racket*, Fairbanks is thoroughly credible in portraying Jimmy as a shrewd, skeptical, world-wise, but still soft-hearted character who is probably supposed to be in his early thirties. He is quite convincing, for example, in the scenes when he argues against printing the milk racket story, showing coolness under pressure and arguing for prudence and common sense. Sure, both professionally and morally, running the story is the right thing to do, but it won't do him or others at the *Globe* any good if, as a result, they wind up dead.

The son and stepson, respectively, of silent film icons Douglas Fairbanks, Sr., and Mary Pickford, Fairbanks (1909–2000), had already been acting in silent and early sound films for nine years when he made *Love Is a Racket*. Afterward, he enjoyed a busy career as an actor and producer in both the United States and the UK, appearing in scores of films and then television programs over the next half-century. His final appearance was in the 1981 supernatural horror film *Ghost Story*, in which he played a central role opposite Fred Astaire, Melvin Douglas, and John Housman.

As Stanley, Lee Tracy brings both engaging comic touches and real empathy to his thinly written role. He is quite good, for example, in expressing his confusion about Jimmy's role in Shaw's death and the morality (or lack of morality) of it all as well as his deep concern for his friend's welfare.

Tracy (1898–1968), best-known for his early roles as fast-talking newsmen, press agents, lawyers, and salesmen, acted continuously in films and then on television until the 1960s. Near the end of his career, he was nominated for both an Academy Award and a Golden Globe for his supporting role in the big-budget 1964 political drama *The Best Man*, his final film.

As Sally, Ann Dvorak makes something memorable out of what is perhaps the most scantily written role in the film, portraying her character as intelligent, charming, caring, and basically quite decent. It's always fascinating to watch an actor who can turn an almost-non-existent character into someone notable and engaging, because most actors simply can't

Two of the pluses of *Love Is a Racket* are the lively, witty performances of Lee Tracy and Ann Dvorak as, respectively, Stanley and Sally (Warner Bros. Pictures/Photofest).

do it. Dvorak, though, was quite special, and watching her in this film, we marvel at how much she could do with so little to work with. She is particularly good, for example, at non-verbally communicating her feelings for Jimmy to the audience and at sparring verbally with the other characters.

Dvorak (1911–1979) is probably most fondly remembered today for her many fine pre–Code performances. After playing small, uncredited parts in more than thirty films between 1929 and 1931, she had her break-out year in 1932, delivering, in addition to her work in *Love Is a Racket*, highly praised performances in such films as *Scarface* with Paul Muni, *The Crowd Roars* with James Cagney, *The Strange Love of Molly Louvain* with Lee Tracy, and *Three on a Match* with Bette Davis and Joan Blondell. Another highly praised pre–Code role is her turn as the second lead in Mervyn LeRoy's *Heat Lightning* (1934). After mid–1934, she acted in a variety of films throughout the 1930s and 1940s, usually playing supporting roles. She retired after playing a key role in the intriguing noir western *The Secret of Convict Lake* in 1952 and (in a move reminiscent of fellow actress, Dorothy Mackaill) relocated to Hawaii to live.

As Mary, Frances Dee does a fine job of portraying a character who is outwardly sweet but at her core quite ambitious and manipulative. She shines in the scenes when she subtly enlists Jimmy in efforts to solve her various personal problems.

First appearing in films in 1930, Dee (1909–2004) had her break-out year in 1931 when she played a featured role in Josef von Sternberg's film of Theodore Dreiser's acclaimed 1925 novel *An American Tragedy*. For the next twenty-three years, she played a variety of characters in more than forty films. Her more notable film credits include roles in George Cukor's *Little Women* (1933), Frank Lloyd's *If I Were King* (1938), and her wonderfully nuanced portrayal of nurse Betsy Connell in Jacques Tourneur's poetic horror film *I Walked with a Zombie* (1943).

Finally, as Aunt Hattie, character actress Cecil Cunningham does a fine job of making her small role quite memorable. She is especially good, for example, when she expresses her very firm convictions that Mary not get involved with a reporter and that there was really only one way to deal with Shaw.

Cunningham (1888–1959) came to Hollywood from the stage in 1929 and, for the next seventeen years, appeared in more than eighty films, often in roles at "know-it-alls."[25] She also appears very briefly, and memorably, as the madam to Dorothy Mackaill's Gilda in Wellman's *Safe in Hell*.

*

One aspect of *Love Is a Racket* that many commentators like about the film is the number of witty, quotable lines the script contains. Examples abound. Some of the best of these lines, for example, come from Dvorak's character, Sally. When Mary, after being introduced to her at Sardi's, says "How do you do?" to her, Sally responds "Very well, thank you—just a slight touch of leprosy." A little later, when Stanley admits to having a romantic interest in her, she fires back, "If you loved me half as much as you love that steak, I'd break down and surrender to you out of pity" (pre–Code for giving him sympathy sex). Fairbanks' Jimmy has his share of zingers, too. When he considers publishing the story about Shaw's milk racket and the gangster's response, he says "That boy would have me on a slab in an undertaker's parlor quicker than a magician could palm a rabbit." And finally, there's Tracy's Stanley, who, when he hears some startling news in one scene, says "Well, I'll be a double-jointed son of a Bulgarian acrobat."

While most of these lines are enjoyable to listen to, especially when delivered by Dvorak and Tracy, nearly all of them seem to lack a characteristic essential to good scriptwriting. By themselves, these lines are clever, and they may even suggest that the characters saying them are clever, yet they often seem forced, and they rarely serve to differentiate or illuminate character, offer insights into other characters, or even underscore basic themes of the story. In fact, many of these lines could easily have been delivered by one or another of other characters in the film or even inserted into another film altogether. In many respects, this kind of writing is much like a common practice we see in sub-par television situation comedies—that is, writers trying to make poorly developed characters more appealing by giving actors cute and clever lines to recite. In addition, this kind of writing is probably one of the key reasons why a significant number of *Love Is a Racket*'s twenty-first-century viewers see the film as both enjoyable to watch and easy to forget.

*

If there is a bottom line to a discussion of *Love Is a Racket*, it might very well be, as pre–Code historian Danny Reid has noted, that the film is "a time capsule, … an unnerving portrait of its own era, where everything in society is broken, save the ever-resilient heart."[26] The story might be slight, the characters thinly drawn, and the prevailing attitudes bleak, but underneath all the cynicism and dark humor is a solid layer of Wellman-infused humanity. Yes, the times are hard and many people leave much to be desired, but, while a better time may currently seem like a dim light in the distance, it is still worth focusing on and moving toward.

8

"The tougher the going, the more you love 'em"
The Purchase Price and *The Conquerors* (both 1932)

Next up for Wellman were *The Purchase Price* and *The Conquerors*, two flawed but, in certain ways, very interesting efforts focusing on characters who, like many Americans in the 1800s and early 1900s, traveled west in search of new opportunities. Both films clearly have their share of weaknesses. In *The Purchase Price*, these include a disjointed script, some unfortunate directorial choices, and an inappropriately cast major character. And in *The Conquerors*, a major issue is the film's unabashed support of the largely discredited nineteenth-century U.S. belief in "manifest destiny"[1] that drives the film's story. At the same time, though, both films are peppered with excellent elements, ranging from a compelling Barbara Stanwyck performance in *The Purchase Price* to some ingenious visuals to communicate major historical transitions in *The Conquerors*. Although these two films aren't among Wellman's better known pre–Code efforts, they are, nevertheless, worth seeing to appreciate the seemingly endless inventiveness he brought to even his less promising projects.

In addition, both *The Purchase Price* and *The Conquerors* have their share of distinctively pre–Code elements. These are more evident in *The Purchase Price*. When the film opens, for example, we learn that the story's heroine has been involved sexually with a well-to-do criminal who is also married. Then, near the end of the story, she borrows $800 of his ill-gotten gains to help save her and her husband's farm. Neither, though, suffers the consequences of these socially frowned-upon actions the way they would in films made after the Code's enforcement. In addition, the heroine is repeatedly propositioned by a lecherous neighbor, who, other being rejected by her, doesn't face consequences, even a reprisal as light as social embarrassment. Although a little more subtle, *The Conquerors* has several hard-hitting pre–Code touches ranging from a mass hanging to a shocking moment when a woman gives birth an instant after her husband (and the baby's father) commits suicide.

*

The Purchase Price is based on a short story that first appeared in the *Saturday Evening Post* in late 1931 called "The Mud Lark," which at the time was a slang term for a person who scavenges in river mud for items of value. Its author was Arthur Stringer (1874–1950), a Canadian-born writer, who, in addition to poetry and stage plays, produced more than forty works of fiction, his stories ranging from formulaic crime and adventure tales to more serious pieces about life on the rugged Canadian prairie. Veteran screenwriter Robert Lord, who had recently collaborated with Wellman on *So Big*, was assigned to develop the adaptation. And, once again, Sid Hickox was on board to handle the cinematography.

For the third time in about a year—and to his great delight—Wellman would also be working with Barbara Stanwyck, and rounding out the cast were Warner Brothers contract players George Brent as the male romantic lead and Lyle Talbot as the heroine's shady earlier love interest.

Shooting took place in the spring of 1932 at the Warner studios in Burbank as well as at various Southern California farming and rural locations. For the most part, the production phase went smoothly, but a couple of interesting anecdotes have been passed down. One involves scenes late in the story when a wheat field is set afire and Stanwyck and Brent's characters must save it. Stanwyck didn't like the way her stand-in acted and convinced Wellman to let her do the dangerous scenes herself. He obliged, and, while the scenes proved to be quite exciting, she received several serious burns on her legs. Although Wellman was concerned, she never complained, the burns healed, and his admiration for both her fearlessness and her intense commitment to her craft only grew. The second story involved a bar-room fight between Brent and Talbot's characters. Before shooting the scene, Wellman approached the two actors separately and told them to let the other guy "have it." The actors worked out the choreography beforehand so the fight would look fearsome but neither would get hurt. When Talbot was hit back against a wall at one point, however, his head struck a slightly protruding nail. As the actor recounted in an interview decades later, "It just bled like mad. They had to take me over to the infirmary and sew me up. Wellman loved it. He said, 'Talbot, what a scene! That was great.'"[2]

For film trivia aficionados, *The Purchase Price* also opens with Stanwyck singing the torch song, "Take Me Away," marking the first time the actress ever sang in a film.

8. The Purchase Price *and* The Conquerors *(Both 1932)*

*

The story of *The Purchase Price* opens in New York. Nightclub singer Joan Gordon (Stanwyck) has left her boyfriend, a wealthy criminal named Eddie Field (Talbot) and is now engaged to Don Leslie (Hardie Albright), a nice young man from an upstanding, well-to-do family. When Don's father learns that Joan has been with the disreputable Eddie, however, he forces his son to break the engagement. After briefly returning to Eddie, Joan leaves town for Montreal and resumes performing, this time under another name. After one of Eddie's men spots her, however, she realizes that she must leave Montreal as well. Her solution is to trade places with Emily, her hotel maid, who has just confessed to using Joan's picture when writing to Jim Gilson (George Brent), a North Dakota farmer who is seeking a mail-order bride. Offering the maid one hundred dollars for the farmer's address, Joan, with only a vague idea of the hardships of farm life, especially during the economically depressed 1930s, sets out to become Gilson's wife.

Joan and Jim immediately marry, but their relationship gets off to a rocky start. On their first night, she rejects his advances and forces him to sleep elsewhere. In the morning, she apologizes, but he keeps his distance. Over time, she falls in love with him, but he remains aloof. Meanwhile, Jim is informed that he will lose his land if he cannot pay his overdue mortgage. He has developed an excellent strain of wheat and is sure that it will bring a profit, but he has no way to forestall foreclosure long enough to plant and harvest a crop. Neighboring farmer Bull McDowell (David Landau) offers to buy Jim's land if Joan will clean his house and, as clearly implied, provide sexual services. Joan turns him down, and Jim is adamant about not selling, especially to Bull.

Later, Joan, who has now become a very capable farmer's wife, visits a neighbor who has just given birth to a boy with only her adolescent daughter, Sarah (Anne Shirley), to help her. Joan cleans the home, prepares food, turns an old dress into diapers and calms the frightened Sarah. She braves a snowstorm to return home only to learn that Eddie, who had told Jim that he was lost in the storm, has arrived. She pretends not to know Eddie, but he tries to convince her to return with him. Jim, figuring things out and now quite angry with Joan because of her checkered past, tells her to go with Eddie. She refuses and later privately asks Eddie for a loan of eight hundred dollars to save Jim's land, telling Eddie, who wonders why she sticks with Jim, that she loves him despite all the difficulties the two have had. "The tougher the going, the more you love 'em," Eddie says with some grace and a touch of envy. He adds, "Just a natural mud lark," alluding, of course, to the scavengers who search for items of value in the most improbable of places.

In *The Purchase Price*, Jim (George Brent) and Joan (Barbara Stanwyck) struggle with the challenges of farm life and their problematic marriage (Warner Bros./Photofest).

The loan, which Jim thinks is an extension from the bank, enables them to stay on the farm until after the harvest. Joan continues to stand by him, but he remains distant. Then, one night, one of Bull's men torches some of the crop. Joan and Jim are able to save it, however. Jim is proud of what Joan has done, and, at long last, he kisses her with real affection and passion.

*

Opening in theaters on July 23, 1932, *The Purchase Price* was greeted by both so-so box office and a cool-to-tepid critical reception. In his review, the *New York Times*' Andre David Sennwald called the film's script "one of the weirdest scenarios within the memory of man" and "totally incomprehensible," adding with a touch of sympathy that the whole experience must have "seemed a bit hard on the cast."[3] Sennwald did note, though, that, in the midst of all the confusion, "many of [the film's] individual scenes are undeniably good."[4] *Variety* declared that Stanwyck and Brent were "both 100% miscast."[5] In a slightly more positive appraisal, however, the *Kansas City Star* chimed in with a couple of intriguing insights, first observing

8. The Purchase Price *and* The Conquerors *(Both 1932)* 113

that the film "has more entertainment value than the plot has logic" and then praising Stanwyck for "her uncanny ability to make the most phony [sic] heroines seem like human beings."[6]

As was true with *So Big*, twenty-first-century reviewers are pretty much aligned with their 1932 counterparts on the subject of *The Purchase Price*. Glenn Erickson, for example, calls the script "oddly structured" and the film "probably the weakest" of the six Wellman pre–Code features he was reviewing in his article.[7] And film writer David Nusair heartily concurs, calling the effort "slow-moving," "mostly uneventful," and "thoroughly forgettable."[8] Despite such derision, however, he does note that the film greatly benefits from the "efforts of its charismatic star," adding that "Stanwyck's engrossing, magnetic performance [goes] a long way towards sustaining the viewer's interest through the narrative's less-than-enthralling stretches."[9]

*

It doesn't take much to understand why the script for *The Purchase Price*, as well as some of the directing choices Wellman made when filming the story, have baffled viewers both in 1932 and in more recent years. Several scenes, while they serve to give us additional glimpses into character, don't advance the plot. The scene when Stanwyck's Joan goes to visit a neighbor who has just given birth is certainly one. While it may serve to show Joan's growing maturity, it comes out of nowhere and then goes nowhere. The relationship between Joan and Sarah, the baby's teenage sister, is quite interesting, but then, when Joan leaves, the relationship just ends. We never see Sarah again. Other scenes, such as Joan and Jim's wedding, may have directly inspired Sennwald's comment about the film having "one of the weirdest scenarios within the memory of man." This scene is played for laughs, but it is still—with everything from one witness stirring cake batter to the other ogling the bride in a very creepy way—more disconcerting and bizarre than funny. This, incidentally, is one of several scenes in which Wellman treats the rural people as louts, buffoons, or—as in the case of the man who confronts Brent's Jim with wolf howls—moronic crazies. Again, the intention is probably to inject some farcical humor into relatively lifeless situations, but the result is just embarrassing.

To Wellman's credit, however, some scenes in *The Purchase Price* come across beautifully. Again, an excellent example is the scene when Joan visits the neighbor who has just given birth, the teenage Sarah, and the baby boy. Yes, this scene does nothing to advance the action of the main story, but, as a vignette, it is a compelling showcase for the abilities of both Stanwyck and the young Anne Shirley as Sarah. The situation is very real, the dialogue is honestly written, and both Stanwyck and Shirley perform with great feeling and integrity. At the end, we really believe that the caring and competent Joan has proven to be the model Sarah needs so that she can now handle the job of helping her recovering mother care for her new baby brother. If *The Purchase Price* contained more scenes like this one, especially if they served to advance the main action, it would have been a much better film.

*

It's interesting that the *Variety* review from 1932 declares that both Stanwyck and Brent are "100% miscast." This is certainly true, especially at a time when viewers expected to see Stanwyck in the sassy, streetwise, take-no-guff roles she played throughout the pre–Code era and Brent in his suave, sophisticated leading-men turns. There is, however, a fascinating difference in the results. While Brent seems out of place because of the miscasting, Stanwyck manages to overcome it, playing against type, as well as playing an inconsistently written character, and pulling it all off remarkably well. Yes, she certainly did have, as the *Kansas City Star* noted in 1932, an "uncanny ability to make the most phony heroines seem like human beings."

Let's begin with Stanwyck, whose character of Joan goes through some very far-fetched changes. She starts off as a wealthy criminal's pampered mistress/nightclub singer in New York and eventually escapes to rural North Dakota to be the mail-order wife of Jim, a well-meaning but rough-edged farmer. When Jim forcibly tries to have sex with her on their wedding night, she rejects him, hurting his feelings, and the marriage remains unconsummated. Despite this setback, however, she seems highly motivated to adapt to this hard new life: putting in long days of manual labor, putting up with loutish neighbors, traveling all day in freezing weather to pick up coal, and doing everything else she can to help Jim keep the farm solvent. In the process, she also falls for Jim and tries to win his favor. As a story arc, the journey from pampered mistress to gritty farmer seems difficult to buy, yet Stanwyck makes Joan credible every step of the way by infusing her character with a very honest and relatable humanity as well as a strong desire to find real love, even if it is with an awkward farmer in North Dakota.

The casting of Brent as Jim is quite another matter. Although Brent gamely tries to play a rough, rustic character, the actor's natural polish and sophistication can't help but come through in scene after scene. In a way, watching Brent play Jim (especially in one scene he shares with a pig) is a little like watching a suave Ronald Colman or Herbert Marshall attempt to play the very rustic Pa Kettle.[10] When cast in the right kind of role, however, Brent, who had a full career playing mostly in romantic leads

8. The Purchase Price *and* The Conquerors *(Both 1932)*

opposite Stanwyck, Bette Davis, and other actresses, could be quite effective and compelling. (We will discuss him a bit more in the next chapter.)

Another actress who needs a mention here is the young Anne Shirley, who does standout work in the one fairly brief sequence she shares with Stanwyck. Only fourteen years old when the scenes were filmed, she is both in total control of her character and disarmingly honest. Her performance is excellent.

Shirley (1918–1993), who also appeared briefly in Wellman's *So Big* as the young Selina Peake, was, at the time she made *The Purchase Price*, right on the cusp of more substantial roles and greater notoriety. Born Dawn Evelyn Paris, she began as a child performer in silent films at age four, using the professional name Dawn O'Day. After the industry transitioned to sound films, she remained in demand, usually to play small parts. Then, in 1934, she was cast in her break-out role—the lead in the popular film adaptation of the novel *Anne of the Green Gables*—and, as a nod to the character she played in the film, Anne Shirley, she took the name to use professionally. The following year, she gave a memorable performance co-starring with Will Rogers in John Ford's *Steamboat Round the Bend* (1935). And for her work (once again with Stanwyck) in King Vidor's *Stella Dallas* (1937), she received a Best Supporting Actress Oscar nomination. After an acclaimed co-starring role in the classic film noir, *Murder, My Sweet* (1944), she announced that she was tired of film acting and retired. At the time, she was a film industry veteran with twenty-two years of experience and more than sixty film roles to her credit, and she was just twenty-six years old.

*

The Purchase Price is a noteworthy example of how resourceful professionals working on an early–1930s assembly line coped with a problematic script. For Wellman, the results this time were mixed. He directs some scenes with imagination, vigor, and real integrity, but he also—perhaps in desperate attempts to inject life into other scenes—resorts to cheap, unnecessary, and sometimes embarrassingly bad comic bits. Stanwyck, however, fares somewhat better. And the main reason was her talent to turn a poorly written role into something interesting by infusing a thinly drawn character with a very real and relatable humanity. In the entire history of film, very few actors have managed to do this both well and consistently, and Stanwyck was one of them.

*

Wellman's next project was a film called *The Conquerors*, a sprawling story that follows an American banking family for nearly sixty years, from the financial panic of 1873 through the Wall Street Crash of 1929. For this effort, he worked, not with Zanuck and Warner Brothers, but with David O. Selznick, then an in-house producer at RKO, who'd negotiated with Warner Brothers to "borrow" the director from the rival studio to make this film.

Like Zanuck and others in Hollywood, Selznick was looking for opportunities to capitalize on the enormous commercial success of *Cimarron* the year before, and *The Conquerors* seemed like an excellent choice. The film is based on a story by Howard Estabrook, who had also written the screen adaptation for *Cimarron*, and—from the story's multi-generational structure to its focus on the great westward expansion in the United States during the late 1800s and early 1900s—it shares many elements of the previous film. With its unabashed cheerleading for American grit, ingenuity, and resiliency, *The Conquerors* is also an attempt to boost morale for movie audiences, who, in 1932, were living through the darkest days of the Great Depression. For the project, Wellman brought with him Warner Brothers contract writer Robert Lord to develop the screenplay. And, in hopes of increasing the chances that *The Conquerors* would be another *Cimarron*, Selznick recruited—along with Estabrook and others associated with the earlier film—its leading man, actor Richard Dix; one of its featured supporting players, Edna May Oliver; the composer of its musical score, Max Steiner; its film editor, William Hamilton; and its cinematographer, Edward Cronjager.

In addition, Selznick and Wellman cast two other actors in significant roles. One was theater-turned-film actress Ann Harding to play the female lead. And the other was popular character actor Guy Kibbee to play a key supporting role.

Among all of these contributors, perhaps the best-known today is Selznick (1902–1965), who won back-to-back Best Picture Oscars for producing the classics *Gone with the Wind* (1939) and *Rebecca* (1940). At the time he produced *The Conquerors*, he was head of production for RKO, the studio that had hired him in 1931 after he had served relatively brief stints at both MGM and Paramount. In 1933, he returned to MGM to work in a senior production role, but, in only two years at RKO, he had left an indelible mark on the once-struggling studio. In addition to turning its financial fortunes around, he (among numerous other contributions) recruited respected director George Cukor, signed actors Katharine Hepburn and John Barrymore, helped to bring the megahit *King Kong* (1933) to the screen, and approved the screen test for a balding Broadway song-and-dance man with, as Selznick once wrote in a memo, "enormous ears," "a bad chin line," and "tremendous charm."[11] His name was Fred Astaire. Long craving to be an independent producer, Selznick finally

8. The Purchase Price *and* The Conquerors *(Both 1932)*

formed his own film company in 1935 and continued to produce films under his own brand until the 1950s. In addition to *Gone with the Wind* and *Rebecca*, these include such classics as *The Prisoner of Zenda* (1937), Wellman's *A Star Is Born* and *Nothing Sacred* (both 1937), and Alfred Hitchcock's *Spellbound* (1945) and *Notorious* (1946).

Of all the contributors to *The Conquerors*, however, perhaps the person most responsible for why classic cinema buffs still discuss this film today is painter; illustrator; and film montage, editing, and special effects specialist Slavko Vorkapich. To note the passage of time in the story, Vorkapich created a series of highly effective montage sequences to show events and other developments occurring in the United States at the time. Sometimes literal, sometimes metaphorical (such as growing mountains of money to depict prosperous times and toppling coins to convey economic crashes), these montages visually convey a great deal in very striking, highly efficient ways. They are clearly among the film's highlights.

Born in Serbia, Vorkapich (1894–1976) migrated to the United States in 1920, roamed the country for about a year, and arrived in Hollywood nearly penniless in July 1921. After beginning his film career as a painter and an actor, he quickly earned fame as a montage developer, special effects expert, and cinematic artist. And, between the 1920s and 1940s, he made significant contributions to dozens of films from creating special effects for MGM's lavish Joan Crawford musical *Dancing Lady* (1933) to designing montages for Frank Capra's classic *Mr. Smith Goes to Washington* (1939). Afterward, he left the movie industry but not the film world, becoming the chair of the Department of Film Studies at the University of Southern California and then a professor at the Belgrade Film and Theater Academy in Yugoslavia.

Filming for *The Conquerors* took place in mid–1932 both on the RKO lot and on location in the abandoned Central California community of Cooperstown. Cooperstown, incidentally, was a popular site to shoot Hollywood westerns during the studio era. Among other notable efforts filmed there were Victor Fleming's *The Virginian* (1929) with Gary Cooper and Michael Curtiz's *Dodge City* (1939) with Errol Flynn.

*

The Conquerors begins in New York City in 1873. Roger Standish (Richard Dix) is fired from his job as a bank clerk for courting Caroline Ogden (Ann Harding), the daughter of the bank's president. When the bank fails in the Panic of 1873, however, Caroline's father becomes penniless and dies. Still very much in love, Roger and Caroline marry and head west to find new opportunities.

As they travel through Nebraska on a raft, however, Roger is shot by

Caroline (Ann Harding, left) and Roger (Richard Dix) appreciate the gesture of trust when Matilda (Edna May Oliver) deposits her money in Roger's newly opened bank in *The Conquerors* (RKO. Moviestore Collection Ltd/Alamy Stock Photo).

a gang of bandits and taken to the nearby town of Fort Allen. There, Doc Blake (Guy Kibbee), a chronic drunk but still a competent physician, operates successfully, and his wife Matilda (Edna May Oliver), who runs the local hotel, welcomes the young couple into the community. Later, however, the same bandits who shot Roger attack Fort Allen. Roger exhorts the community to pursue them. Still recovering from his gunshot wound, however, he is unable to lead the pursuit. Eventually, the townspeople catch up with the bandits and hang them *en masse*. Soon, the Standishes open a bank, and, with the help of the Blakes, it is an immediate success. On the same day, Caroline also gives birth to twins, a girl and a boy.

Over the years, both the Standishes' bank and Fort Allen prosper. The railroad comes through the town, offering the promise of even greater growth and prosperity. On the day the railroad station is opened, however, tragedy strikes: both Doc Blake and the Standishes' young son die in a buggy accident.

Although devastated by the loss of their son, the Standishes press on, and years later their daughter, Frances (Julie Hayden), marries Warren

8. The Purchase Price *and* The Conquerors *(Both 1932)*

Lennox (Donald Cook), who works at Standish's bank. Soon afterward, though, a major economic downturn hits, and, partially due to Warren's incompetence, the bank is forced to close and Warren kills himself at, ironically, the exact moment that his and Frances' son is born. Undeterred, Roger vows to pay all his depositors back, presses on, and eventually does fulfill his promise.

Frances' son, Roger Standish Lennox (also played by Dix) grows up and becomes a decorated fighter pilot during World War I. But, as the family watches him march in a victory parade after the Armistice, Caroline, whose heart has weakened with age, collapses and dies.

With the elder Roger now quite old, young Roger becomes an ever-more-important leader at the bank, and, during the 1920s, the bank and the family—like the country—thrive. With the stock market crash of 1929, however, young Roger faces a situation similar to the one his grandfather had faced decades before. To keep the bank solvent, young Roger asks his grandfather to sign papers to dissolve his five-million-dollar trust fund, and, as the elder Roger signs the papers, he shares his optimism, that, just has the country has always recovered from setbacks and then risen to new heights, it will certainly do so again.

*

Opening in theaters on November 18, 1932, *The Conquerors*, turned out to be a major box-office disappointment for Selznick and RKO, recording an overall loss after expenses of $230,000.

Critics at the time were generally mixed. In his review, for example, the *New York Times*' Mordaunt Hall, wrote that, while the film "has much that holds one's attention, the levity during certain interludes (namely the comic moments involving Oliver and Kibbee) is overdone."[12] The review in *Variety* was a bit harsher, saying that the film lacked "the epic sweep"[13] of *Cimarron* and that it "measures up at a little better than fair screen material, its failings being in the conception rather than in the production or acting of its people."[14] At the same time, however, the critic from the *Galveston Daily News* found the film quite stirring, saying that "one emerges from the theater with a courage to face any task, an ambition to surmount any barrier, and a faith to conquer any problem."[15]

Over time, though, *The Conquerors* has been reconsidered and praised for a number of its elements. Wellman biographer Frank T. Thompson, for example, has declared that it "remains one of Wellman's most intriguing films, not for the rah-rah you-can't-lick-America theme but for the boldness of its images and the sincere, unpretentious approach to what is, after all, a simple love story."[16] Pre-Code historian Cliff Aliperti has generally seconded this sentiment. While seeing *The Conquerors* as essentially propaganda, he observes that "every time the movie threatens to drag, it manages to weave in ... surprising moments ... to at least quicken the heartbeat if not the overall pace."[17] It's worth noting, too, that, while both Thompson and Aliperti acknowledge that *The Conquerors* was made mainly to capitalize on the success of *Cimarron*, it is actually, according to Thompson, a "far finer,"[18] and Aliperti, the "superior," film. In fact, Aliperti even stresses that, although it was "a knock-off," this "doesn't mean that it wasn't an improvement as well."[19]

*

Although *The Conquerors* is not as distinctively Wellman-esque as most of the director's other pre–Code films, it does contain several of his characteristic, and quite vivid, touches.

Perhaps the most striking is the sequence leading up to and including the mass hanging that occurs about a half-hour into the film. The Slades, the same gang of bandits that robbed and shot Roger on the river boat, have descended upon Fort Allen, robbed as many people as they could, committed murder in the process, and departed. Roger exhorts the townspeople to pursue the gang and catch them, saying, "The Slades owe me a debt, and I'm going to collect. Are you with me?" He tries to ride out with the rest of the townspeople. Still weakened from his gunshot wound, however, he falls from his horse. The others stop to see if he is all right, and, from the ground, Roger asks rhetorically, "Well, what are you going to do now?" Another man resolutely answers, "Just what you would ... if you could." In the next scene, Roger is back indoors and resting, he and Caroline discuss the idea of starting a bank so people can keep their money in a safe place, Doc Blake comes in to provide a touch of comic relief, and, after a final bit of levity, the picture fades to black. Then, as the picture slowly fades back in from the black, we see a campfire in the wilds at night. The men from the town who went to pursue the Slades are sitting around it. Soon, about ten of them with ropes in their hands stand up, walk toward a long horizontal tree branch that extends over what appears to be a gulley, toss their ropes over the branch, wrap one end of each rope around the saddle horn of each of several horses facing away from the tree branch, and mount the horses. After this, one man gives a signal, the horses move forward, and, as they do, the ropes pull about ten men up from the gulley, each with a noose wrapped around his neck. A few of these men kick for a second or two in vain, and, in a final shot, we see only the legs of the horses holding the ropes firm as the hanged men are being strangled by the taut nooses. Again, the picture fades to black. Then, after a beat, the action returns to Fort Allen. It is a bright new day sometime later, and we learn that the Standish Bank is now open for business.

8. The Purchase Price *and* The Conquerors *(Both 1932)*

This whole sequence (which immediately conjures up associations with Wellman's 1943 western, *The Ox-Bow Incident*, which also centers on a lynching) is the director at his purest and finest. After the Slades rob the town, we assume that the townspeople are acting as a posse who will catch the culprits and bring them back to face justice in the hands of the proper authorities. As they pursue the Slades, however, the action cuts back to the Standishes and the Blakes and a bit of comic relief. Then, we see the resolution, the captured culprits are not brought back to face justice but brutally hanged. This scene takes only about a minute of screen time, but it is riveting, eerie, and devastating. No one says a word. All we hear are the sounds of the horses moving forward as they pull the hanged men off the ground. The ten or so hangmen all perform each action in the process simultaneously. The scene is choreographed deliberately to give the occasion a sense of ceremony, of ritual, of solemnity. Needless to say, this is one scene that would never have been included in exactly this way if this film were released after the Production Code was fully enforced.

One fascinating aspect in this sequence is the line of dialogue the man delivers to Roger just before the townspeople ride out in pursuit: "Just what you would ... if you could." This, of course, begs the question: What is Roger's attitude about what ultimately happens here? Is he just as bloodthirsty as the other townspeople? Or, if he had been able to ride out after the Slades, would he have argued that these outlaws should be turned over to the proper authorities? And what, in the end, is his responsibility in the matter? He is, after all, the one who stirred the passions of the townspeople and exhorted them to go after the Slades. In true Wellman style, the story simply moves on and these issues are never discussed. We are, however, left with an extremely intriguing ambiguity: Is Roger every bit the decent, fair-minded, law-abiding person we see elsewhere throughout the story, or not?

A second interesting aspect of this sequence is the choice of cutting to the comic relief scene after the pursuers leave town but before the actual hanging. As first-time viewers, we are totally caught off-guard. We relax, assuming that the charged drama of the previous few minutes has passed. Then, of course, we are hit with perhaps the film's most electrifying, and horrifying, scene. Wellman loved to play with viewers' assumptions and expectations, suggesting one thing and then hitting them with something else altogether. In this sequence he plays this card exceedingly well.

Another characteristic Wellman touch was to show the paradoxes and ironies of life in very succinct, elegant cinematic ways, and in *The Conquerors*, he does this in several scenes. One of the most effective of these is the scene when Roger and Caroline's grandson, young Roger, is born at just one second after his father, Warren Lennox, shoots and kills himself. In true Wellman fashion, both events take place off-screen and we listen to, rather than see, what's happening. This time the camera is placed in a hallway. As it faces the door to the room where Lennox is, we hear the gunshot. Immediately, the camera pans to the next door down the hall, and we hear the cries of the newborn. The scene is so powerful because the enormity of these two events, and immense tragic irony implicit in them, are both conveyed with such simplicity.

*

The transition montages are, of course, another highlight of *The Conquerors*. And, along with Slavko Vorkapich, Wellman; the film's editor, William Hamilton; and its cinematographer, Edward Cronjager, also deserve high praise for the effectiveness with which these montages convey both the relationship between industrial progress and prosperity and the cyclical nature of a capitalist economy. Among the sequences in the film, perhaps the most gripping is the one leading up to the Wall Street Crash of 1929. At first, we see images depicting a rising stock market juxtaposed with shots of happy investors. Then, one side of a steep mountain is superimposed on charts of the rising stock values, tracking with the rise. Ultimately, we see the top of the mountain. After this, the joy on the investors' faces turns to concern, the mountain begins to crumble, the investors' faces turn to panic, and then the faces themselves unnervingly melt into non-existence before our eyes. From here, the images turn to reality as we see shots of closed factories, unused ships sitting in harbors, unemployed workers standing in a relief line, and so on. The sequence is a spellbinding mix of both metaphorical and literally images that is just as gripping to viewers today as it surely was to movie audiences experiencing the Great Depression first-hand in 1932.

*

Offsetting its strengths, *The Conquerors* does have more than its share of weaknesses, and they no doubt have been instrumental in relegating the film over time to relative obscurity.

At the top of the list is the film's "manifest destiny" perspective, one reinforced by its pompous title. Today, a great many Americans do not see the westward expansion of mostly white settlers in the 1800s as anything resembling the glorious undertaking that many of their ancestors once did. And today, much of the film's story and some of its attitudes can strike audiences as naïve and dated if not downright chauvinistic.

Related to this is the film's attempt to tell a story with such epic sweep in under ninety minutes. Although the montages are fascinating and usually help in this process, the overall result is akin to taking a survey course

8. The Purchase Price *and* The Conquerors *(Both 1932)*   123

that covers sixty years of U.S. history in just two forty-five-minute lectures: it's virtually impossible to give any character or significant event adequate depth, and we come away with the feeling that the experience has all been very superficial.

Another weakness is the film's acting. Although leading man Richard Dix is markedly better in this film than he was in *Cimarron* (which is not saying much), he is still tedious and boring. A major star in silent films, Dix (1893–1949) would soon experience a precipitous decline in his career fortunes, spending most of the 1930s and 1940s acting in low-budget genre films. As Caroline, Ann Harding is also quite unengaging. One of many stage actors who migrated to Hollywood with the advent of sound, Harding (1902–1981) retains many of her theatrical mannerisms and her portrayal often comes across as affected and dated. The film's two most interesting actors, character players Edna May Oliver (1883–1942) and Guy Kibbee (1882–1956), do the best they can in underwritten semi-comic roles, but they often resort to mugging and their work here is far from their best. (We will discuss Kibbee in a bit more detail in this book's next chapter.)

*

After directing *Rebecca* for David O. Selznick eight years after Wellman worked for the producer on *The Conquerors*, Alfred Hitchcock remarked that, ultimately, *Rebecca* wasn't a Hitchcock film but a Selznick film. This observation is well worth noting. Selznick was one of a handful of "auteur producers" in Hollywood during the classic era who infused the films he worked on with his own views and preoccupations and, as a result, put his own very distinctive personal stamp on them. As strong-willed directors with very distinctive personal styles and points of view such as Hitchcock and Wellman soon learned, working for Selznick—who often preferred stories with an epic sweep and overly sentimental and/or overwrought romance—was not without its challenges. In the end, of course, the films were usually much more a reflection of the producer's, rather than the director's, perspectives and contributions.

This is clearly the case with *The Conquerors*. Although Wellman brings some amazing, and very characteristic, moments (such as the mass hanging scene) to the finished product, this is, for all intents and purposes, a Selznick film with Wellman working as the hired hand.

As noted, Wellman and Selznick would work together again later in the 1930s on two films, *A Star Is Born* and *Nothing Sacred* (both 1937). Although both efforts were critical and commercial successes, these two very strong-willed personalities, acknowledging that they did not complement each other well, opted never to make another film together again.

*

With *The Conquerors* completed, Wellman returned to Warner Brothers, where he reunited with Zanuck and met another very strong-willed artist, an idiosyncratic and demanding actress, who at first refused to work with him, but who would soon be starring in not one, but two, Wellman features.

9

"It may be the wrong way, but it's going to be my way"
Frisco Jenny (1932) and *Lilly Turner* (1933)

After completing *The Conquerors*, Wellman returned to Warner Brothers, where Zanuck—true to form—wasted no time before summoning the director to his office to receive his next assignment.

The first bit of news Zanuck had for Wellman was quite heartening. His new project was a melodrama centering around a fascinating female character, a San Francisco madam who turns bootlegger while also concealing from the upright, up-and-coming son she had given up for adoption that she is, in fact, his real mother. Colorfully titled *Frisco Jenny*, it had been co-written by a playwright hired by the studio just a year before named Wilson Mizner. Though they hadn't officially worked together yet, Wellman and Mizner—both rebels who often clashed with authority figures—had become fast friends at Warner Brothers. Wellman told Zanuck he already knew about the story, loved it, was delighted at the prospect of working with his pal Mizner, and was ready to jump into the project.

Ready to leave, he asked, "Is that all you're going to tell me?"

"No," Zanuck said, "the star's coming in."[1]

The producer buzzed his outer office, the door opened, and in walked Ruth Chatterton. An acclaimed Broadway actress who had begun working in films in 1928, achieved stardom with her 1929 hit *Madame X*, and recently left Paramount for Warner Brothers, Chatterton had also brought along her reputation for being a diva.

When Chatterton sat, Zanuck began to talk to her and Wellman about the production, but she quickly interrupted him, saying that she—apparently having heard about Wellman's own reputation for being difficult—would not work with the director. At this, Wellman said that he wouldn't work with her, either. Then, without missing a beat, Zanuck declared, "I've got news for you. You're both going to work together or you can look for another job. And it isn't going to be easy to find, when I get through [with you]."[2]

With this stern warning, the two settled down. When shooting began, both were absolutely professional. After three days, Chatterton looked at Wellman and said, "Truce?" The director responded, "Yep. Truce." And from that moment, according to Wellman, "we became nothing but pals."[3] In fact, soon after *Frisco Jenny* was completed in late 1932, the two worked together again in another female-centered melodrama, 1933's *Lilly Turner*. And later that year, the two briefly teamed up for a third time, Wellman directing seventeen scenes of the now-acclaimed pre–Code comedy *Female* before being assigned to another project, a football film called *College Coach*.

Their collaboration filming scenes for *Female* aside, Wellman's working partnership with Chatterton resulted in two fascinating films. And today, both are well worth watching for their sympathetic takes on the challenges many women faced leading up to and during the early 1930s; bravura performances by Chatterton, now a virtually forgotten talent; and, of course, Wellman's ability to make the most with tight budgets and minimal resources.

We'll start with *Frisco Jenny*, an effort Chatterton would later pick—from among the twenty-six Hollywood films she made—as her favorite.[4]

*

Although Zanuck and Wellman only discussed the director's writer-friend, Wilson Mizner, during their kick-off meeting for *Frisco Jenny*, the story and screen adaptation have no less than five parents. The original version was a short story titled "Common Ground" by a writer named Gerald Beaumont (1880–1926) that first appeared in *Redbook Magazine* in 1926. And Mizner was only one of four writers who received screen credit for the film adaptation. Two other longtime Hollywood script writers, John Francis Larkin and Lillie Hayward, prepared the scenario, and, along with Mizner, scriptwriter Robert Lord (discussed in Chapter 6), developed the film's screenplay. Larkin (1901–1965) was a producer as well as a writer, whose Hollywood credits range from scripting Charlie Chan mysteries in the 1930s to producing seventy episodes of the acclaimed television crime series *M Squad* in the late 1950s. And Hayward (1891–1977) began writing for silents in 1917 and remained active in films and then television until the early 1960s, her credits ranging from the suggestively titled pre–Code drama *They Call It Sin* (1932) to the fine noir western *Blood on the Moon* (1948), to the Disney comedy *The Shaggy Dog* (1959).

Of all the writers involved with developing the story and then the

9. Frisco Jenny *(1932) and* Lilly Turner *(1933)*   127

script for *Frisco Jenny*, though, by far the most colorful, and at times notorious, was Mizner (1876–1933). A playwright and short story writer turned screenwriter, he was also, at various times, a professional gambler; a con-man who swindled prospectors during Alaska's Nome Gold Rush of 1899; a hotel manager; a real-estate developer; a prize-fight manager; an art forger who copied his rich wife's Rembrandts and Picassos and sold the counterfeits, claiming they were the originals; and a co-owner and the manager of the storied film industry gathering place, the Brown Derby Restaurant.

In addition, he was quite a raconteur, minting such memorable one-liners as "Be nice to people on the way up because you'll meet the same people on the way down"[5] and "When you steal from one author, it's plagiarism; if you steal from many, it's research."[6] Among his one-liners, some of the most scathing were those directed at the film industry. He sometimes referred to his years in Hollywood, for example, as "a trip through a sewer in a glass-bottom boat,"[7] and he likened his experience at Warner Brothers in particular to "fucking a porcupine—it's a hundred pricks against one."[8] The screenwriter Anita Loos—who claimed she based the character of Blackie Norton, the professional gambler played by Clark Gable in the MGM film *San Francisco* (1936), on Mizner—once described him as "America's most fascinating outlaw."[9] It's quite easy to understand why Loos felt this way, and why, when Mizner joined Warner Brothers, Wellman instantly took a liking to him.

All his colorful, scoundrel-like behavior aside, Mizner, as some of his one-liners suggest, was also quite a talented screenwriter. In his very short stint at Warner Brothers, for example, he worked on only about a dozen films, and, in addition to *Frisco Jenny*, among these are such pre-Code triumphs as *20,000 Years in Sing Sing*, *One Way Passage*, and *Heroes for Sale*.

Another fascinating addition to the *Frisco Jenny* production team, of course, was its star, Ruth Chatterton. Headstrong and supremely confident of her abilities, Chatterton (1892–1961), became an actress in her mid-teens after she criticized another actress' performance and friends told her to stop complaining and become an actress herself. Soon, she dropped out of school to pursue a stage career, and, in October of 1911, when she was eighteen, she debuted on Broadway in a play called *The Great Name*. She moved to Los Angeles in 1925 and continued to act in stage plays there until she was recruited by silent film star Emil Jannings to play a featured role in the now-lost Paramount film *Sins of Our Fathers* (1928). This, in turn, led to *Madame X*, stardom, and the first of two consecutive Best Actress Academy Award nominations. (The second was for her work in the 1930 drama *Sarah and Son* helmed by pioneering female director Dorothy Arzner.) After several more hits, she moved, in 1932, from Paramount to Warner

Brothers. In addition to her acting, she also has the distinction of being one of the top female aviators in the United States at the time, making several solo cross-country flights and sponsoring a number of competitive aviation events. Sadly, however, Chatterton's star declined almost as quickly as it had risen. Very likely because of her age (she had just turned forty when both *Frisco Jenny* and *Lilly Turner* were released) and the various studios' preferences for younger female stars, her films were less popular and she received fewer film offers. She did deliver one excellent later performance, though, as the spoiled, unfaithful wife of the title character in William Wyler's fine adaptation of Sinclair Lewis' novel *Dodsworth* (1936). She retired from films in 1938, acted occasionally on the stage and later for early television, and then, in 1950, reemerged as a best-selling novelist with her book *Homeward Borne*. Over the next decade, she capitalized on her new-found literary success, publishing four more novels.

In addition to Chatterton, two actors assigned to key roles in *Frisco Jenny* were Louis Calhern and Donald Cook. Calhern (1895–1956), who had aristocratic looks and bearing, alternated between stage and films in a career that spanned between 1921 and 1956. During this time, he was especially effective at playing polished, seemingly upstanding people who were, in reality, scoundrels. And today, he is probably best remembered for playing Alonzo Emmerich, the main villain in John Huston's film noir classic *The Asphalt Jungle* (1950). Cook, whom we've discussed earlier in this book, was now appearing in his fourth Wellman film in less than two years, and here would be used to great effect in one of the film's closing scenes.

Two notable behind-the-scenes contributors to *Frisco Jenny* were cinematographer Sid Hickox (working on his sixth Wellman film in slightly more than a year), and editor James Morley, who collaborated closely with Wellman and Hickox to piece together the film's impressive re-creation of the 1906 San Francisco earthquake.

Filming took place in late 1932 at the Warner Brothers studios in Burbank.

*

The story of *Frisco Jenny* begins in San Francisco in April 1906. Jenny Sandoval (Chatterton), who works in her father's saloon, is pregnant by the saloon's piano player, Dan McAllister (James Murray). Both are in love and want to marry, but Jenny's father (Robert Emmett O'Connor) is furious and opposes the match. In the midst of this personal conflict, however, the city is struck by a devastating earthquake and fire. Both Jenny's father and Dan are killed, and afterward, Jenny gives birth to a son, whom she names Dan.

9. Frisco Jenny *(1932) and* Lilly Turner *(1933)*

With the help of a slick but disreputable lawyer named Steve Dutton (Calhern), Jenny becomes a madam, procuring women for well-heeled San Francisco politicians, businessmen, and others. Making the decision to embrace this kind of work, seemingly the best realistic choice she believes she has, she stoically says, "It may be the wrong way, but it's going to be my way."

Both during this time and afterward, the only real friend and confidant Jenny has is Amah (Helen Jerome Eddy), a Chinese woman who initially helps her care for young Dan and then stays at her side during both good times and bad.

In *Frisco Jenny*, Louis Calhern plays shady lawyer Steve Dutton and Ruth Chatterton is madam-turned-bootlegger Jenny Sandoval, two underworld allies who eventually become adversaries (Warner Bros./Photofest).

At a party both Jenny and Dutton attend not long after she enters the vice business, Dutton catches a gambler cheating at cards in a back room, the two fight, and Dutton shoots him. Jenny, the one person who knows what actually happened, offers to help Dutton out of the jam by covering for him, but neither her story or Dutton's quite adds up to the police, who remain suspicious. Both are questioned, but ultimately neither is charged with any crime. There is a scandal, though, and the local child welfare society threatens to take young Dan away from his disreputable mother. To avoid this, Dutton suggests that they temporarily give Dan to a respectable, well-to-do couple in nearby Oakland, who are willing to care for Dan until Jenny can safely take him back. Reluctantly, Jenny agrees.

Three years later, Jenny has made enough to retire from the vice business and leave town with Dan. When she goes to the couple in Oakland, however, Dan—clinging to the only parents he knows—resists. With great sadness, Jenny allows him to remain with them and leaves. As the years go by, she watches Dan's life from afar, saving newspaper clippings showing that, among other things, he has gone to Stanford University, starred in football there, graduated, and become an assistant district attorney in San Francisco.

As all this has occurred, the United States has also entered the era of Prohibition, and, in addition to running her vice operation, Jenny branches out into bootlegging.

Soon, the ambitious and idealistic Dan (now played by Donald Cook) runs for district attorney. His opponent is Tom Ford (Edwin Maxwell), a corrupt politician who winks at Jenny's bootlegging activities and often avails himself of Jenny's call girls. Most everyone assumes that Jenny will back Ford in the race, but she arranges for the police and press to find Ford at a party with call girls. Scandal follows, and Dan, previously the underdog, handily wins the election.

Once in office, Dan goes on a mission to clean up corruption in the city, and, when Dutton, misjudging Dan, offers him a bribe in hopes of a favor, Dan arrests him. Dutton is quickly bailed out and pressures Jenny to blackmail Dan into dropping the charges by telling him that she is his real mother, a revelation that could destroy his political future. When Jenny refuses, Dutton threatens to tell Dan himself, and, as he is about to enter Dan's office to share the information, Jenny shoots and kills him.

Dan has no choice but to arrest and prosecute Jenny, who refuses to defend herself, and she is sentenced to be executed by hanging. As she awaits the gallows, Amah begs her to tell Dan the truth, believing that, if he better understood her reasons for shooting Dutton, he would arrange for a more lenient punishment. Then, Dan, sensing that there is something more behind Jenny's actions—something he is missing—comes and begs her to tell him what that is. Seeing Amah once again, Jenny reaffirms her wishes, insisting that Amah never reveal the truth to Dan. She also whispers something private into Amah's ear.

In the film's final scene, Jenny has now been executed. Amah sits beside a small blaze in a fireplace, and we learn what Jenny had whispered into her ear. Her loyal friend is now carrying out a request to burn the newspaper clippings about Dan that Jenny had so lovingly saved over the years, clippings that, if they ever fell into the wrong hands, could hurt him and his career.

*

Frisco Jenny premiered in theaters on December 30, 1932, and, according to film writer Frank Miller, did not perform as well at the box office as Warner Brothers had hoped. Apparently, because of key plot similarities between this film and Chatterton's 1929 hit *Madame X* (such as the protagonist-mother making the ultimate sacrifice for the well-being

9. Frisco Jenny *(1932) and* Lilly Turner *(1933)*

of her child) many viewers saw this film as simply a rehash of the previous film and received it less than enthusiastically.[10] The critics at the time were also mixed. While praising *Frisco Jenny*'s earthquake sequence early in the story, Mordaunt Hall noted that the rest of the film "does not live up to" its promising beginning.[11] And, while calling the story "hokum" overall, the reviewer for the *New York Herald Tribune* praised Wellman for keeping the story "marching along" through the "use of colorful atmosphere, effective costuming, and the logic with which he unfolds this episodic tale."[12]

As has happened so often with Wellman's pre–Code films, however, film historians and contemporary critics have tended, after reevaluation, to see *Frisco Jenny* in a much more favorable light. In addition to praising Wellman's direction as "solid and impressively frank and authentic throughout,"[13] for example, film writer Stuart Galbraith IV was especially impressed with the film's honest, mature, empathetic, and tolerant nature, noting:

> The depiction of that era's vices is neither romanticized nor scorned; the film basically doesn't pass judgment on Jenny's willingness to do whatever it takes to feed her son and build a new life for herself—an attitude the Production Code would in no way have permitted just a few years later. The argument could be made that the film's tragic, bitterly ironic ending—a genuinely emotionally devastating one that must have left 1932 audiences shell-shocked—*could* have permitted such a film to be made post–1934, but I doubt it. The picture is emphatically on Jenny's side, no matter her bootlegging and procuring.[14]

Several contemporary writers have also been impressed with Chatterton's fearless, no-holds-barred portrayal of Jenny, a strong woman determined to be master of her destiny long before women's liberation entered the mainstream of American life. As film writer Mark Fusion observes:

> The real draw is Ruth Chatterton.... The role is a great fit for her and she makes the most of it, putting her charm and charisma to good use throughout. I love the scene where she works hard to cover up a murder, as she is so expressive and brings a great sense of dark humor to the sequence. The movie greatly benefits from her presence, and I don't think many actresses could fill the role in quite the same way, with such a unique, bad ass brand of charisma. The rest of the cast is solid, but no one can keep pace with Chatterton, which is no surprise.[15]

*

Looking more closely at *Frisco Jenny*, it becomes clearer why recent appraisals of the film have generally been more positive than earlier ones.

One reason is a greater (and still growing) appreciation for Wellman's many contributions to the effort.

A fine example of the director's handiwork is the film's earthquake and fire sequence. Although not quite as impressive as the rendering of the disaster in the big-budget MGM spectacular *San Francisco* (1936), this low-budget depiction nevertheless holds up quite well. The sequence here is an amalgam of stock footage actually shot in San Francisco in 1906, footage from the Warner Brothers silent drama *In Old San Francisco* (1927), and models and live-action scenes shot specifically for this film. And, with the help of cinematographer Hickox, editor Morley, and other technicians, Wellman pieced all this together to convey—and quite well, too—the suddenness and enormous scope of the disaster both at the personal and the large-scale levels. Within seconds, Jenny sees her father killed and his saloon destroyed and, fearing for her own safety, runs into the street. Then, we see other buildings destroyed, some massive structures collapsing like houses of cards. After this, we see one explanation for the cause-and-effect relationship between the earthquake and the ensuing fire: oil spills out into the street, sparks from broken electric power lines set the oil on fire, and entire buildings burn as we hear the incessant clang of fire bells. The holocaust is complete. What's amazing is that all of this is so succinct, clear, and, at the same time, evocative: in only two minutes of screen time, all hell has broken loose and we see just enough to imagine how destructive and horrifying the actual 1906 earthquake and fire must have been.

Another intriguing Wellman contribution to *Frisco Jenny* is how some large-scale group scenes are so beautifully and richly presented that they suggest a film with a much larger budget. An excellent example is the makeshift camp Jenny wanders through in the aftermath of the earthquake. As we see her trying to find out about her lover's fate, she passes several groups of people, each group with a distinct character and suggested backstory—a large gathering of African Americans listening to one man sadly singing a spiritual, a couple of nuns quietly praying, a madam giving a pep talk to a group of working girls, and a mother in an open-air bed tenderly playing with her newborn. It's a lovely, very poignant few moments that also conveys the great range of people affected by the tragedy.

Finally, Wellman's unusual camera angles and other creative shooting choices throughout *Frisco Jenny* help keep viewers keenly engaged in the proceedings. One good example is the camera position he chooses in order to emphasize the growing conflict between Dutton and Dan after the former offers the latter a bribe. For their climactic stare-down, the director places the camera to capture a close-up of both Dutton and Dan's profiled faces, a shot in which these two profiles take up most of the screen, and then leaves it there as:

9. Frisco Jenny *(1932) and* Lilly Turner *(1933)* 133

- Dutton says, very threateningly, "You'd better go slow. You're putting yourself in a spot, my boy."
- The two continue their stare-down for a tense silent moment.
- Dan bravely replies, "I'll risk it."

The other element that gives this moment great dramatic irony, of course, is that Dan doesn't fully understand what Dutton's threat of putting him in a spot (that is, making it public that the notorious Jenny is his mother) actually means.

In addition to Wellman, several of the actors in *Frisco Jenny* made notable contributions to the film.

Foremost among them, of course, is Chatterton, who, despite some acting affectations she brought to films from her stage work, is an imposing presence on the screen. In some of her other film performances, she clearly, as the saying goes, "chews the scenery," but in *Frisco Jenny* she, more often than not, commands through understatement. It's difficult to tell whether the decision to underplay the role of Jenny was hers, Wellman's, or one they mutually agreed on, but, whichever is the case, the decision was the right one. Both Chatterton and her director were smart enough to realize that Jenny's story is, in its own right, such a tearjerker that the actress wouldn't need to beg for additional tears from viewers. In fact, the underplaying actually helps to elicit more of an emotional response, leaving it to viewers to imagine for themselves what Jenny is feeling and then, perhaps, to feel more deeply for her. We see this approach used to greatest effect in many of the story's most poignant moments such as when Jenny opts for the vice business because it's the only way that she can realistically support young Dan; when she realizes she can't in good conscience take young Dan back from the adoptive parents he's bonded with; and when, in her jail cell awaiting execution, she refuses to tell Dan why she killed Dutton.

Chatterton is also quite good at pulling off another big challenge of the role: playing Jenny from the time she is a young woman of about twenty in 1906 to a woman in her mid-forties in 1932, twenty-six years later. The actress—who turned forty just a week before the film's release—might not be entirely believable as the twenty-year-old in the earlier scenes, but she is fairly credible, playing the still-somewhat-innocent character with real feeling and conviction. When playing characters much younger than they were, many actresses of the era came across as self-conscious and forced. Chatterton, on the other hand, meets the challenge quite well.

In key supporting roles, both Louis Calhern and Donald Cook also deliver fine performances. As the charming, smarmy, and totally unscrupulous Dutton, Calhern eases into the part so naturally and smoothly that we can see why he was cast in these kinds of roles so often during his long Hollywood career. He is especially good, for example, in the scene when Dutton tries to bribe Dan. When Cook's Dan challenges him, Calhern quickly drops Dutton's amiable façade and, in a very calm, calculating way, becomes quite threatening, quietly emphasizing that Dutton is not a person to be trifled with. As the adult Dan, Donald Cook at first comes across as a self-righteous stuffed-shirt, but, during Dan's prison cell chat with Jenny, he very convincingly portrays Dan as a person possessing much more insight and emotional depth than we might have expected. Dan's sensitivity toward her is a big part of what makes this scene, contrived as it is, perhaps the most compelling in the entire film.

*

Although *Frisco Jenny* has many strengths, it does have its share of weaknesses. Perhaps the most glaring, especially to contemporary viewers, is its manipulative and melodramatic storyline about a mother who will do anything for her child, even give up her life to keep him from learning about his disreputable heritage. While both Chatterton and Cook are quite affecting in their prison cell scene, for example, the situation here is, nevertheless, a bit much to swallow. In addition, the film sometimes suffers from a hyperactive camera. While Wellman's creative camerawork usually energizes the storytelling, it can sometimes detract. This occurs, for example, in the final courtroom scene when, during Dan's closing arguments, the camera moves from character to character sitting in the room. Rather than undercutting, reinforcing, or otherwise commenting on what Dan is saying, these shots are confusing and distracting.

All things considered, though, *Frisco Jenny* is well worth seeing, especially for Wellman's inventive and vigorous style of storytelling and for Chatterton's self-assured and masterly star turn. The actress was truly one of a kind, and this is clearly one of her best film performances.

*

Soon after completing *Frisco Jenny*, Wellman and Chatterton again joined forces, and again the project was to bring a woman-in-distress melodrama to the screen.

This film was titled *Lilly Turner*, and it was based on a stage play of the same name by Broadway impresarios George Abbott and Philip Dunning, which had recently completed a respectable run at New York's Morosco Theater. Both Abbott (1887–1995) and Dunning (1889–1978), who frequently collaborated both as playwrights and stage producers, had storied Broadway careers. And today, Abbott especially—who also acted and directed in a career that spanned eighty years—remains a towering

9. Frisco Jenny *(1932) and* Lilly Turner *(1933)*

figure in American theater. Just a few of his many, many hits include *Pal Joey* (1940), *On the Town* (1944), *The Pajama Game* (1954), *Damn Yankees* (1955), and *A Funny Thing Happened on the Way to the Forum* (1962). Abbott was active in films as well, working in various capacities on forty projects between 1918 and 1958. His screen credits range from writing the screenplay for the classic 1930 version of *All Quiet on the Western Front* (for which he received an Oscar) to directing the screen versions of *The Pajama Game* (1957) and *Damn Yankees* (1958).

After securing the screen rights to the story of *Lilly Turner*, Warner Brothers assigned two in-house writers, Gene Markey and Kathryn Scola, to the project. Markey (1895–1980), who wrote either scenarios or screenplays for thirty-seven films and served as either producer or associate producer for another seventeen between the 1920s and 1950s, was well known in social circles during his Hollywood years as a captivating conversationalist and ladies' man. Married four times, his first three wives were actresses Joan Bennett, Hedy Lamarr, and Myrna Loy. Scola (1891–1982) contributed writing to about three dozen films during the 1930s and 1940s, and among her credits are screenplays for the pre–Code classic *Baby Face* (1933) and the sparkling Henry King musical *Alexander's Ragtime Band* (1938). Apparently, Wellman appreciated Markey and Scola's work on *Lilly Turner*, because he turned to them again a few months later to develop the screenplay for another of his women-in-distress films, *Midnight Mary*.

To handle the cinematography for *Lilly Turner*, Wellman enlisted veteran cameraman James Van Trees, who had previously worked with him on *The Star Witness* and would soon collaborate with him on both *Heroes for Sale* and *Midnight Mary*.

In addition to Chatterton, *Lilly Turner* also features three of the more interesting actors from the Warner Brothers stock company of the period. These include George Brent, who had recently played roles in Wellman's *So Big* and *The Purchase Price*; perennial scene stealer Guy Kibbee, who had recently appeared in *The Conquerors*; and character player Frank McHugh.

Most of the shooting took place in early 1933 at the Warner Brothers studios in Burbank, and, with Wellman directing, it was, once again, a highly efficient, tightly managed affair.

*

The film version of *Lilly Turner* opens on the title character's wedding day. Lilly (Chatterton) is about to marry a handsome glad-handing vaudevillian named Rex Durkee (Gordon Westcott), but many of her family and friends have concerns about his character. The two follow through with the ceremony, though, and, as they depart on their honeymoon, Rex tells Lilly that things are pretty tough in vaudeville right now and that he will have to take work wherever he can find it. Rex does find work at a carnival and recruits Lilly to help him in his magic act. We are also introduced to Dave Dixon (McHugh), a good-hearted carnival barker with a serious alcohol problem. Soon, we see what Lilly's family and friends had feared: Rex steps out with another woman from the carnival.

After six months, things between Lilly and Rex reach a low point. By now, she is on to his bad behaviors, and he is pretty much done with her. In the midst of an argument, she tells Rex that she is going to have a baby, and he is infuriated. Then, Lilly finds out that Rex, in addition to his lying and philandering, is also a bigamist and that her marriage to him isn't valid. Immediately afterward, Dave tells her that Rex has skipped town, but not to worry because he will take care of her. To give the baby legitimacy, Lilly and Dave marry, a friendly but chaste arrangement. Dave's drinking, though, continues. Then, just after Lilly gives birth, the baby, a girl, dies. As Dave consoles her, Lilly says that in a way she's glad that the baby didn't live. "What chance would she have had?" she adds.

Eventually, the two find work with a traveling medicine show run by Doc McGill (Kibbee), where Dave continues to work as a barker and Lilly performs as a woman who was once sickly and deformed and now credits McGill's advice and treatments for her health and beauty. Here, we meet another performer, Fritz (Robert Barrat), a muscular, weightlifter who also tells audiences that his good health is entirely due to McGill's program. Fritz is also quite smitten with Lilly, although she sees him as an oaf and shows no interest in him.

Soon, Fritz has what appears to be a mental breakdown. As a medical doctor examines him, Lilly meets and is immediately attracted to a handsome young cab driver named Bob Chandler (Brent). Bob is drawn to her as well. When the doctor says that Fritz must be taken to an asylum, Fritz resists and is sedated. Lilly asks Bob to help carry Fritz to his cab to go to the asylum, and Bob proves to be surprisingly strong. To be closer to Lilly, Bob quits his cab-driving job and joins the show as the new strongman. Quickly, the two fall in love. During this time, Bob also reveals that he is a civil engineering graduate from Columbia University and has been looking for work in that field, but, because of the hard economic times, he must take any kind of a job he can get to make ends meet.

Meanwhile, Fritz escapes from the asylum and comes searching for Lilly. About this time, too, Bob receives a telegram from a company based in Denver offering him a civil engineering job. When he shares the news with Lilly, he tells her that he wants her to come with him, and she agrees. Now, however, Fritz finds Lilly in her hotel room and grabs her. Both Bob and Dave try to subdue him, but, in the fracas, Fritz pushes Dave through a second-story window. Dave isn't killed, but his spine has been fractured,

9. Frisco Jenny *(1932) and* Lilly Turner *(1933)*

Working in a carnival medicine show, Lilly (Ruth Chatterton) falls for Bob Chandler (George Brent), who joins the act as a strongman, in *Lilly Turner* (Warner Bros./Photofest).

and, before he is taken to the hospital, he asks Lilly to stay with him. She agrees to this and tells Bob that, because of the ways things are now, she'll have to stay with Dave but that he must follow up on his job opportunity. She adds that she'll love him no matter where she is. After she leaves, though, Bob decides that he, too, must stay to be with Lilly.

*

Opening in theaters on May 13, 1933, *Lilly Turner* did well at the box office but received a lukewarm response from critics. Calling the film "a drab, uninspired story," for example, Mordaunt Hall felt that Chatterton was "not in her element" here and "obviously far better suited for a more sophisticated subject."[16] Hall did, however, praise Guy Kibbee for playing Doc McGill "remarkably well."[17] The reviewer from *Variety* shared similar sentiments, writing that the film "fails to measure better than fair."[18] This reviewer, though, was kinder toward the film's leading lady, noting that the effort is "Miss Chatterton's all the way, [the] star making every effort to [compensate for] what the story lacks...."[19]

It's curious that, while many of Wellman's pre–Code films have gained in stature with the passage of time, *Lilly Turner*, while quite interesting to many contemporary film critics and historians, remains a mixed bag to them as well. After declaring that *Lilly Turner* "falls shy" of the great films Wellman would later make in 1933, for example, pre–Code historian Danny Reid writes that the film "is still a down-and-dirty character piece, filled to the brim with atmosphere and a wry smile on its face."[20] Reid also observes, "The movie is still fun to watch as an example of a slice of life that gets glossed over now, one about surviving near-constant treachery and yet still remaining open and alive.... It's a movie made for dark times, and, some days, it doesn't seem like we'd ever left."[21] Film writer James Travers sees the film along similar lines, saying, "The smallness of the budget and the absurdities of the plot are to a large extent masked by the generally excellent performances and the oppressive mood that Wellman and his cinematographer James Van Trees manage to create...."[22] Travers then adds that, for an early–1930s film, *Lilly Turner* has an unusually modern feel to it, one which, he suggests, anticipates the claustrophobic atmosphere and futility found in many films noir of the 1940s and 1950s:

> A thick air of fatalism hangs over this film.... Although Chatterton gives her character plenty of spunk, she [Lilly] is far from in control of her destiny—social and economic forces will determine her future happiness. That said, you can't help sensing in the film's wonderfully ambiguous ending that Lilly Turner will get what she wants, eventually.[23]

*

Although the script of *Lilly Turner* contains its share of melodramatic contrivances and thinly written characters, Wellman and the featured actors all sportingly worked to do the best they could with the material they had.

As usual, Wellman shoots many of the scenes in *Lilly Turner* from visually interesting, and sometimes arresting, camera angles and keeps the action moving at a brisk pace. One excellent contribution is his use, once again, of the Warner Brothers rain and wind machines. In this film especially, the choice to set several scenes in the rain achieves multiple ends and often to great effect. One—when coupled with a long succession of scenes inside cramped, shabby carnival tents—is to visually underscore the oppressive, claustrophobic nature of Lilly's existence. Simply put, she is trapped in an unsavory, low-life world, and, for much of the film, there seems little hope of her finding an escape from it. Another, curiously, is to help reinforce the idea that Bob may offer her the security, comfort, and hope she craves. We see this in the scenes when Lilly and Bob's truck gets stuck in the mud during a rain storm and, while others go for help, the two use the opportunity to make love for the first time in the cozy, nest-like

9. Frisco Jenny *(1932) and* Lilly Turner *(1933)*

area they've carved out for themselves in the back of the vehicle. Here, the presence of the pouring rain outside contrasts with—and, in doing so, actually serves to highlight—both the relative warmth and pleasantness inside the dry truck and the positive prospects associated with Bob. This sequence works quite well.

The main actors, too, turned in fine work.

Much as she did in *Frisco Jenny*, Chatterton delivers a forceful performance throughout *Lilly Turner* while also—and quite skillfully—underplaying, especially in scenes when Lilly is feeling great sorrow or loss. One excellent example is the scene is when Lilly and Dave ride away from a hospital in a cab and we hear that she has lost her baby. Every line Chatterton speaks is matter-of-fact, understated. But underneath, we can sense that Lilly feels great pain and loss. At the same time, too, Chatterton's Lilly is no pushover. She more than stands her ground, for example, in scenes when Fritz and Doc McGill make advances toward her, putting them both in their place gently, sometimes teasingly, but also firmly. Finally, Chatterton again brings her distinctive personal stamp and charisma to Lilly, truly making the role her own.

Worthy of kudos, too, are three actors who support Chatterton in *Lilly Turner*: George Brent, Guy Kibbee, and Frank McHugh. The handsome, personable Brent had a talent for bringing intelligence and emotional depth to thinly written characters. And here, cast in a role much better suited to his talents than the oafish farmer he played in *The Purchase Price*, he does a nice job of doing just that. He and Chatterton, who had recently married, also have great chemistry on screen, and we can absolutely see why his Bob offers Lilly the only glimmers of real hope and happiness that she has in the film. Kibbee, who reveled in playing colorful supporting roles throughout the 1930s and 1940s is clearly in his element here. His Doc McGill is simply a con-man, but Kibbee manages to give him elements of vulnerability and empathy that round out the character more fully. Finally, Frank McHugh (1898–1981), who played sidekicks and/or loveable drunks in films from the late 1920s to the late 1960s, brings real depth and dimension to the part of Dave, the incorrigible alcoholic who marries Lilly so her baby can be legitimate. His Dave hasn't just done a pal a favor: he truly loves Lilly while also knowing that she will never feel the same way toward him. At the same time, too, his Dave is also needy and often annoying, a major ongoing burden for Lilly. In lesser hands, Dave could simply have been played as a clichéd stock character, but McHugh handles the role quite adeptly, making Dave more sensitive, nuanced, and, in the process, human than he might otherwise have been portrayed.

*

Although *Lilly Turner* lacks some of the production gloss and stylings of *Frisco Jenny*, it does have its fair share of elements—such as its in-your-face grittiness, relatively casual attitudes about sex, portrayals of people living a hand-to-mouth existence, and ambiguous ending—that make it classically pre–Code. In many ways, this film is a time-capsule that enables us to glimpse into the hard lives many people lived during especially hard times. At the same time, it also more than holds its own as an engaging, skillfully crafted entertainment, a film well worth watching, especially for viewers with an interest in all things pre–Code.

*

In the end, perhaps it is best to see both *Frisco Jenny* and *Lilly Turner* as intriguing, if not flawless, examples of the work of the two artists who made the most significant contributions to them: Wellman and Chatterton. Wellman's imprint, from the cynical tone and sympathetic characterizations to the fast pacing and visceral energy of both films, is very much in evidence. In addition, these films are both excellent examples of the work of Chatterton, an actress who radiated, as film critic Mick LaSalle has written, "a vision of total female authority, circa 1930."[24] Yes, this woman could command the screen, riveting viewers with her magnetic presence, intelligence, charm, and wit. And, for an actor from any era, that is no small feat.

10

"Whoever he is, he's flirting with the undertaker"
Central Airport (1933)

After the enormous success of *Wings* in 1927 and 1928, the great fanfare that followed pilot Charles Lindbergh's solo flight over the Atlantic Ocean in 1927, and other developments, the still-nascent field of aviation quickly became a ripe subject for Hollywood. And, by the early 1930s, stories about the daredevils of the air and their personal (and usually romantic) struggles on the ground had become a distinct subset of the action-adventure genre. One of the most lavish efforts of the time is *Hell's Angels* (1930), an independent production about World War I fliers produced and directed by the eccentric multi-millionaire Howard Hughes. A second is *The Dawn Patrol* (1930), another World War I adventure epic produced at Warner Brothers; directed by Howard Hawks, who had served in the war as a flight instructor; and co-starring actor Richard Barthelmess, an experienced pilot in his own right. These films didn't confine themselves to the wartime exploits of fliers, either. Still another entry into mix is John Ford's *Air Mail* (1932), a story about intrepid U.S. Postal Service pilots who often braved treacherous weather conditions to assure that the mail did indeed go through.

After *Wings*, Wellman made two aviation follow-ups at Paramount. The first, as noted earlier, is the lost film, *The Legion of the Condemned* (1928), another well-received effort focusing on World War I fliers and the first film to star Gary Cooper, who had played a small but quite affecting role in *Wings*. The second is *Young Eagles* (1930). Relying on aerial footage Wellman had shot for *Wings* but ultimately didn't use, and saddled with a bad script, this film was poorly received, "a mass of wild and absurd incidents,"[1] as Mordaunt Hall put it, and did poorly at the box office.

The failure of *Young Eagles* didn't discourage Wellman from wanting to make more aviation films, though. As previously mentioned as well, one of the first projects he proposed after he arrived at Warner Brothers was a feature film about a dirigible, or blimp. This project, however, never came to pass. And it's curious—considering the great interest in aviation films at the time, Wellman's obvious love for the subject, and (*Young Eagles* aside) his talent for bringing these kinds of stories to the screen with great gusto—that he didn't get the chance to direct at least a few of them during his three years with the studio.

He did, however, make one, his first release of 1933, a programmer called *Central Airport*. Today, this film has the special distinction, according to aviation film historian Michael Paris, of being "the first feature to look seriously at civil aviation" and is, Paris continues, notable for showing "something of the background of the development of air transport and the workings of a busy commercial airport."[2] Today, however, this film is also, and sadly, nearly as neglected as *Young Eagles*.

One reason for *Central Airport*'s obscurity has been its inaccessibility, a frequent problem with many pre–Code films that, like this one, deal openly with sexual situations. With the enforcement of the Production Code in 1934, the film was kept under wraps for more than sixty years before *Turner Classic Movies* began to air it from time to time in the mid-1990s.

Another reason is *Central Airport*'s reputation. Wellman biographer Frank Thompson has called it one of the director's "more minor flying films."[3] And, considering that Wellman also directed *Wings*, *Island in the Sky* (1953), *The High and the Mighty* (1954), and other extremely well-crafted aviation features, this is a fairly reasonable claim to make.

All this duly noted, *Central Airport* is much more than simply a minor movie. The personal story, which revolves around two brothers—both commercial fliers, and both in love with the same woman—has its share of clichéd elements, and there is one unfortunate major casting choice. But the film also has a great deal going for it. Despite a few hackneyed moments, for example, the love story is handled with a level of pre–Code-era candor, maturity, and emotional investment that make it especially engaging. The acting of the film's two leads, Richard Barthelmess and Sally Eilers, is quite strong and moving. The flying sequences, all orchestrated by Paul Mantz, a leading Hollywood stunt pilot at the time, are impressive and often quite exciting to watch. And Wellman's great talent for clear, succinct visual storytelling as well as his abiding love of flight are on full display. Although *Central Airport* may be one of Wellman's "more minor" aviation films, it is also skillfully made, briskly paced, brimming with vitality, and—from beginning to end—very entertaining. Far from being undistinguished, it is, in fact, quite accomplished.

*

10. Central Airport *(1933)*

Jim Blaine (Richard Barthelmess) climbs aboard one of the many early 1930s airplanes flown in *Central Airport*. An experienced pilot in real life, Barthelmess was often cast as a pilot in films (Warner Bros. Album/Alamy Stock Photo).

The story and script for *Central Airport* were put together in typical Warner Brothers assembly-line fashion. The film is based on an original story titled "Hawk's Mate" by John C. ("Jack") Moffitt (1901–1969). Credited with about twenty-five original stories and screenplays for Hollywood films between 1931 and 1955, Moffitt also made notable contributions to such efforts as Michael Curtiz's World War II adventure drama *Passage to Marseille* (1944) and Andre De Toth's noir western *Ramrod* (1947). Then, two other Warner Brothers staff writers, Rian James (who had written the novel upon which Wellman's *Love Is a Racket* is based) and James Seymour, put the story into screenplay form.

To help film the story, Wellman assembled a talented production team. This group ranged from frequent collaborator, cinematographer Sid Hickox, to actor Richard Barthelmess, a major silent film star then under contract with Warner Brothers, and, as noted, an experienced flier, who had turned in a fine performance in 1930's *The Dawn Patrol*. Perhaps the most interesting addition, though, was widely respected air racing pilot and flying consultant Paul Mantz (1903–1965), who was working as a Hollywood stunt pilot at the time. Mantz's job here was to direct and fly in the film's aviation scenes and, on many levels, it was quite a formidable undertaking. First, he needed to gather an impressive array of early–1930s aircraft—in this case: the Alexander Eaglerock, American Eagle A-101, and Stearman C3 biplanes; a Fairchild 71 bush plane; a Pitcairn PA-5 Mailwing mail carrier; and four Ford Tri-motor three-engine airliners—to tell the story credibly. Then, he had to execute several hazardous feats that included numerous stunt-flying scenes (one in which he flies a plane up-side-down) and two plane crashes. All didn't go smoothly, either. In one of the crash scenes, for example, Mantz broke his collarbone when he rolled out of the careening plane and was hit by its tailwheel. In fact, aviation film historian Stephen Pendo has noted that, out of many the films Mantz flew in, *Central Airport* "proved to be one of [the] most dangerous."[4]

In addition to the Warner Brothers studios, production for *Central Airport* took place at the United Airport in Burbank, a facility now known as the Hollywood Burbank Airport. Most of the shooting was done in the winter of 1933.

*

In typical Wellman fashion, *Central Airport* opens with a treacherous thunderstorm. At an airport, various people anxiously wait for news about an incoming commercial flight piloted by highly respected airman Jim Blaine (Barthelmess). When no news comes and the plane doesn't show up at the airport, a massive search is launched. Jim is found hurt, but alive. All his passengers, however, have perished. After recovering, Jim returns home to his parents and younger brother Neil (Tom Brown), who is just beginning to work as an air pilot. All ask Jim when he is returning to the air, but Jim is convinced his flying career is over. "When a commercial flier cracks up, he's through," he glumly tells his family. "No, I couldn't get another passenger run right now if I was the last pilot in the world."

Disheartened, he takes a job as a bank teller. Soon, however, he meets Jill Collins (Eilers), a bright and beautiful parachutist who works with her brother, a pilot, traveling around giving exhibitions of flying and performing aeronautical stunts or, in the parlance of the time, "barnstorming." Jim is immediately attracted to Jill, and when her brother is killed in a freak crash, he reveals his past and volunteers to replace the brother in their act. She accepts, and, as they tour throughout the Southwest, the two become romantically involved. Soon, Jill wants marriage, but Jim believes that their dangerous profession doesn't allow him the luxury of a wife and family, telling her, "People like ourselves have got to get our happiness where we can find it, like we're getting it right now." As she listens, however, Jill begins to reassess their relationship.

10. Central Airport (1933)

The next morning, Jim's brother Neil runs into them. Immediately, he is attracted to Jill as well, but he also respects his brother's relationship with her. Then, however, a freak accident puts Jim in the hospital for a prolonged convalescence, and, when Jim catches up to Neil and Jill again, he finds them married and in bed together. Angry and bitter, he leaves, becomes a soldier of fortune, and—in the process of flying dangerous missions in various countries, often in support of revolutionary causes—loses an eye and two ribs and damages a leg.

After many months, Neil and Jill are living in Havana, where Neil is now based. After Jill bids Neil goodbye as he takes off on his latest flight assignment, she notices a very flashy flier coming into the airport. Both apprehensive about, and impressed by, his daring, she tells a person with her, "Whoever he is, he's flirting with the undertaker." When the plane lands, we see that the pilot, of course, is Jim, now wearing an eyepatch and walking with a limp.

Later, Jim and Jill meet and, since Neil is away, agree to have dinner together. Despite his flying antics, Jim is now calmer and humbler, interested in Jill and Neil's happiness. Although Jill assures Jim that all is good with her and Neil, she clearly hasn't lost the deep feeling she has long had for the older brother. During the evening, Jim, with a bit of Wellman-esque dark humor, also tells Jill that his current lifestyle has resulted in his leaving souvenirs around the world, "Yes, an eye in Nicaragua, a heel in China, a couple of ribs in Chile. It's been a habit. Wherever I go, I leave them something to remember me by."

That same evening, they hear that Neil's plane has gone down in a storm over the Gulf of Mexico. As the only one with any chance of saving Neil and his passengers, Jim offers to fly into the storm. After finding the downed aircraft and saving all aboard, he flies back. Now, however, heavy fog has set in, Jim cannot see well enough to land, and, to add to his troubles, his plane is running out of fuel.

The townspeople down below have an idea, though. Word is sent out via radio asking everyone with a car to go to an old emergency airfield, and, with the help of their car headlights and horns, Jim brings the plane in through the fog and lands safely.

Realizing how much Neil loves Jill, Jim decides that it would probably be better if he left them again. This time, though, he departs on better terms with them and, it seems, a bit more at peace with himself.

*

Premiering on April 15, 1933, *Central Airport* was an immediate hit with audiences. Although its budget was approximately $421,000, which was unusually large for a Wellman early–1930s programmer, it performed quite well at the box office, bringing in $747,000, and earning a hefty profit for Warner Brothers.

The critics, however, were not as enthusiastic as the film's audiences. Although praising the work of Eilers, complimenting some of the film's technical accomplishments, and finding the final air-sea rescue sequence "moderately effective," Mordaunt Hall called *Central Airport*'s story "a most obvious affair."[5] The review from *Variety* pretty much followed suit, saying, "There's a thrill in *Central Airport*'s flying moments, and just enough of those moments to cover up deficiencies in practically every other department, from story to cast."[6]

In more recent years, however, film historians and critics have generally taken a much more positive view of the film, especially the love story at its center. Glenn Erickson, for example, writes:

> *Central Airport* is an unappreciated little gem. World War I flier William Wellman lends the production his usual accuracy in the aviation sequences. Impressive stunt scenes include a biplane buzzing a speeding train and the usual wild look-the-loops low over the runway. Flying pictures of this sort usually hang their plots on a contrived romance, and resolve conflicts with a big action scene and a sacrificial gesture. Wellman made his share of those, but *Central Airport* uses its pre–Code freedom to posit a frank and realistic love triangle. Jim and Jill risk their necks together in the air and naturally gravitate toward one another.... Wellman respects their out-of-wedlock sex life and so do we.[7]

Another aspect of the story some contemporary writers have better understood is how well the film depicts Jim Blaine's complex relationship with his chosen profession, specifically how the life of a flier can be both thoroughly exhilarating and achingly lonely. As Danny Reid (also using that wonderful word "gem") quite elegantly sums up the film:

> *Central Airport* is kind of a forgotten gem. Another well-made Wellman film with sex, death, and spectacle, as well as a genuine pathos that takes an old love triangle plot and makes it fresh and poignant. That's because the triangle isn't just about Tom, Neil, and Jill, but about that big beautiful sky up there. How it can make everything else seem so small in comparison, but also about how empty it can be.[8]

At the same time, many contemporary critics acknowledge that, despite the super-sophisticated special effects in today's films, the various technical contributions to *Central Airport* still hold up quite well. As Jeff Stafford, writing for the Turner Classic Movies website, puts it, "*Central Airport* is distinguished by its first-rate aerial photography and stunts [and] model set miniatures of landscapes and airfields."[9]

Various online bloggers and reviewers have also expressed quite positive opinions about *Central Airport*. "It's a small film and so I didn't go in with big expectations," writes one, "but I was pleasantly surprised at how entertaining it was."[10] "Anyone who likes early aviation [will] love this film," writes another, "and it's very rewarding for anyone who likes good solid entertainment, love, tears, and non-stop action all combined in a kind of delectable Wellman omelet."[11] "Not only is this film daring sexually," writes still another, "it is still quite interesting and exciting today, especially the aerial sequences. Highly recommended if you like good action films and pre–Code cinema."[12]

*

Despite *Central Airport*'s relatively brief shooting schedule, it is amazing how well this so-called "small film" is made, and much, if not most, of the credit for this must go to Wellman. Ever the visual communicator, he delivers, in scene after scene, images that both engage and quickly advance the story.

One especially intriguing sequence is at the very beginning of the film. We see the manager of a commercial airport arriving at the facility in the early morning in the middle of a serious thunderstorm. He checks the posted flight schedule and then the clock. We see that a certain flight—one we soon learn is Flight 127—is now about thirty minutes late. He checks the reports, expressing great concern. He then hears messages coming from the air traffic controllers—still no news on Flight 127. People throughout the airport—other pilots, the cook and the waitress at the airport restaurant, and other workers—are concerned. A few express their confidence in the flight's skilled, experienced pilot, Jim Blaine, but their words aren't enough to diffuse the sense of foreboding they all feel. That day, a large-scale search is organized: pilots are called back to duty, planes are dispatched, and soon a crashed plane and an injured Jim Blaine are found. Taking only about four minutes, this series of events immediately draws us in with its sense of urgency and keeps us absorbed with its visual cues; hints about this talented pilot, Jim Blaine; and anxiety about the fates of both Jim and his passengers. It's tightly paced, thoroughly engaging, and—because it makes us wonder about Jim's future—quite evocative. What's ahead for him now? Will he be able to fly again? If not, what will he do? And how will he handle this tragedy emotionally?

Another superb sequence is Jim and Jill's reunion in Havana near the end of the story. As Neil departs on a flight and Jill bids her goodbye at the airport, she sees a showy flier coming in and, perhaps being reminded of Jim, says "Whoever he is," this airman "is flirting with the undertaker." The plane lands, we see that, yes, the pilot is Jim, and we follow the two, unaware of each other, as they both check into their rooms (which coincidentally are next to each other) at the same hotel. Later, as each prepares to have dinner alone, we see them both readying themselves on opposite sides of the same wall. She hums a tune she's long associated with him and their relationship. He hears it, finds it quite delightful, and whistles the same tune in response, something that clearly intrigues her. Then, they both leave their rooms, finally spot each other, agree to have dinner together, and have a warm, very tender conversation, discussing their lives, her relationship with Neil, and other subjects. It is clear that, while Jill is fond of Neil, she has never gotten over Jim. Here, the dialogue is simple and straightforward, never too clever or cute, and the two actors, Barthelmess and Eilers, both deliver their lines with great sincerity. This entire interaction is filled with genuine sentiment without ever slipping into contrived sentimentality. There's an interesting touch of ambiguity here, too. Since this is pre–Code, we wonder if, with Neil away, the two are going to rekindle their sexual relationship as well. Both are certainly tempted. But, as they embrace later that evening, each overwhelmed with feelings for the other, they hear the news that the lives of Neil and his passengers are in danger, and the action dramatically shifts. Jim must now play the action hero, and Jill must be the dutiful wife. Again, this is a beautifully rendered piece of filmmaking.

Jim (Richard Barthelmess) and Jill (Sally Eilers) are tempted to rekindle their relationship, even though Jill is now married to Jim's younger brother, Neil, in *Central Airport* (Warner Bros. Album/Alamy Stock Photo).

10. Central Airport *(1933)*

Finally, of course, there's the superb final air-sea rescue sequence that even Mordaunt Hall found "moderately effective." With Jill beside him, Jim realizes that he's the only one who can save his brother and his passengers and sets off for the downed plane's location in the Gulf of Mexico. Then, the action cross-cuts between the downed plane and the desperate people on board, Jim flying to it, and the airport where Jill and others anxiously await news. At last, Jim spots the plane, rescues Neil and the other survivors, and flies back to Havana. Back in Havana, however, there is now dense fog to contend with. How can the plane get through it and land safely? In time-honored Hollywood fashion, the community on the ground pitches in as we see instance after instance of people hearing the calls to drive to the old airfield and dutifully responding. Altogether, it's not difficult to see how complex all of this would be to plan, film, and edit seamlessly together in a way that never seems too rushed but that also never drags, yet Wellman, cameraman Hickox, and the film's editor James B. Morley pull it all off with great assurance.

In addition to these and other well-rendered sequences and scenes, Wellman peppers the story with inspired visual touches that elegantly convey important pieces of information. One, which would have been impossible to get by censors after mid–1934, is when Jim and Jill, for the sake of propriety, enter their adjoining rooms in a hotel and Jim quickly, and eagerly, opens the door to Jill's room and enters. As we look through the door, seeing them embrace passionately, the door—as a result of Jim's nudging, slowly (and quite artfully) closes, blocking our view. Everything that we need to know here has been communicated visually, naturally, and with great economy. Another is when Jim gives his speech about why aviators shouldn't marry and Jill secretly places a paper cigar-wrapper ring on her marriage ring finger. This brief, eloquent gesture is all we need to know about her feelings on this subject.

*

Another of *Central Airport*'s assets is the acting of Barthelmess and Eilers. As an on-screen couple, the two have great chemistry, and, as actors, they both show real respect for the characters they play and the dilemmas those characters face during the story.

A major silent film actor who played opposite Lillian Gish in the D.W. Griffith masterpieces *Broken Blossoms* (1919) and *Way Down East* (1920) and then starred in Henry King's enormous hit *Tol'able David* (1922), Barthelmess (1895–1963) never quite caught on in talking pictures. Although he remained busy during the pre–Code era, he worked much less frequently in the late 1930s (mostly in supporting roles) and retired in 1942. In all, he made about eighty films, and many of his silent efforts are now lost. Soon after *Central Airport*, he starred in what is arguably his best pre-Code film, Wellman's *Heroes for Sale*, which we will discuss in this book's next chapter. And, after that, he did have one significant professional last hurrah, playing a pilot intent to prove that he is not a coward in Howard Hawks' great aviation film *Only Angels Have Wings* (1939).

As Jim in *Central Airport*, Barthelmess is quite good at playing a haunted man trying to put his life back together after being unfairly blamed for a tragic accident. Although he sometimes reverts to his silent film acting habits, such as his slightly overexaggerated reactions in some scenes, he brings an air of gravitas, sensitivity, and basic decency to the role. He is especially winning, for example, in the scenes when Jim and Jill are first in love and then when they reconnect in Havana, excellently conveying how much Jim sees Jill as a lifeline to a happier, more fulfilled life.

Even for many seasoned film buffs, Sally Eilers (1908–1978) is not a household name, but she appeared in about seventy films between 1927 and 1950. At her height in the early 1930s, she was featured in numerous comedies and crime melodramas and was known for her liveliness and charm. Increasingly, though, she received fewer film offers and retired in her early forties after playing supporting roles in the low-budget westerns *Coroner Creek* (1948) with Randolph Scott and *Stage to Tucson* (1950) with Rod Cameron.

For those who have never seen Sally Eilers in a film, her Jill in *Central Airport* is a revelation, and, seeing her at work here, one has to wonder why she didn't have a more successful Hollywood career. As well as sexy—"a real sizzler,"[13] as one online reviewer puts it—her Jill is smart, self-respecting, and quite sensitive to the needs of both the men in her life, and Eilers acts the part in an honest, straightforward, unaffected way, an approach that certainly must have appealed to the no-nonsense Wellman. We have no problem understanding why both Jim and Neil instantly fall for Jill.

Tom Brown (1915–1990), who plays Neil, began his career as a child actor in silents and continued in films and then television until the mid-1970s, playing guest roles on such well-known series as *Perry Mason*, *The Untouchables*, and *77 Sunset Strip*. While a competent actor, he is totally unconvincing in the part of Neil, lacking both any sexual chemistry with Eilers and the air of authority any airplane passenger would want from a pilot. A big part of this problem was his age. He was just eighteen when he played this part, and, when we first see him, he looks like he's about sixteen. Later, in an effort to make him appear older, Wellman has him sport a mustache, which only makes him look younger, more like a fifteen-year-old with a fake mustache in the high school play. Eilers was just seven years older than Brown, but she had such maturity and presence

10. Central Airport *(1933)*

that, when the two are together on screen, they resemble—to use contemporary slang—a seasoned cougar and her latest cub. It's a shame that Wellman could not have cast a more suitable actor in the role of Neil, but *Central Airport* was a low-budget, fast-turnaround programmer, and the director may not have had a great selection of casting options to choose from.

*

Despite the casting of Brown and a few other shortcomings, *Central Airport* is quite an intriguing film overall. And, to its great credit, it becomes more interesting with repeated viewings that enable us to see more of what Wellman the craftsman does to make the story consistently entertaining, intensely human, and—during the flight scenes especially—thrilling.

*

After *Central Airport*, it wasn't until 1938—when he produced as well as directed the lavish Technicolor adventure *Men with Wings* with Fred MacMurray and Ray Milland—that Wellman made another aviation film. Ultimately, he directed nearly a dozen of these flying features during his career. And, apart from *Wings*, perhaps the best known is *The High and the Mighty* starring John Wayne. Although *The High and the Mighty* has its clichéd and dated elements today, it did receive six Academy Award nominations, including a Best Director nod to Wellman, in 1955. In addition, it was eventually quite influential, its air disaster storyline serving as the plot template for *Airport* (1970); its three sequels; and other examples from the enormously popular disaster film genre of the 1970s such as *The Poseidon Adventure* (1972), *Skyjacked* (1972), *Earthquake* (1974), and *The Towering Inferno* (1974).

For most of the rest of 1933, Wellman focused on his next four releases, which rotated between two woman-in-distress melodramas, *Lilly Turner* and *Midnight Mary*, and two hard-hitting social dramas, *Heroes for Sale* and *Wild Boys of the Road*. Although the year would be marked by increasing tensions with his superiors at Warner Brothers, the director would—from these four assignments—be able to create three of his most widely praised, and enduring, pre–Code films.

11

"It may be the end of us, but it's not the end of America"
Heroes for Sale (1932)

Perhaps the most significant contribution Warner Brothers made to U.S. film history during the pre–Code era was a substantial body of work that examined—sometimes unflinchingly—the severe economic conditions and enormous social upheaval of the early 1930s. Under the guiding hands of Zanuck and others, these so-called "message pictures" tackled such subjects as widespread unemployment, crime, drug addiction, corruption in law enforcement, cruel business practices, and the especially difficult challenges for women. And, although many of these films could be quite bleak (and some a bit more than a bit preachy), the best could also be filled with enormous energy, good humor, a keen awareness of life's ironies, a genuine empathy for ordinary people caught in the grip of daunting forces, and, above all, a stubborn hopefulness. Instead of offering the unabashed escapism that MGM, Paramount, and other Hollywood studios routinely delivered in their films, these strove to mirror the moment in vivid and often provocative ways. And this commitment, along with the greater artistic freedom filmmakers had before the Production Code's enforcement, are perhaps the main reasons why so many of these efforts continue to captivate film students, historians, and aficionados nearly a century later.

During this period, Wellman, of course, was in the thick of it, churning out films that assessed the hard times and doing so in his own inimitable style. But, in 1933, he, Zanuck, and the fast-and-loose pre–Code era would all be facing major turning points. Zanuck's came first. After a salary dispute with the Warners, he left the studio in April of that year to form his own independent production company, Twentieth Century Pictures. Wellman followed that autumn. Tired of the grind of assembly-line production, interference by executives, and other in-studio working realities, he departed to pursue a career as an independent director who developed his own projects. And, as the year progressed, more and more filmmakers throughout Hollywood saw the proverbial writing on the wall: soon the film industry's very restrictive Production Code, the set of regulations many of them had so casually mocked and disregarded, would be fully and faithfully enforced. The times were certainly changing.

In the meantime, though, there was still much to be done. And, for Wellman, the work would include three new films, which—along with *The Public Enemy*, *Night Nurse*, and *Safe in Hell*—would establish him as one of the U.S. film industry's most fearless and exhilarating directors of the period: *Heroes for Sale*, *Midnight Mary*, and *Wild Boys of the Road*.

Among these, perhaps the most daring is the first, *Heroes for Sale*, which depicts a Job-like character's harrowing personal journey from the trenches of World War I to the economic depths of the Great Depression. Along the way, the film explores a range of social ills and issues from drug addiction to widespread hunger and homelessness, the harshness of capitalism, and the insensitivity and cruelty of law enforcement. It does all this with great passion and urgency as well as a deep feeling for its main characters and a keen understanding of human frailties and hypocrisy. And it is filled with wonderful performances, both from its star, Richard Barthelmess, and from actors in key support roles such as Aline MacMahon, Loretta Young, and Gordon Westcott. Perhaps its most remarkable aspect, though, is its ability to give viewers so much to process in such a short time. A mere seventy-one minutes in length, it covers such an incredibly wide range of material that it sometimes seems like an *Odyssey*-style epic. And, as opposed to the more didactic message films of the era, this is among a small sub-group of these films, which, as writer Jay Carr notes, "ring more true, more powerful, strike a deeper chord precisely because they are less self-consciously message films, and more like daily newspapers being slammed out under deadline pressure. They simmer with tabloid vigor, fielding the realities as they unfolded in America's collective experience."[1]

*

While the vast majority of Wellman's films are based on source material such as novels, plays, or Zanuck's favorites: sensational news stories "ripped from the headlines," *Heroes for Sale* has a slightly different origin. In the first week of January 1933, Zanuck met with screenwriter Robert Lord, telling him that he needed a new story for a film starring Richard Barthelmess. In the discussion, the subject turned to "the forgotten man," a term in popular use in the early 1930s to describe men, many of whom had served in the U.S. military during World War I, but who were now without jobs, neglected, and often in desperate need of help. Very likely, the producer and the writer agreed that this subject would be a good fit for Barthelmess, an actor who, while not particularly good at comedy, could excel at playing long-suffering heroes much like his Jim Blaine in Wellman's *Central Airport*. Lord then met with his writing partner for this project, the colorful Wilson Mizner, and the two developed a story outline titled "The Forgotten Man" and submitted it to Zanuck on January 24. After Zanuck approved the outline, they wrote the first draft of a feature-length screenplay, which they now called *Breadline*. Wellman was brought in, and both he and Zanuck made changes which were then incorporated into the script. For Lord, who was moving into producing, this was his fourth and final collaboration with Wellman. And for Mizner, this was his second (following *Frisco Jenny*) and also his last. He died on April 3, roughly two months before *Heroes for Sale* was released.

It's interesting, too, that Zanuck and Lord apparently had no qualms about getting as much mileage as they could out of the forgotten man idea. At the same time that *Heroes for Sale* was being developed and shot, so was *Gold Diggers of 1933*, a sassy, exuberant musical that Lord produced under Zanuck's supervision. This film's finale, an elaborate Busby Berkeley production number, is keyed to the strains of a moving song by composer Harry Warren and lyricist Al Dubin. The song is about men who'd fought in World War I and who were now out of work and desperate, and, yes, it is titled "The Forgotten Man."

To shoot the film, the studio assigned cinematographer James Van Trees, who had previously worked with Wellman on *The Star Witness* and *Lilly Turner*.

Rounding out the cast were several of Warner Brothers' very talented contract players. One of these was Aline MacMahon (1899–1991), a stage actress who had made her film debut in 1931 in the drama *Five Star Final* and would continue to deliver vivid, memorable portrayals mostly in character roles both in films and on television until her retirement in 1975. Another was Gordon Westcott (1903–1935), who had very effectively played the title character's disreputable first husband in *Lilly Turner* but whose promising career was sadly cut short when he died from a head injury following a polo accident less than two and a half years after *Heroes for Sale* was released. Still another was Robert Barrat (1891–1970), a versatile character actor with a special talent for accents who had played Fritz, the mentally unbalanced weight lifter, in *Lilly Turner*. Finally, there was the radiant Loretta Young, who, while miscast in Wellman's *The Hatchet Man*, is quite compelling here. (We will discuss Young at some length in the next chapter.)

Wellman began shooting *Breadline* on March 6, 1933. This was the

11. Heroes for Sale (1932)

day, incidentally, that newly inaugurated U.S. president Franklin Roosevelt ordered the nation's banks closed and three days before he signed the Emergency Banking Act, a federal law granting the president and other federal officials broader regulatory authority over the country's banking system. Many historians consider these days to be among the darkest of the Great Depression, and it is likely that the national mood had an impact on Wellman and others associated with the film during the shoot. Whether or not this was the case, Wellman proceeded in his usual, highly efficient manner. Most of the filming took place at the Warner Brothers/First National Studios in Burbank, and certain exteriors were shot at nearby locations such as the Warner Ranch in Calabasas, California. After twenty-three days of filming, the shoot wrapped up on March 31. At some point during this time, too, the film's title was changed from *Breadline* to the more cynical and evocative *Heroes for Sale*.

*

Heroes for Sale begins on the World War I battlelines, Tom Holmes (Barthelmess) and his fellow soldier and home-town friend Roger Winston (Westcott) are ordered to go on an extremely dangerous mission behind enemy lines to capture a German soldier (preferably an officer) and bring him back to obtain intelligence from him. When they must act, however, Roger cowers in fear, so Tom bravely goes alone. He captures a German officer and delivers him to the trench where Roger waits. Just as he arrives, though, Tom is shot in the back. In what appear to be his dying words, he tells Roger to take the prisoner in. Then he collapses. Roger returns and is greeted as a hero. He tries repeatedly to give Tom the credit for capturing the soldier but can't muster the courage to do so. In the meantime, Tom is found and treated at a German hospital, and, to relieve him from the intense pain he now suffers from his wound, his doctors give him morphine.

When the war ends, Tom and Roger run into each other on a transport ship headed back to the United States, and Roger, seeing Tom, is shocked and ashamed that he has been given the honors that should have gone to his friend. Tom is just happy that they are both alive and promises to keep the real story of the capture to himself.

Back in their home town, Roger is welcomed as a hero, and Tom is thrilled to be reunited with his loving mother. By this time, though, Tom has become addicted to the morphine he has been taking. Roger gets Tom a job at his father's bank, but soon Tom's addiction leads to erratic behavior and he is sent to a local treatment center to rid himself of the morphine habit. After many months pass, Tom is declared free of the addiction and returns home.

Now, however, Tom's mother has died, and, desiring to start a new life elsewhere, he moves to Chicago. There he meets several people. The first is Mary Dennis (MacMahon), a caring, common-sense woman who, with her father (Charley Grapewin), runs a diner and rents several rooms upstairs to tenants. She immediately takes a liking to Tom and rents him a vacant room. Another person is Ruth Loring (Young). Also a tenant in the building, she works at a local laundry. And another, a third tenant, is an eccentric German inventor with communist sympathies named Max Brinker (Barrat). He hates all capitalists and constantly rants about how they exploit the sheepish masses. With Ruth's help, Tom gets a job driving a delivery truck for the laundry. He soon shows a talent for coming up with ideas that help the business and his kindly boss (Grant Mitchell) gives him more responsibility and added pay to go with it. Tom and Ruth fall in love, marry, and soon have a son. This is a bittersweet turn of events for Mary, who also loves Tom, but from afar.

About this time, Max, the communist inventor, comes up with an idea for a machine with the potential to greatly reduce the time and effort it normally takes to wash and dry clothes. Tom brings the idea to his fellow

Mary Dennis (Aline MacMahon, left) introduces Tom Holmes (Richard Barthelmess) to Ruth Loring (Loretta Young) in *Heroes for Sale* (Warner Bros. / Photofest).

11. Heroes for Sale (1932)

employees and convinces them to contribute toward the machine's patent. The owner is thrilled with the idea and adopts the machinery, agreeing to Tom's stipulation that the technology doesn't put any of the plant's employees out of work.

After several years, however, the owner dies and the new owners break the deal, further automate the laundry, and fire Tom and most of the other workers. Furious and resentful, the fired workers march on the plant to destroy the machines. Tom does his best to stop them, but the mob turns into a riot. The police are called in, and, in the ensuing chaos, Ruth—who has gone to the scene in hopes of helping Tom—is killed. To make matters worse, Tom is singled out as a mob ringleader, convicted, and sentenced to five years in prison.

Ironically, as Tom serves his prison time, the machine he promoted and Max invented continues to sell widely, putting countless people out of work and delivering substantial royalties to both of them. This development has also transformed Max, turning him into an unrepentant capitalist. And, when Max visits Tom in prison to update him on these developments, the two have a very frank exchange:

> Tom: I thought you hated all lawyers and capitalists.
> Max: I despise them. I spit on them. (He spits.) But I'm willing to get rich with them.
> Tom: I couldn't take a profit on people starving to death.
> Max: There's only one thing important in the world—to have money. Without it, you are just garbage. With it, you are a king.
> Tom: You used to hate the capitalists.
> Max: Naturally. That was before I had money.
> Tom: All right, you can keep my money if you think so much of it. Throw it away. Give it away. Do anything you want with it.
> Max: I'll put it in the bank. While you're recovering from your insanity, it can be drawing interest.

When Tom is released from prison, it is 1932 and the United States is in the depths of the Great Depression. He still refuses to take any of his royalties, which now come to more than $50,000. Instead, he turns all the money over to Mary to help feed the endless line of hungry people who seek handouts at her diner. Tom is also thrilled to finally spend some time with his son Bill.

His troubles continue, though. Because he was considered a ringleader in the riot that led to his going to prison, he is being watched by the local "Red Squad," which scrutinizes the activities of suspected communists. Then, when leftist riots break out near him, he is pressured to get out of town and again leaves young Bill with Mary.

Now jobless and homeless, Tom is effectively a hobo constantly pushed from one town to another. In the midst of this existence, though, he counters another hobo's pessimism about the state of the nation, saying: "It may be the end of us, but it's not the end of America. In a few years, it will go on bigger and stronger than ever.... It takes more than one sock in the jaw to lick a hundred-and-twenty million people." He also has a chance encounter with Roger Winston, who, despite being part of a once-wealthy family, is now homeless and penniless.

Back at the diner, as the money Tom gave Mary helps to feed a long line of hungry people, Mary and young Bill look at a wall plaque that honors Tom for making this mass food service possible. Filled with pride, Bill declares that that, when he grows up, he wants to be just like his dad.

*

Heroes for Sale opened in theaters on June 17, 1933, to both lackluster box office and mixed critical notices. As the reviewer for the *New York World Telegram* put it, "It is hardly likely that the film will be popular and gross a lot of money."[2] This reviewer's counterpart in the *New York Herald Tribune* shared similar sentiments, writing about the film's "grim bitterness" and adding that its "occasional notes of good cheer will annoy those who might have been stirred by its frank facing of the unpleasant facts of recent life."[3] Future screenwriter Frank Nugent, then a newly hired reviewer at the *New York Times*, found the viewing experience "bewildering" mostly because he saw the film as essentially two stories: one about Tom's war experiences, drug addiction, and recovery and the other focusing on his life after he moves to Chicago. "If there be any connection between these stories," Nugent adds, "it is only that of Tom's unbroken misfortune."[4]

*

In recent years, however, film writers and historians have looked upon *Heroes for Sale* far more favorably, often downplaying its quirky, or perhaps jarring, aspects and focusing on its strengths, especially the contributions that Wellman brings to the effort.

In one appraisal, for example, film writer Sheila O'Malley sums up the film, paying special attention to the director's ability to avoid excesses and keep the proceedings clear-eyed and down to earth:

> Wellman does not tip his action over into melodrama. This is a drama, end-stop. It shows its characters, flaws and all, and follows them on their bumpy journey through life, and through a time of great upheaval in American history. [The years] 1918 to 1933 saw a lot of changes, and the worst was yet to come, but *Heroes for Sale*, while it could be seen as a piece of propaganda, ... is also an examination of the economics and transformations that went down

during that time, all seen through the eyes of people we come to care about deeply.[5]

In another, Ben Sachs of the *Chicago Reader* writes about Wellman's ability to communicate a great deal with great efficiency, noting that he "crams an astonishing amount of narrative incident into the short running time, with more developments every ten minutes than most contemporary Hollywood productions cover in their entirety."[6]

In his critique, film writer Sean Axmaker points out the director's uncanny ability to balance, and often synthesize, the narrative's many opposing elements with such seeming ease:

> The schizophrenic tone twists as much as the plot—light comic relief is slammed by brute tragedy and no good deed goes unpunished—but Wellman's gritty sensibility makes it simmer. His direction of a labor riot is harrowing. Yet for all the injustice and hypocrisy (not just the judgmental authority figures, but a raving communist who transforms into an arrogant capitalist and blames the poor for their poverty the minute he strikes it rich), the film is also filled with generous folks and honest people, all sorts of men and women just trying to get by in bad times and offering a hand out to those in need. The film ends on the grim march of homeless armies tramping the rails for work in the depths of the Depression, but, after all of that, Tom is still optimistic and he sticks out his chin to walk on, just daring fate to take another poke at it.[7]

Finally, in another, and quite insightful, analysis, one writer, who uses the *nom de plume* "Just Another Film Buff," expresses a great appreciation for the many positive and uniquely characteristic contributions Wellman makes to the film:

> Wellman brings a lean muscularity to *Heroes for Sale*, which possesses a novelistic sprawl without ever turning labored or precious. The film hurtles from one genre, one setting to another, making vast leaps in time that are all the more striking in that they are executed with straight cuts without transitions.... There's [also] something about Wellman's style that makes it free of value judgments about what is being depicted.... The riot sequence in *Heroes for Sale* is a good example. The strikers wreck the laundry and hurl stones at the police, who fire back. The camera pushes through the fighting mass to pick up Tom's wife, who has come to look for him. A barely perceptible blow ... knocks her down dead. Since the previous shot shows both the rioters and the police wielding batons, we are not sure who [has] delivered the blow. Wellman's staging and editing of the action takes no sides, shifting the emphasis from assigning responsibility to describing results. A riot took place, blows were exchanged, a woman was killed.[8]

*

As these last four perspectives suggest, Wellman's contributions to *Heroes for Sale* are many, varied, and often quite significant. In the hands of a less-talented director, the story, which is so episodic and far flung, could have easily lost focus, veered into melodrama, or both. Wellman, however, again acting much like a master conductor leading an orchestra in the performance of a complex symphony, synthesizes these seemingly discordant elements with great deftness and authority.

A very significant contribution Wellman made, for example, was tying together the two stories that make up the film's shooting script, the same two stories, of course, that perplexed Frank Nugent in his 1933 review. Nugent concluded that the only element that appears to connect them is Tom's "unbroken misfortune." But, when we look at the film more closely, there are several other elements that help to reinforce, and strengthen, the connection in ways similar to how Wellman addressed similar script challenges in *Night Nurse*, which is also basically two separate stories. One is his decision to shoot both the film's early scenes of the soldiers on the World War I battlefield and, later, the scenes of the forgotten men walking from town to town in the darkness and rain. These scenes not only connect Tom's misfortunes but they also reinforce the idea that, like Tom, all the forgotten men have endured great hardship both during the war and during the dark economic times. Also, the reemergence of Roger Winston, Tom's cowardly friend and fellow soldier, near the film's end is both a tie-back to the first part of the film and a kind of closure: Roger has received his comeuppance, his character arc is now complete, and his conversation with Tom in the hobo camp is somewhat cathartic for them both. (It can be argued, of course, that Roger's unexpected reemergence was the decision of the scriptwriters. This may be so, but it is also such a characteristically Wellman-esque touch that it's hard to imagine that the director wasn't involved in coming up with this idea or, at the very least, supportive in developing it.)

Another important Wellman contribution to *Heroes for Sale* is the film's seeming absence of didacticism. This could have easily been a very preachy film, but—with the possible exception of a little pro–Roosevelt flag waving at the end—it isn't. The comments by Just Another Film Buff about the director's ability to depict scenes in ways that appear to be objectively rendered and free of value judgements are well taken. In this respect, Wellman reminds us of the work of a director such as Otto Preminger who emphasized showing rather than telling—depicting actions in ways that were as unprejudicial as possible and letting viewers make their own value judgements. The riot scenes in *Heroes for Sale* are, of course, among of the film's most vivid examples of Wellman's talent for achieving this objective. But, many other scenes in the film also do this quite effectively. Among these are the scenes depicting the "suicide" mission Tom and Roger undertake during the war, Tom's morphine addiction, and finally Tom's life as a jobless transient.

Tom Holmes (Richard Barthelmess) leans against a roadside billboard that bluntly sums up prevailing Depression-era attitudes towards him and other jobless transients in *Heroes for Sale* (Warner Bros./Photofest).

*

In addition to Wellman's many contributions, *Heroes for Sale* benefits greatly from the work of several talented Warner Brothers' contract players.

Heading the list is Barthelmess, who could be especially effective when playing characters who struggle to maintain their self-respect and sense of self-worth even after they have endured some form of public disgrace. While quite good in this kind of role in *Central Airport*, he is even better in *Heroes for Sale*. The actor could at times appear stiff and uncomfortable showing his emotions, but, as in *Central Airport*, these traits only help to suggest the intense, complex feelings swirling about within characters facing immense personal challenges. In *Heroes for Sale*, for example, he is especially good in the scenes when Tom struggles with his morphine addiction, grieves over the loss of Ruth, and, after being kicked out of town by the Red Squad, faces life as a transient.

While Barthelmess is quite good as Tom, Aline MacMahon is nothing less than superb in the role of the kind, funny, self-assured, and no-nonsense Mary. In fact, MacMahon steals nearly every scene she's in with her intelligence, charm, and humanity. And, in one scene especially, her acting aligns perfectly with Wellman's directorial choices to create one of the film's most eloquent moments. From the instant Mary meets Tom she is smitten him but never too obvious about it. Tom, of course, is also very much in love, but with Ruth. One night, the three decide to go out together. Mary, however, needs to fix the hem of her dress. When she finishes and is dressed and ready, she opens the door to the next room, only to see Tom and Ruth in a romantic embrace. Wellman photographs MacMahon from the back, letting us only imagine the expression on Mary's face and the feelings she is experiencing. After a moment, MacMahon, her face still looking away from us, closes the door and speaks through it to Tom and Ruth, making an excuse and recommending that the two go on without her. Then, she turns toward the camera and stands in silence, her body sinking a bit and her face expressing feelings of great disappointment and sadness. The scene is heartbreaking, and especially so because it says so much so simply and quickly.

Gordon Westcott, who had played a much smaller role in *Lilly Turner*, gets a much meatier opportunity in *Heroes for Sale*, portraying the cowardly, self-loathing, and conscience-stricken Roger Winston. It's a challenging role, a flawed, complex character who is not easy to like, yet Westcott inhabits the character so thoroughly and makes him so real that it's difficult not to empathize with him, at least to some extent. This is another excellent performance.

Character actor Robert Barrat plays a highly entertaining Max, the eccentric communist inventor who becomes a rabid capitalist once his invention makes him rich. In a serious story, Max supplies much of the comic relief, and Barrat, reveling in the colorful role, clearly has fun with it. He plays Max with great energy, stealing many of the scenes in which his character appears. The performance is deliberately over the top, perhaps a little bit too much so at times, but it is always enjoyable.

As Ruth, Loretta Young is both quite engaging as Tom's love interest and then absolutely riveting when she goes to the site of the riot out of concern for Tom and then is struck fatally on the head. The scene in which she lies dead, her open eyes staring blankly up, is, even by today's standards, both horrifying and spellbinding. And, needless to say, after the Code's enforcement, it would have been impossible to get this scene in its current form past the industry censors. Wellman and cinematographer James Van Trees certainly deserve to share in the credit for this moment's compelling staging, but, ultimately, it is Young's fine acting that makes it so unforgettable.

Finally, another person who deserves enthusiastic kudos for making significant contributions to *Heroes for Sale* is Van Trees. Working

11. Heroes for Sale *(1932)* 163

closely with Wellman, he was able to achieve a remarkable look to several of the film's sequences—among them the World War I battle scenes, riot scenes, and the scenes of the homeless transients near the end of the film. In these scenes, director and cinematographer simultaneously mix elements of realism and expressionism[9] to produce a complex and often powerful viewer reaction. On one hand, these scenes have a gritty, almost-documentary-like quality about them. On the other, they are lit and staged in ways that convey a sense of oppressiveness, suggesting the great emotional weights characters living through those moments must be bearing. They are quite striking and effective.

*

Heroes for Sale is widely considered to be one of Wellman's top three or four pre–Code masterpieces, a ranking few, if any, film historians or aficionados will quibble with. It tells a moving story that captures many of the dark realities people in the United States experienced between the late 1910s and early 1930s with a frankness and no-holds-barred honesty that would not have been possible after the Production Code was enforced. The writing by Lord and Mizner is lean, hard-hitting, often sharply ironic, and always to the point. The acting—especially the work of Barthelmess, MacMahon, Westcott, and Young—is quite good and at times exceptional. Van Tree's cinematography is at times stunning. And, at the center of the entire effort is the work of Wellman, the maestro who fused all of these and other elements into a harmonious whole. While still very much a product of its time, *Heroes for Sale* speaks to viewers today with great conviction and authority. For fans of pre–Code films, this is must-see cinema.

*

After completing *Heroes for Sale*, one might imagine that, by now, Wellman would have had the degree of freedom at Warner Brothers he'd longed for ever since he'd first signed with the studio in 1930. He quickly learned, though, that his blunt, sometimes combative personal style was again contributing to tensions between him and his studio's executives: tensions that would soon lead to an assignment he viewed as a firm slap on the wrist—one he would then transform into yet another pre–Code gem.

12

"Now what do you suppose made me think of sex?"
Midnight Mary (1933)

"We were both being punished," Loretta Young recalled in an interview in 1995.[1]

The other half of the "we," of course, was William Wellman.

Although it's unclear why the powers that be at Warner Brothers were upset with their young female star, their displeasure with their ornery contract director is well documented. After completing *Lilly Turner*, Wellman had gone to the studio's executives and ranted about all the women-in-distress films he had been making for them, how sick he was of these kinds of pictures, and that he wasn't going to make any more of them. He had a point. Beginning with *Night Nurse* and *Safe in Hell* more than a year before—and continuing through *So Big*, *The Purchase Price*, *Frisco Jenny*, and *Lilly Turner*—he had directed more than his fair share of these. Instead, he now wanted to do one of the signature aviation projects he'd been thinking about since his early days at Warner Brothers, a story about a dirigible. To no one's surprise, none of the executives took kindly to this outburst. Wellman, after all, was on the studio payroll and, as such, was expected to be a compliant employee who didn't grouse about assignments. So, to put him in his place, they loaned him, Young, cinematographer James Van Trees, and several others from the studio out to MGM's B-picture unit to work on a programmer about—of all subjects—a woman in distress.[2]

The result, *Midnight Mary*, is—and quite surprisingly, considering the circumstances that brought the director and the project together—one of Wellman's best and most under-appreciated pre-Code films. This unassuming gem does not delve as deeply into the societal ills of the early 1930s as, say, *Heroes for Sale* does, but it doesn't pull any punches in depicting that life, especially for young women who must fend for themselves in a largely uncaring world, could be quite difficult and at times brutal. In many respects, this is a Cinderella story amply sprinkled with pre–Code hard knocks, cynicism, sex, and melodrama. The heroine gets her prince, but only after she's endured the premature loss of her mother, a stint in a juvenile correction center, life as a gangland moll, three years in an adult women's prison, a beating by her hoodlum lover, and the trauma of being put on trial for her life. In addition, the film is unusually well crafted, incorporating Wellman's trademark in-your-face storytelling style and visual flourishes; a tight, sharply written script; an unusual and very creative flashback design; fine cinematography; and excellent performances in the key roles from Young and co-stars Ricardo Cortez and Franchot Tone.

William Wellman, Jr., has noted that *Midnight Mary* "is considered the only time MGM made a Warner Brothers picture."[3] It's interesting to view the film this way, but it is probably more precise to see it as the embodiment of the strengths of *both* studios, namely the fast pacing, sassy scripts, and hard edges of Warner Brothers films combined with the glamour and elegant costumes and sets of MGM films—a rare, if not unique, blending of Warner-style realism with MGM-style escapism.

Finally, *Midnight Mary* is a tribute to both Wellman and Young's professionalism (and perhaps perfectionism). Neither, of course, was happy about being farmed out to MGM's B-picture unit as a punishment, and they both could have easily done the minimum needed to deliver a routine programmer. But they didn't. Instead, they both put all they had into making it the best film they could, and their effort shows. In the late 1990s, Young, then well into her eighties, told both Wellman, Jr., and film writer Mick LaSalle of her very high regard for *Midnight Mary*, confiding to LaSalle that it was "one of the best pictures I've ever made."[4] This certainly suggests that, even more than six decades after she'd worked on it, this largely forgotten film still remained a source of great personal pride.

*

The development of what eventually became *Midnight Mary* took almost as many twists and turns as there are in the final story's plot.

The initial inspiration for the film was a series of newspaper articles titled "By a 'Gunman's Moll'" that appeared in the *San Francisco Examiner* (and perhaps other newspapers in the Hearst chain) in May and June of 1932. Writing credit was given to a Margaret Murray, and each installment was reportedly based on her real-life experience as a moll and mob informant. To draw readers in, each installment also included the lurid subtitle, "Margaret Murray, Who Was the 'Bright Eyes' (the Lookout) for Stephen Sweeney's Hold-Up Gang, Reveals the Secrets of Life in the

Underworld—a Hunted, Miserable Existence, With Death or Disaster Always Threatening."[5]

Seeing the screen potential in these articles as well eyeing a romantic vehicle for rising stars Jean Harlow and Clark Gable, MGM assigned Anita Loos (1888–1981)—the author of the hugely popular 1925 comic novel *Gentlemen Prefer Blondes* and at the time one of the studio's top screenwriters—to adapt the material into a story suitable for a feature film. Loos jettisoned the informant part of Murray's story and submitted a treatment called *Nora, Girl Delinquent*. Then, when both Harlow and Gable rejected the project, MGM decided to go in a totally different direction and import outside talent. Wellman, Young, and Van Trees came over from Warner Brothers. Gene Markey and Kathryn Scola, the writing team who had recently worked with Wellman on *Lilly Turner*, also took over the script development and made numerous changes, including retitling the story *Lady of the Night*. In addition, Actors Ricardo Cortez and Andy Devine were borrowed from Paramount and Universal, respectively, to play major parts. This didn't mean, though, that MGM supported the entire effort with imported talent. In addition to other staff members, two of the studio's respected contract players, Franchot Tone and Una Merkel, were assigned important roles, and in-house film editor James Gray and costume designer Adrian also made major contributions.[6]

Filming took place at MGM during parts of April and May 1933, lasting about four weeks. As he nearly always did, Wellman worked fast and efficiently, and, according to Young and others, the production went quite smoothly. One of the few hitches involved the film industry's censors, who, when they saw the film's first preview, objected to the title *Woman of the Night*. To accommodate them, the title was again changed, this time to the more acceptable (but also more suggestive and intriguing) *Midnight Mary*. Then, on July 4, 1933, the film was released.[7]

This title change, incidentally, is an excellent example of just how weak censorship was as long as the Hays Office lacked an effective enforcement mechanism over the film studios. *Midnight Mary* is sprinkled throughout with moments of violence against women, sexual suggestion, moral ambiguities, and other elements that would clearly have been removed if it had been released after the Production Code went into full force in mid-1934. In fact, among the roughly twenty Wellman-directed feature films released during the pre–Code era, we can make a solid case for *Midnight Mary* as being one of the "most pre–Code" in style, spirit, and subject matter of them all.

*

12. Midnight Mary (1933)

Midnight Mary begins at a moment of reckoning in a courtroom. Young, beautiful Mary Martin (Young) is on trial for murder. The prosecutor gives a passionate summation calling for her conviction and execution. Then, the jury is sent to deliberate, and, as it does, the kindly court clerk (Charley Grapewin) allows Mary to wait for the verdict in the comfort of his office. Once inside, she notices that all his records, going back more than thirty years, are neatly bound and placed on bookshelves in chronological order by year. She notices the book labeled "1910," the year of her birth. Then her eyes skip to "1919," and the story flashes back to her and her friend Bunny (Una Merkel) as nine-year-old girls scavenging in a junkyard. It is here when Mary learns that her mother has died. Her eyes then skip to "1923." A thirteen-year-old Mary, in a department store, goes to pick up a wallet Bunny has tried to steal but dropped and is arrested for shoplifting and remanded to a juvenile detention facility.

The years of Mary's life continue to go by. Mary and Bunny, now in their late teens and out for a good time one night, are picked up by aspiring hoodlum Leo Darcy (Cortez) and his henchman Angelo (Warren Hymer). Very quickly, both Mary and Leo and Bunny and Angelo become involved. Bunny seems fine with the moll lifestyle, but Mary, who sincerely wants to be a good person, is increasingly uncomfortable. At one point, after Leo gives her fifty dollars for acting as a lookout in a robbery, for example, she doesn't feel right about it and donates the money to the Salvation Army.

At the scene of another Leo-led robbery, this time a clandestine gambling parlor, Mary meets Tom Mannering, a suave, well-connected lawyer who is immediately captivated by her beauty. The robbery is botched, however, and, when the police arrive, Tom helps Mary flee the scene and the two have a late-night meal at his well-appointed home. There, she tells him of her desire to find respectable work, and soon, with Tom's help, she goes to secretarial school and gets a job working in his law firm. During this time, she also develops feelings for him. Leo catches up with her, though, and so does a policeman who saw her at the botched robbery. To protect Tom from any connection to Leo and his gang, she breaks up with him, turns herself over to the policeman, refuses to implicate Leo or others who took part in the robbery, and goes to jail for her involvement.

Three years later, Mary is released from jail and once again cannot find respectable work. Then, like the proverbial bad penny, Leo shows up, thanks her for not implicating him in the robbery, and tells her she's welcome to come back and resume her relationship with him. Reluctantly, she accepts. Leo also learns that she has feelings for Tom and doesn't like it one bit. After sending men out to kill Tom and then learning that they mistakenly killed Tom's friend Sam (Andy Devine) instead, Leo sets out to kill the right person this time. To save Tom, Mary shoots Leo, killing him.

In *Midnight Mary*, the notorious Leo Darcy (Ricardo Cortez) and the beautiful young Mary Martin (Loretta Young) have a complex and decidedly less-than-healthy relationship (MGM/Photofest).

Now back in the courtroom after the jury has deliberated, Mary hears the verdict—guilty. Just then, however, Tom enters and speaks, admitting to the world that he and Mary are in love and that she killed Leo because it was the only way she could save his life. He pleads for a new trial based on this and other new revelations, and the judge agrees.

Now, Mary will get her new trial and probable acquittal, and both she and Tom can be free to find happiness together. As Tom tells her, "Life is just beginning for us both."

*

When *Midnight Mary* was released, the popular and critical response to it was mixed. Especially for being a low-budget programmer, the film performed quite well at the box office, Young later noting that it was

MGM's big money maker for the first two weeks it was out.[8] The critics, however, were generally dismissive. Among the most flip was Andre David Sennwald of the *New York Times,* who called the film "an average specimen of its type" (its "type," of course, being a lowly programmer) and remarked sarcastically about finding a strategy to help stifle "the tremendous yawn which is always threatening to interrupt the recital of Mary's sufferings."[9] While calling the film "hokum pure and unadulterated," the *Hollywood Reporter* did concede that it was nevertheless hokum that "breezes along with a fine, tense speed" and that Young's work "hits a high level in the very first scenes and never drops for a moment."[10]

*

In the last few decades, however, attitudes toward *Midnight Mary* have changed greatly. One on-line blogger calls it "a great watch, worth your seventy-four-minute investment for Loretta Young's performance alone,"[11] another "sparkling and compelling,"[12] and still another "pre–Code bliss par excellence!"[13] Concluding his assessment of the film, pre–Code historian Danny Reid calls it "a breezy gut punch that never gets old."[14] Film writer Jay Steinberg notes that the film is "well worth rediscovery, as a crisply told tale of Depression-era desperation showcasing Loretta Young at the height of her beauty, with plenty of Wellman's signature motifs and touches in play."[15] And film historians Jeffrey Vance and Tony Maietta have even gone as far as to say, "The combination of Wellman's vigorous direction, sharp dialog, ... the cut-to-the-chase structure, and the always-glamorous MGM production values make this dynamic film one of Wellman's best."[16]

*

What do contemporary viewers see in *Midnight Mary* that Sennwald and others writing in 1933 missed?

Perhaps the best place to begin this discussion is with Wellman's many contributions. And an excellent starting point comes in the film's opening few minutes: a brilliant storytelling set-up in terms of its economy and creativity.

We enter a crowded courtroom, and, as we do, Wellman puts us, the audience, right in the jury box. "Mary Martin has killed a man," the prosecutor says with ferocious intensity, and for this crime she must pay with her own life. Along with the jury, we are being asked to pass judgement on this young woman. What verdict does she deserve? And how, we might even ask, has she come to this point?

Quickly, Wellman moves to Mary sitting behind the prosecutor, and rather than hanging on his every word as we might expect, she is, seemingly indifferent to the proceedings taking place, casually reading a copy of *Cosmopolitan Magazine*. Immediately, we are curious: is she really that jaded and cynical, or is she simply putting up a tough-girl front?

When the jury is sequestered and Mary goes to the court clerk's office to await the verdict, we, along with Mary, see that the clerk is disarmingly kind and thoughtful. She relaxes a bit, and we see a more sensitive, vulnerable person beneath her façade.

Along with Mary, we also see the many bound volumes of court records, volumes dating back to before her birth, lined up in strict chronological order on bookshelves in the office. Mary begins to look at certain years that have meaning in her life, and we move into the first of several flashbacks that offer us glimpses of her story, the "how" she has come to this point.

As a general rule, Wellman didn't like to use flashbacks in his films because he felt they tended to disrupt the flow of the story, but, for *Midnight Mary*, he breaks his rule, and, interestingly, in very creative fashion by employing a couple of his stylistic flourishes. One, of course, is using the years—1910, 1919, 1923, etc.—on the bound court records to cue us as to when these events occurred in Mary's life. This technique is quite clever in two respects. First, it uses information logically rooted in the story to avoid the cliché of simply recapping Mary's life by putting one particular year after another on the screen to keep a chronology clear in viewers' minds. Second, it also keeps viewers anchored to the present, and focused on the grim reality that Mary has been tried for murder and is now anxiously awaiting the jury's verdict. The other Wellman flourish is the use of horizontal "wipes"—transitions used in editing in which one shot replaces another by moving or "wiping" from one side of the screen to another—to move to and from the flashback scenes or sequences. In traditional film language, a flashback is almost always cued by a "dissolve"—a transition between scenes in which one scene fades into another—and, to emphasize that the story is flashing back to another time, the dissolve is normally slow. Because the use of wipes is so novel and unusual in *Midnight Mary*, the effect makes the story more interesting visually and, as a result, seem fresher. Even today, viewers are fascinated by the way Wellman and the film's editor, James Gray, managed this.

Another personal rule Wellman broke when making *Midnight Mary* involved the use of actors to play characters at different times in their lives. Although he often portrayed characters as both children and then adults to give viewers a more well-rounded sense of these people, he preferred, as he does in *The Public Enemy*, *So Big*, and other films, to use different actors to portray the same characters as children and as adults. In *Midnight Mary*, he makes an exception. In the scenes when Mary is nine and thirteen, he uses both the twenty-year-old Young and the twenty-nine-year-old Una Merkel to play Mary and Bunny, respectively. To everyone's great credit, Wellman, the actresses, and cinematographer Van Trees pull off this feat quite well. Young and Merkel are especially effective conveying the gestures and expressions of young girls, and, by placing the camera slightly above the actresses' heads, Wellman and Van Trees convincingly make them look shorter and, more importantly, younger.

Wellman's visual touches are by no means limited to the first few minutes of the film, either. In one scene later in the story, for example, Mary has reluctantly returned to Leo and his gang. Everyone but Leo decides to toast Mary's return with champagne. Then, in one stunning shot, we see the champagne glasses clinking together then pulling back to reveal a close-up of Leo's face looking intensely at Mary, his expression filled with sexual desire. This visually affirms, of course, that, while the other gang members are happy that Mary is back, Leo has his own reasons for being especially delighted. Later, in the scene when Mary shoots Leo, Wellman has Cortez fall into a sitting position in front of a door. When others in Leo's gang hear the shot that's killed him, they try to push the door open, but, as they do, their actions force Leo's body to twitch back and forth as if he were still alive (an effect reminiscent of the macabre ending of *The Hatchet Man*). Watching this, Mary reacts in shock, her body also twitching in a way that mimics his. The entire bit of business is quite bizarre and shocking, but it also works extremely well to underscore this climatic moment in Mary's story without seeming forced or superfluous.

In *Midnight Mary*, Wellman often develops his visual touches into major story motifs as well. One that's quite effective is photographing Young either behind prison bars or along with shadows that resemble prison bars. At one point, for example, these shadows are the reflection of banister bars on a staircase in a gambling parlor, subtly foreshadowing that her participation in the robbery taking place there will eventually lead Mary to jail. At the end of the story, we see a similar visual image, the shadows of prison bars behind Mary in a prison visiting room as she and Tom discuss their hopeful future together. As the scene proceeds and Mary feels more confident that she and Tom will have good things to look forward to, the bars, slowly and subtly, fade and disappear.

As with all of Wellman's visual touches, the purpose in depicting or suggesting prison bars repeatedly in the film is not just to create an effect but to reinforce meaning. In this case, the bars have represented a largely cold and uncaring justice system that hasn't tried to understand or help Mary but has instead focused on punishment, which, in turn, has impeded her efforts to be a good person and find happiness. Once again, as he has done in films from *Beggars of Life* to *Heroes for Sale*, Wellman emphasizes his preoccupation with justice and the thorny issues that accompany this subject. What, for example, constitutes just treatment? In the real world, is such a thing even possible? Who, if anyone, has the right to judge or dispense justice? Should justice be tempered with mercy? If so, how do we do this? True to form, Wellman doesn't preach but leaves many of these issues open in *Midnight Mary*. As he suggests when he places us in the jury box at the film's beginning, we are the ones who must determine for ourselves what a just verdict, and ultimately Mary's fate, should be.

In addition to the visual touches he brings to *Midnight Mary*, and although he is working from a prepared screenplay, Wellman's wry and playful personality certainly makes its presence known in the finished film's dialog. One scene soon after Mary and Tom meet is a fine example of this:

> TOM: (Looking coyly at Mary) Now what do you suppose made me think of sex?
> MARY: I can't imagine. Most men never do.
> TOM: I'm the intellectual type myself.

Wellman (left) chats with stars Loretta Young and Franchot Tone on the set of *Midnight Mary* (MGM. Album/Alamy Stock Photo).

12. Midnight Mary (1933) 173

MARY: Me too.
TOM: Of course, sometimes my baser nature gets the better of me.
MARY: That's the beast in you.
TOM: How well you understand me.

Again, too, one reason why Wellman thrived during the frank and free-wheeling pre–Code era is that he had the freedom to be uncompromisingly honest, and this is clearly evident in *Midnight Mary*. Soon after Leo picks up the teen-age Mary, for example, we see her tightly intertwined with him, her legs up and exposed, in the back seat of his car. The two will clearly be having vigorous, perhaps rough, first-night sex very soon. Later, when we see Angelo hitting Bunny and, still later, when we hear Leo beating Mary, the outbursts are brutal and disturbing to witness. But then these are not well-adjusted couples—these are vicious hoodlums and their molls in what we would today call sordid (perhaps even somewhat sadomasochistic) relationships—and Wellman was adamant about depicting such behavior as vividly, forcefully, and truthfully as possible. After the Code was fully enforced in mid-1934, of course, scenes such as these would never have passed the censors.

*

Among the actors in *Midnight Mary*, Young, Cortez, and Tone all deliver excellent performances.

Young, especially, is a marvel. Only 20 years old when she made *Midnight Mary*, Young (1913–2000) had been appearing in movies since she was a child, receiving her first screen credit (as Gretchen Young, her birth name) when she was four in the 1917 silent fantasy *Sirens of the Sea*. As she grew into a teenager, filmmakers became increasingly captivated by her striking on-screen presence, and her career received a big boost when the great silent film actor Lon Chaney, Sr., insisted that she play the object of his character's rather disturbing romantic fixation (at the time, Young was fifteen and Chaney forty-five) in the 1928 melodrama *Laugh, Clown, Laugh*. After this, she was cast in numerous films, usually as the hero's romantic interest or in another supporting role. She turned in fine featured performances in some films, especially Roy Del Ruth's *Employees' Entrance* (1933), but continued to be known more for her beauty than her acting ability.

Her performance in *Midnight Mary* was a major step in proving to film colleagues and audiences that she was, to use the well-worn phrase, "more than just a pretty face." She dominates this film, appearing in virtually every scene and credibly portraying Mary as a nine- and thirteen-year-old girl, a young woman on the make, a tough-girl gun moll, an earnest young woman seeking honest work, a prison inmate, an appreciator of beauty and art, a woman in love willing to sacrifice herself to protect Tom, and more. It's intriguing, too, how, when the situation requires, she can transform from, say, the good, sensitive Mary to the tough, gun-moll Mary so quickly, effortlessly, and convincingly. This is a fine performance, more than deserving of the praise she received from critics in 1933 and has received since.

Young would go on to become one of Hollywood's major stars during the 1930s and 1940s, delivering excellent performances in such films as Frank Borzage's pre–Code drama *Man's Castle* (1933), Orson Welles' noirish thriller *The Stranger* (1946), H.C. Potter's comedy *The Farmer's Daughter* (1947), Henry Koster's holiday perennial *The Bishop's Wife* (1947), and Koster's comedy-drama *Come to the Stable* (1949). For both *The Farmer's Daughter* and *Come to the Stable* she received Best Actress Academy Award nominations for her work, winning the Oscar for *The Farmer's Daughter*. Among the first of the major stars to move to television, she hosted *The Loretta Young Show*, a long-running (1953–1961) anthology series, in which she starred in many of the show's 162 episodes, winning three Emmy Awards for her work. After effectively retiring in the 1960s, she returned a quarter of a century later to star in two made-for-TV movies, *Christmas Eve* (1986) and *Lady in a Corner* (1989), receiving Golden Globe nominations for both and winning a Golden Globe for *Christmas Eve*.

Ricardo Cortez, as head honcho hoodlum Leo, also delivers with his trademark blend of charm, slickness, and sleaze. Born Jacob Krantz to Jewish parents in New York City, Cortez (1900–1977) came to Hollywood in the 1920s, and, to capitalize on his handsome Latin-like features in an era when Latin lovers such as Rudolph Valentino and Ramon Novarro were especially popular, was given the professional name of Ricardo Cortez. He began playing romantic leads, but, with the coming of sound, his commanding screen presence and New York accent made him a very effective bad guy, and, during the pre–Code era, he was at his height, appearing in more than two dozen films often as the featured heavy.

His Leo Darcy in *Midnight Mary* is classic pre–Code Cortez: intelligent, suave, magnetically sexy, and very bad. We can totally see why Mary is drawn to him sexually and even willing, to a point, to debase herself in order to stay with him. Simply put, he turns her on, and it doesn't hurt that he also sets her up with a lavish wardrobe and elegant lifestyle. To his credit, Cortez has both the acting capability and the on-screen charisma to pull all this off quite handily. He succeeds in a role that many actors would have had difficulty with.

The pre–Code era marked a career highpoint for Cortez, giving him many of the roles for which he is best remembered today. He continued to act in films, most of them undistinguished, throughout the 1930s and 1940s. Between 1938 and 1940, he also directed seven B-pictures for Twentieth Century–Fox. Retiring from films in the late 1950s, he returned to New York and went to work as a stock broker for the Wall Street investment bank Salomon Brothers. For those who can't resist additional tidbits of classic film trivia, Cortez was also the older brother of the highly respected cinematographer Stanley Cortez (born Samuel Krantz), who was a key contributor to such exceptional films as Orson Welles' *The Magnificent Ambersons* (1942) and Charles Laughton's *Night of the Hunter* (1955).

Finally, Franchot Tone, who had only been acting in films for about a year, brings real strength and substance to the role of Tom Mannering, which, like Leo Darcy, is another role in *Midnight Mary* that is deceptively difficult to play successfully. Born into a well-to-do, socially prominent family in New York state, Tone (1905–1968) went to Cornell, where he was president of the drama club, and then to the New York stage, where he acted from 1927 to 1932. For part of this time, he was a member of the legendary Group Theatre, working with such New York theatrical icons as director and critic Harold Clurman, actors and acting teachers Lee Strasberg and Stella Adler, and playwright Clifford Odets. And it was Odets who, many years later, remarked, "The two most talented young actors I have known in the American theater in my time have been Franchot Tone and Marlon Brando, and I think Franchot was the more talented."[17] In 1932, Tone left the New York stage for Hollywood films and contract work at MGM.

As Tom in *Midnight Mary*, Tone very effectively counterbalances the despicable Leo. He is well-born, fun-loving, highly capable, good-hearted, and quite decent. Initially smitten by Mary's beauty, he quickly grows to value her intelligence, wit, and appreciation for life's finer things. In turn, he has a positive influence on her. To better herself, she, with his help, learns a skill and finds respectable work in his law office. Tone is especially good in the courtroom scene, when he unexpectedly enters, claims that he has new evidence to share, and demands that Mary be given a new trial, one which will prove that she shot Leo to save him. The script here requires a bit of a credibility stretch from viewers, but Tone approaches it with the earnestness, forcefulness, and heart that he makes this stretch easier to make. In a sense, he, just as much as Young, makes the whole Cinderella story work.

A leading man throughout most of the 1930s and 1940s, Tone moved to supporting roles in films and a variety of roles on television shows in the 1950s and 1960s. On television, he appeared as a guest star on many shows, including such classic series as *Alfred Hitchcock Presents* and *The Twilight Zone*, and as a series regular in the second season of the medical drama *Ben Casey*. For his film work, he also received a Best Actor Academy Award nomination for his performance in MGM's 1935 epic production of *Mutiny on the Bounty*, which also starred Clark Gable and Charles Laughton.

Among the main supporting players, Una Merkle as Bunny, Andy Devine as Sam, and Warren Hymer as Angelo, Merkle clearly is the standout, ably playing a character who is both Mary's loyal friend and a person who, unlike Mary, has pretty much learned to live with the compromises one must make to be a gunman's moll. She's excellent, for example, in one darkly comic scene when Bunny tells Mary that she's become pregnant by Angelo and is repulsed by the thought of marrying him—another scene that would not have been kept in the film after the Code's strict enforcement.

*

Also making significant contributions to *Midnight Mary* were cinematographer James Van Trees, film editor James Gray, and costume designer Adrian. Van Trees, who had recently worked with Wellman at Warner Brothers, ably adjusts to MGM's more glamorous presentation style for this project. Especially effective is the way he shoots Young in many of her close-ups, composing them to accentuate her beauty and succeeding admirably. Gray does a marvelous job of editing in *Midnight Mary*, keeping the film humming along at a fast pace without appearing too hurried, orchestrating the film's many "wipe" transitions between present time and flashbacks, and making the film's montages work so well. For example, the montage early on in the film that depicts Mary's frustration at not finding work is marvelous, taking on an eerie expressionistic quality that excellently captures the emotional nightmare the heroine is experiencing. Infusing additional MGM glamor into the film, Adrian's costumes, such as the mostly backless gown and beaded headpiece Mary wears during the botched gambling parlor robbery and then at Tom's home, are stunning and quite alluring. Occasionally, though—such as when Mary, now trying to go straight and without access to Leo's money, wears a very stylish Adrian-designed dress to Tom's office to ask for a job—the glamor seems out of place.

*

After completing *Midnight Mary* on time and under budget, Wellman returned to Warner Brothers with a very different attitude than he'd had when he first arrived in 1930. By now, he had been directing films for a full decade—thirty-six features in all, with one of them winning the Academy Award for Best Picture. He had also directed several of Warner's biggest

12. Midnight Mary (1933)

recent moneymakers, including *The Public Enemy* and *Night Nurse*. And, with *Heroes for Sale*, he had made one of Hollywood's most honest and compelling statements about the plight of the downtrodden in the economically depressed early 1930s. He had more than proven, he felt, that he'd reached the point where he didn't have to plead constantly for stories he wanted to film and better scripts. Perhaps it was time that he left for that long-dreamed-about career as an independent director who could develop his own projects and see them through the way he wanted to.[18]

Before he had the chance to act on any of these impulses, however, Warner Brothers gave Wellman the proverbial offer he couldn't refuse: the chance to direct a film about Depression-era teenagers forced to become hoboes. The story, filled with echoes of his own difficult youth, had affected him deeply. Despite feeling under-appreciated at Warner Brothers, this was much too good an opportunity to pass up. He would, he ultimately decided, stay a bit longer.

13

"What good will it do you to send us home to starve?"
Wild Boys of the Road (1933)

One of the shiny lures Darryl Zanuck had dangled in front of Wellman to entice him to come to Warner Brothers in 1930 was the opportunity to develop more high-quality films that tackled worthwhile subjects and, in the process, get his creative juices flowing—more, if you will, passion projects. Now, ironically, after Zanuck had left the studio, Wellman received what was for him perhaps the ultimate plum assignment of his Warner Brothers years. Not only did he relish the opportunity, but he took full advantage of it, throwing himself unreservedly into the effort.

The result is the gritty drama *Wild Boys of the Road*, a story of struggling teens who, during the height of the Great Depression, roam the United States in search of any work they can find. This may very well be the best of the eighteen features Wellman made during his 1930–1933 tenure at Warner Brothers, and it is certainly one of the best films Wellman ever made. Today, it also stands as one of the highpoints of Hollywood's pre-Code era and is frequently, and favorably, compared to such other similarly themed film masterpieces as John Ford's *The Grapes of Wrath* (1940) and Vittorio De Sica's Italian neorealist drama *The Bicycle Thief* (1948).[1]

One of the main reasons why *Wild Boys* is such a compelling film is Wellman's unflinching commitment to realism. During the story, he depicts disturbing events, ranging from the rape of a transient girl to the mangling and later amputation of another character's leg, with a clarity and honesty that would not have been possible after the Production Code's enforcement only a year later. The finished product, while not always pleasant to watch, is a film that oozes with conviction and authority. It is fiction based on fact, but it sometimes seems so real that, as viewers, we occasionally feel that we are first-hand witnesses to true events.

*

13. Wild Boys of the Road *(1933)*

The production story of *Wild Boys of the Road* begins with a scenario called "Desperate Youth" by Danny Ahearn, a contract writer at Warner Brothers in 1932 and 1933. Very much in keeping with Zanuck's mandate to emphasize films based on stories ripped from the headlines, it was inspired by multiple newspaper accounts of teenagers and young adults who'd left home during the height of the Great Depression to look for work anywhere they could find it. The story was then adapted into the script for *Wild Boys* by Earl Baldwin, who worked as a staff writer at Warner Brothers between 1930 and 1941.

Of the two writers, Baldwin (1901–1970) clearly had the more prolific Hollywood career, developing story scenarios, original screenplays, and screen adaptations for more than fifty films and then numerous television shows between the late 1920s and the early 1960s. In addition to *Wild Boys*, other notable films he contributed to include the horror-thriller *Doctor X* (1932), the crime film *Blondie Johnson* (1933) with Joan Blondell, and the gangster classic *The Roaring Twenties* (1939) with James Cagney. Among his television credits are scripts for such hit series as *Sugarfoot*, *Rawhide*, *My Little Margie*, and *M Squad*.

By far the more unusual and intriguing, however, was Ahearn (1901–1960). In addition to working on films at Warner Brothers and later as a reporter for the left-wing *The Daily Worker* and other newspapers, Ahearn spent much of his life as a career criminal, serving two different prison sentences for fraud beginning in 1934 and later a sentence of twenty years to life for robbery. And today, he is perhaps best known, not for his contributions to such films as *Wild Boys* or another absorbing Warner pre–Code effort, *Picture Snatcher* (1933), but for writing the 1930 non-fiction "how-to" book, *How to Commit a Murder (and all the Major Crimes of the Calendar and Get Away with It)*. In chapters titled "How to Rob a Jewelry Store," "How to Stick Up a Fur Joint," "Taking a Crap Game," and so forth, Ahearn shares both lessons learned from a lifetime of law-breaking and tips for achieving success in this line of work. When it first appeared, the book was greeted by a cadre of stunned reviewers. "We honestly believe that the author, Danny Ahearn, could commit any crime and get away with it," declared the *Wilmington News-Journal*. "A truly dangerous book," noted the *Lansing State Journal*. "Even salacious or sexy trash is less harmful," asserted the *Edmonton Journal*. "The epitome of gangster ideals, if there are any," added the *Nebraska State Journal*. Not to be outdone, the *Victoria Daily Times* perceptively identified what it found to be the book's only two shortcomings. "Danny Ahearn tells everything," its reviewer wrote, "but how to acquire the nerve to kill a man and how to get rid of a guilty conscience after it is done."[2] Despite all the critical concern, though, the book found a wide audience in its time and is still available today in both print and electronic formats.

Once the screenplay for what was eventually retitled *Wild Boys of the Road* was readied, Wellman spent a great deal of time—much more, according to William Wellman, Jr., than he usually did when preparing scripts for shooting—making story changes and adding his distinctive touches.[3] Many of these changes (such as eliminating a plot turn in which the story's main female character is forced into prostitution) were intended to soften some of the harshness and bleakness of Ahearn's original version and Baldwin's screenplay. The main story, which still included a downbeat ending, was, Wellman and others at Warner Brothers agreed, bleak enough.

For *Wild Boys*, Wellman also worked for the first time with veteran cinematographer Arthur L. Todd. Spending much of his career at Warner Brothers, Todd (1895–1942) worked on about 140 films between 1917 and 1942. In addition to *Wild Boys*, among his better-known efforts today are *Monkey Business* (1931) with the Marx Brothers, *Babbitt* (1934) with Guy Kibbee, and *Alibi Ike* (1935) with Joe E. Brown.

Casting the players also presented some interesting challenges for Wellman. Although many familiar faces appear in the film, they belong to character actors such as Grant Mitchell, Charley Grapewin, Ward Bond, and Sterling Holloway, all in supporting roles. For the main roles, Wellman, who was determined to give this film as much of a documentary-like look as possible, picked one somewhat familiar and two virtually unknown players.

The somewhat familiar one was Frankie Darro (1917–1976), who plays the film's lead, Eddie Smith. Starting as a child of six in 1924, Darro had acted in small, often uncredited parts in films. He had worked previously with Wellman in *The Public Enemy*, playing the teenage incarnation of the Matt Doyle character. And, in a career that continued through the early 1970s, he amassed nearly 190 film and television credits, starring in some efforts but increasingly taking small roles and work as a voice-over artist. In addition to playing Eddie in *Wild Boys*, he is perhaps best known for his voice-over role as Lampwick, the unlucky boy who turns into a donkey in Walt Disney's classic animated feature, *Pinocchio* (1940). Born into a family of circus aerialists, Darro was also in demand for much of his career to perform physical stunts (such as spinning on his head) both as an actor and as a stuntman, a talent Wellman would utilize in *Wild Boys*.

Darro's two co-stars, Edwin Phillips and Dorothy ("Dottie") Coonan, were true unknowns. Phillips (1911–1981) who plays Eddie's best friend, Tommy, made his debut in *Wild Boys* and afterward played small parts in only two other films, the comedy/drama *Soak the Rich* (1936) and the Betty Hutton musical *Satin and Spurs* (1954). Coonan (1913–2009), who plays Sally, the hobo girl Eddie and Tommy befriend on their travels, had been

13. Wild Boys of the Road *(1933)*

Wellman's landmark social drama, *Wild Boys of the Road*, focuses on its three young heroes (from left) Eddie (Frankie Darro), Tommy (Edwin Phillips), and Sally (Dorothy Coonan) (Warner Bros. Photographer Mac Jones. First National Pictures/Photofest).

a Busby Berkeley dancer with no desire to act. Wellman met her at Warner Brothers when he was working on *Heroes for Sale* and the two quickly fell in love. Then, when Warner executives were pushing for a more established, glamorous actress to play Sally, Wellman, who felt that Coonan could excellently convey the tomboy qualities he wanted for the part, insisted on her and eventually won over both the studio executives and the hesitant Coonan. Shortly after completing *Wild Boys*, she and Wellman were married, she retired from the film business, and together they had seven children and remained happily married until the director's death in 1975, forty-one years later.

The filming of *Wild Boys*, originally scheduled as a twenty-four-day shoot, started in mid–June 1933. In addition to scenes shot at the Warner Brothers studios, Wellman, insisting upon as much realism as possible, arranged for numerous scenes to be shot on location at nearby sites. Just a few of these sites included the now-defunct American Concrete Pipe Company facilities in the city of South Gate, the train station in Burbank, and the expansive railroad yards in downtown Los Angeles. Although

Wellman had made a habit of bringing films in on-time and under budget, his passion for this project led to his exceeding the original cost estimate by about $29,000.

Before *Wild Boys* was released, however, Jack Warner, believing that the story's conclusion was too bleak for audiences at the time, ordered a new, more hopeful ending. Wellman, feeling that this undercut the story's integrity, strongly objected. But Warner was the boss and, on September 7, 1933, the new ending was shot.

*

Wild Boys of the Road begins with a slice of seeming middle-class normality peppered with teen-age hijinks. It's the "Sophomore Frolic" dance at Hilldale High School, and Eddie Smith (Darro) and Tommy Gordon (Phillips) take their girlfriends, Grace and Harriet, to the event. Tommy can't afford a ticket, so Eddie comes up with a scheme to dress Tommy up as a girl and sneak him in. Tommy's ruse is discovered, he is forced to leave, and, out of loyalty to him, Eddie, Grace, and Harriet all accompany him out. But now Eddie's car is out of gas, so he and Tommy siphon some from another vehicle nearby. Everything rolls along in quite a light-hearted, teens-will-be-teens way.

At one point, though, Tommy confides that he is going to drop out of school and find a job to help support his struggling family. Eddie offers to speak to his father, who works at a cement company, to see about getting Tommy a job there. When Eddie returns home later that night, however, he finds that his father (Grant Mitchell) has just lost his job. As the days pass, Eddie's father continues to look for work but without success. The bills keep piling up, and soon the family is faced with eviction. Rather than being extra burdens on their families, Eddie and Tommy agree to leave, ride the rails, see if they can find work elsewhere and, if so, send money back to their families. Eddie writes his parents a note, and the two boys depart.

Aboard a freight train they meet Sally (Coonan), another teenager, who is hoping that her aunt in Chicago can house her for a while. The three head for Chicago, and, as they do, they meet large numbers of other young people like themselves, riding the rails, looking for any opportunities they can find. When the three arrive at the home of Sally's aunt, however, they learn that it is actually a house of prostitution, and, when it is raided, they must quickly escape through a back window.

Continuing to head east by train, the three witness and experience more grim events. In one instance, a teen-aged girl is caught alone on a train by a brakeman (Ward Bond) and raped. When the other transient youths learn about this, they surround the brakeman and start punching

13. Wild Boys of the Road (1933)

him. Then, quite by accident, he falls in front of another train and to his death. In another instance, Tommy, running from one train, falls across the track in front of second, oncoming train and passes out just before the train runs over his leg. Sadly, the leg must be amputated.

For a while, Eddie, Tommy, and Sally all live with hundreds of other young people in a slum nicknamed Sewer Pipe City. To discourage vagrancy and push the young people out of town, however, the police point a fire hose at the youths and pummel them with a torrent of rushing water. Once again, the three are forced to move on.

Still continuing eastward, the three eventually find a new home in the New York City Municipal Dump. Eddie finally finds work but needs three dollars to pay for a coat he needs for the job. They panhandle to raise money, Sally helping out by doing some slick dancing on the sidewalk to impress passers-by. As they panhandle, two men offer Eddie five dollars to deliver a note to a movie theater cashier across the street. He jumps at the chance, but the note turns out to be a demand for money. The cashier calls for help, Eddie is arrested, and Tommy and Sally are also picked up.

Soon, the three stand before a judge (Robert Barrat), who, while sympathetic to their plight, can't learn anything about them, where they're from, or who their parents are, and he insists that the three must go to juvenile incarceration facilities. At this, an impassioned Eddie tells him:

> I knew all that stuff about you helping us was baloney. I'll tell you why we can't go home—'cause our folks are poor, they can't get jobs, and there isn't enough to eat. What good will it do you to send us home to starve? You say you gotta' send us to jail to keep us off the street. Well, that's a lie. You're sending us to jail 'cause you don't want to see us. You want to forget us. Well, you can't do it. 'Cause I'm not the only one. There's thousands just like me, and there's more hittin' the road every day.... But what's the use? You're not going to believe me, and I don't care whether you do or not. Go ahead—put me in a cell. Lock me up. I'm sick of being hungry and cold. I'm sick of freight trains. Jail can't be any worse than the street. So, give it to me!

At this point, Eddie breaks down in tears. His words, however, have moved the judge, who has a change of heart, promising to get Eddie's job back for him and to help Tommy and Sally as well. The judge also tells them that things will be getting better and that their parents will also be going back to work soon. Heartened by this news, the three youths leave the courtroom with—for the first time in a long time—a sense of hope.

(In the film's earlier ending, the one Jack Warner insisted upon changing, the judge does not have this magnanimous change of heart. Although he is sympathetic to the three youths, he still sends them to the juvenile incarceration facilities.)

*

When *Wild Boys* opened in theaters on October 7, 1933, it was a major box-office disappointment. Largely because of its grim subject matter, audiences shied away, and the film never even came close to recouping its $203,000 production budget.

The film was also the recipient of mostly negative reviews. Although appreciative of the film's artistic strengths, the critic for the box-office-minded *Variety*, was baffled by its harsh storyline and obvious lack of commercial appeal. "Indeed, the very merits of [the film] are its difficulties," the writer declared. "The acting is so gripping and the incidents so graphic that they conspire to make the hour's running of the subject one of considerable discomfort to the spectator."[4] A staffer for *Screenland Magazine* likened *Wild Boys* to the 1931 horror film *Frankenstein* and then focused in depth on the horrific scene when the train runs over Tommy's leg, lamenting that the viewing experience "succeeded only in upsetting us."[5] Finally, in a stinging review, Frank Nugent of the *New York Times* called the film "disappointing" mainly because it "might have been at once tragic, dramatic, and a stirring call for remedial action."[6] Instead, he continues, "Its tragedy has been over-sentimentalized, its drama is mostly melodrama and, by endowing it with a happy ending, the producers have robbed it of its value as a social challenge."[7] Continuing further, Nugent adds considerable salt to the wound, declaring, "The responsibility for its weakness, therefore, must be laid at the door of the director, William A. Wellman. He has taken a theme with broad social implications and has converted it into a rather pointless yarn about three wandering youngsters."[8]

It's interesting to note, too, that, while all three of these critics responded negatively to *Wild Boys*, and for very different reasons, all their reviews have an unusually striking emotional intensity about them, as if the film really unnerved them, eliciting, not just a negative reaction, but also a visceral one. It's impossible to pinpoint the precise what and why of this, of course. But one possible explanation might be that the film presented them with a perspective so unexpectedly original, raw, and real that they didn't quite know how to respond to it, let alone articulate a calm and measured response. Perhaps this was a viewing experience that might require some time and distance for each of them to process internally. Perhaps not. In any case, these critics' very charged reactions are fascinating to speculate about.

*

Fortunately for Wellman and *Wild Boys*, however, the vast majority of twenty-first-century reviewers have responded to the film far more positively.

13. Wild Boys of the Road (1933)

Film historian Gwendolyn Audrey Foster, for example, reserves special praise for the film's uncompromising honesty, a quality which she believes has also contributed to its enduring relevance and appeal:

> Of all the films made during the Depression, *Wild Boys of the Road* is perhaps the most realistic and unsparing, due in no small part to Wellman's penchant for unvarnished realism. Much of the film looks like a newsreel, and the scenes of local police breaking up the hobo encampments ... as well as the footage of riding the rails—often presented with an air of romance in escapist films of the period, but here shown to be exactly what it was—desperate, dangerous, and violent—combine to create a film of ... astonishing honesty....
>
> [The film] stands as a warning that the social fabric of society is delicate indeed, and that, when tough times come, no one is really ready for them....
> [It] is absolutely essential viewing both then, and now—perhaps even more so today, lest we forget the lessons it can teach us.[9]

Speaking of enduring relevance, a very astute observation comes from Mick LaSalle, who, at the height of the worldwide Covid pandemic in the summer of 2020, wrote:

> There is something special about movies that are made about a national crisis while it is still taking place. There's an immediacy there and an awareness of suffering. There's urgency. And there's something else: Such films have the ability to touch us when we, too, are going through a national crisis.
> *Wild Boys of the Road* is an amazing depiction of the Great Depression, a film about a real-life phenomenon. Young teens, not wanting to be a burden on their financially strapped parents, were leaving home and riding the rails, living the lives of vagabonds....
> Of course, things eventually got better, but in 1933, when this film was made, no one knew when or if they ever would. So, the movie is an expression of concern and courage in the midst of a terrible time, and it's worth seeing, for the connection and for the sense of understanding we experience while watching it.[10]

Numerous online bloggers have also added to the general acclaim for *Wild Boys*. One, for example, calls it a "huge emotional epiphany" and adds, "Brutal and raw, this is a journey you, too, must take. A page of America's history told so expertly as to make you laugh and cry simultaneously."[11] Another laments that, after all these years, a film of this quality is still "criminally underseen."[12] Still another declares, "[Y]ou could not find a more heart-wrenching and emotionally stirring depiction of the brutal reality and its effect on the human spirit."[13]

*

Especially when we factor in that *Wild Boys of the Road* was intended to be a low-budget, fast-turnaround programmer, the finished product is a truly remarkable achievement, and Wellman and his various collaborators deserve high praise for their efforts.

One critically important facet of *Wild Boys* that sets it apart from many of Wellman's other pre–Code efforts is the strong, solid construction of its story. In many respects, *Night Nurse* and *Heroes for Sale* contain two different stories within the same film. Likewise, *So Big* and *The Purchase Price* have meandering storylines and arbitrary endings. In contrast, *Wild Boys*, even with its many episodes, is driven by a focused, forceful, and credible plot. Actions lead to consequences and additional actions, and, in the process, the film's main characters, especially Eddie and Tommy, go through significant changes, both growing sadder but wiser. It was an excellent decision, for example, to begin the story with the scenes at the high school dance. These moments show where the two boys have come from, vividly capturing the innocent, "footloose-and-fancy-free" nature of their lives before far harsher realities overtake them. In doing so, the stark contrast between these scenes and many of the scenes that follow greatly enhance both the story's drama and the sympathy viewers feel for the characters.

Yes, *Wild Boys*' Jack Warner–imposed ending, in which the judge decides to help the three heroes rather than punish them, may somewhat compromise the film's integrity. Yet, even though Wellman obeyed Warner's order, he added a beautiful bittersweet note that almost compensates for the compromise. As the three leave the courtroom, Eddie literally jumps for joy, performing some acrobatics on the sidewalk. Then, he looks at Tommy leaning on his crutch and realizes that, even though things may be looking up, Tommy's life has been profoundly and irrevocably changed by the experiences they have been through.

While striking and certainly memorable, this is only one of the many characteristic touches Wellman adds to *Wild Boys* that enrich the proceedings on both literal and symbolic levels.

Another of these occurs early in the film as Eddie returns home from the dance. The first thing he does is go to the refrigerator and take out a full-size pie with a little more than half of it still remaining on its plate. Very carefully, he cuts what we assume will be a respectably modest-size piece of it for himself. What he does, however, is put the small piece back in the refrigerator and take the enormous remaining piece for himself, a decision (and a humorous one) a hungry teen-age boy might easily make. At that moment, he spots his parents in another room, puts his large piece of pie down, and goes to greet them. As they talk, he learns that his father has been laid off from his job and that the family may soon be in dire straits financially. Somberly, he leaves and goes back to the kitchen for his pie, and now, instead of eating the enormous piece he has cut for himself, he eats the much smaller piece—a recognition that he knows he must economize and is willing to do so without being asked. This is a superb piece of Wellman-esque business. First, it shows on a literal level both Eddie's understanding that realities have greatly changed and that he must now adapt. Second, it serves as a symbolic bridge between light-heartedness of the film's first few scenes and the seriousness of the scenes that will follow—a bridge that reinforces the fact that both Eddie and the story are entering new territory.

Still another fascinating, and quite distinctive, Wellman touch occurs in the scenes when the police—after other tactics have failed—resort to the use of a powerful fire hose to drive the youths out of Sewer Pipe City. As they attach the fire hose to a hydrant in the effort, one of the seemingly anonymous policemen says to another, "This is a rotten trick, if you ask me." Nodding, the other responds, "How do you think I feel, with two kids of my own at home?" This short exchange is jolting and quite memorable for a couple of reasons. First, in films made during Hollywood's classic era, we almost never hear police personnel express sympathy for undesirables in large-scale crackdown scenes such as this. Instead, these enforcers of the law are almost always portrayed as a committed, monolithic unit doing the dirty work because, quite simply, it's part of the job. Second, the brief exchange reinforces to viewers that, beneath the surface, this particular situation is fraught with complexity and ambiguity. No, the police, as portrayed here, aren't simply the heartless enforcers. At least some of them feel deeply for these homeless youths and wish that there were better ways to resolve the problems at hand. By showing these two policemen as reluctant enforcers, Wellman adds depth and nuance to the dramatic situation, enhancing the drama while also reducing the chances that the scenes will slip into stock melodrama.

Yet another excellent Wellman contribution to *Wild Boys* is the way in which he handles interactions between key characters, in this case two close male friends, in moments of great loss. In a number of his films, he's quite successful in portraying these male-male interactions—especially when one or both of the men face an extreme situation and both, while trying hard to appear strong and manly, still show great feeling and vulnerability. In *Wild Boys*, he does this superbly, and perhaps the film's best example is the scene between Eddie and Tommy just before, and when, the doctor amputates Tommy's leg:

> (As the preparation for the amputation proceeds off-camera, the scene centers mostly on shots of the two boys' faces.)
> EDDIE: You're not scared, are you, Tommy?
> TOMMY: What's there to be scared of?
> EDDIE: Nothin'. Only I thought ... oh, you know, sometimes a fella gets kind of nervous.

Frankie Darro's Eddie (center) leads the defiant youths of their makeshift home, "Sewer Pipe City," as they retaliate against the police, who are intent on driving them out in *Wild Boys of the Road* (Warner Bros. Photo 12/Alamy Stock Photo).

> TOMMY: Shucks. What do I care about an old leg? Just think. From now on, when I get a new pair of shoes, I'll only have to break in one of them.
> EDDIE: Sure.
> TOMMY: And won't I laugh at Harriet? I won't have to argue with her any more about dancing. I won't even have to learn.
> EDDIE: That's right.
> TOMMY: And another thing. I won't have to run errands for mama, or bring up coal.
> EDDIE: I know you won't, Tommy. You'll get out of doing a lot of things.
> TOMMY: Sure. I'll get out of doing a lot of things, like kickin' footballs, playin' basketball, goin' ice skating, tumbling, walking…
> (At this, the two boys, now unable to restrain their feelings, start crying, clutch each other's hand, and hug each other tightly.)

In all of Wellman's films, this brief scene is easily one of the most heart-wrenching expressions of both great affection between two characters and the sadness they share during a tragic moment. And, as befits the director's personal style and artistic preferences, it is rendered in a simple, straightforward, and beautifully underplayed manner. The two young

13. Wild Boys of the Road (1933)

actors, Frankie Darro and Edwin Phillips, certainly deserve great credit for performing the scene with such intensity and emotional honesty. But, as we watch the two actors deliver this great screen moment, it's difficult not to see the guiding hand of Wellman getting the most from his film's two main players.

Finally, Wellman took unusual care shooting numerous other scenes throughout the film. Whether they are serious or light-hearted, involve crowds or intimate interactions, or take place in bright sunlight or (Wellman's specialty) heavy rainstorms, there is something special, and especially heartfelt, about nearly all of them. There is no doubt that, especially in light of Wellman's own troubled youth, he had a special connection with this story and its young heroes.

*

Although *Wild Boys* features no established Hollywood stars, the actors do fine work throughout.

Clearly the film's best performance is by Frankie Darro, who is essential to making Eddie the story's most fully realized and compelling character. Smart, sassy, hopeful, resourceful, resilient, caring, and deeply loyal, Eddie is the natural leader of any group he is part of and, from start to finish, the heart and soul of the story. We see all these qualities in him in his first scenes as a carefree high school student, and we see these qualities evolve as Eddie matures. Throughout, Darro excels at giving him both the Cagney-like swagger and the youthful naivete and vulnerability required to make him both credible and captivating. He is especially riveting as Eddie, for example, during the character's scenes with his father, the scene when Tommy's leg is amputated, and when he delivers his heart-wrenching statement to the judge near the end of the film.

Although their parts are not as complex as Eddie's, the film's other actors do fine jobs as well. Edwin Phillips is quite good, for example, in the scenes when Tommy's leg is amputated and afterward when he struggles to live his life with only one leg. Likewise, Dorothy Coonan brings plenty of spunk and charm to her portrayal of Sally. (And it's lots of fun to watch her dance as part of the youths' panhandling routine in one of the film's New York scenes.) Among the film's smaller character parts, Grant Mitchell is quite moving as Eddie's father, exquisitely conveying the personal despair and concern for loved ones of an older man who has been laid off from his job, can no longer provide for his family, and has no prospects of finding work again soon. When given the opportunity, Mitchell, who also shined in Wellman's 1931 hit, *The Star Witness*, could—and almost always did—deliver marvelous performances, and this is definitely one of them.

*

Finally, the contributions to *Wild Boys* of both cinematographer Arthur Todd and film editor Thomas Pratt deserve special praise. Obviously, Wellman and Todd worked closely to get the desired, starkly realistic look of certain scenes and ultimately the entire film. And obviously, the director had a big say about camera set-ups, lighting, the blocking of actors, and other considerations. It was up to the cameraman, though, to make it all work and please his demanding boss, and, in this film, Todd does an outstanding job of fulfilling this requirement. The film's editing, very much in the fast, hard-driving Warner Brothers style of the time, is also quite good, and Pratt, who spent virtually all of his thirty-year career at the studio, wins kudos for keeping the proceedings moving briskly while also varying the fast-moving action with slower, often intimate, moments that serve as emotional exclamation points.

*

For the rest of his life, Wellman regarded *Wild Boys of the Road* as one of his best films. And, with the benefit of hindsight, it's easy for us to assume that its completion might have been have been the perfect time for him to leave Warner Brothers on a high note and begin his long-dreamed-of career as an independent director.

This, however, was not to be the case. When *Wild Boys* turned out to be anything but a hit with both moviegoers and critics, Wellman, perhaps hedging his bets, chose to stay at Warner Brothers a bit longer. Almost immediately, he picked up two other projects coming down the studio assembly line: the first, a comedy already in production, and the second, a college football story with echoes of his first Warner Brothers effort, 1930's *Maybe It's Love*. Although neither of these films was a personal passion project to near the degree that *Wild Boys* had been, the director still managed to make his presence known in the finished products, both of which radiate with distinctly Wellman-esque—and unmistakably pre-Code—irony, irreverence, and cynicism.

14

"How'd you like to stick your finger in her coffee?"
Female and *College Coach* (1933) and *Looking for Trouble* (1934)

After *Wild Boys of the Road*, Wellman worked on three more films that were released before full enforcement of the Production Code took effect in 1934. The first two of these, a Ruth Chatterton comedy called *Female* and a college football story called *College Coach*, turned out to be the last two he would be involved with during his time as a contract employee at Warner Brothers. The third, a crime melodrama called *Looking for Trouble* with Spencer Tracy, was both the first of his new career as an independent director and a reunion of sorts with his fellow Warner Brothers alumnus Darryl Zanuck.

*

Of the three films, *Female* is the one that, by far, attracts the most attention today. The story of a brilliant, accomplished woman who runs an automobile company by day and relaxes at night by seducing a succession of compliant "boy-toy" employees, it is, even by pre–Code standards, radical in concept. It is also, for much of its running time, very funny. And it has the extra advantage of Chatterton, who delivers yet another commanding, memorable performance.

The source material for *Female* is a 1933 novel of the same name by Donald Henderson Clarke (1887–1958), a writer whose fiction often focused on less-than-upright characters ranging from bootleggers to women of dubious morals. The novel focuses on the rise of one of these women from the back alleys of New England to married life on Park Avenue. In 1935, this novel also earned the distinction of being declared obscene by Brooklyn Appellate Division of the New York Supreme Court. The film version, which only admits to being "suggested" by the novel is, of course, quite different. Written by the Warner Brothers in-house team (and former Wellman collaborators) Gene Markey and Kathryn Scola, it retains little from the book, other than the heroine's penchant for libertine behavior.

*

The production of *Female* was, to say the least, an often chaotic experience. The shooting began with Warner staff director William Dieterle at the helm, Chatterton and leading man George Brent in the main roles, most of the other actors who appear in the finished film in their supporting roles, and cinematographer Sid Hickox behind the camera. Then, after just ten days of shooting interiors, it was clear that Chatterton and Dieterle weren't getting along. The star was consistently late for work, and, to add to the director's frustration, she didn't like the script and started rewriting scenes on her own. The studio resolved this problem by shutting down production, announcing that Dieterle had been taken ill, and bringing Wellman in to complete the film, which, by this point, meant shooting mostly exteriors. In the process, the studio also swapped out cameramen, bringing in Ernest Haller to replace Hickox. After Wellman finished his scenes, the production wrapped up, and he started work on his next assignment, *College Coach*.[1] In the meantime, however, Jack Warner saw the rough cuts of *Female*; disliked the performance of actor George Blackwood, who played one of the heroine's boy-toys; and ordered that Blackwood be replaced and the handful of scenes he appeared in be reshot. Another actor, Johnny Mack Brown, was assigned the role. And, since Wellman was now shooting *College Coach*, Michael Curtiz was called in to direct reshoots of scenes involving the character Brown was now playing as well as several other interior scenes that Dieterle had shot.[2]

In the end, the credits were given (and withheld) in a very curious way. Curtiz received the sole directing credit, and Hickox received the sole credit for cinematography. Neither Dieterle nor Wellman was given credit for making a significant directing contribution, and Haller received no recognition for his cinematography work. While uncredited contributions were commonplace in films made during the studio era, there was usually no issue about giving shared credits to those who had—such as Wellman and Haller (and perhaps Dieterle) in this case—made significant contributions to a film.

*

The film opens in the executive boardroom of Drake Motors, a major automobile manufacturing company. We quickly learn that its president is a woman, Alison Drake (Chatterton), an extremely capable, hard-driving leader who inherited the company from her father. We quickly learn, too, that, instead of settling down with one man, she prefers to have casual sex with various men, often her employees. When the flings are over, she routinely pays the employees bonuses and, if they are disgruntled, also has them transferred to company facilities in other cities. As she says when her long-time friend Harriet asks her about romance:

ALISON: Me? Haven't got time.
HARRIET: Aren't you ever going to fall in love?
ALISON: It's a career in itself. It takes too much time and energy. To me, a woman in love is a pathetic spectacle. She's either so miserable that she wants to die, or she's so happy that you want to die.
HARRIET: Aren't you ever going to marry?
ALISON: No thanks, not me. You know, a long time ago I decided to travel the same open road that men travel. So, I treat men exactly the same way that they treat women.
HARRIET: Apparently, you don't have much respect for men.
ALISON: Oh, I know that, for some women, men are a household necessity. Myself? I'd rather have a canary…. Men? Oh, I see lots of men. But I've never found a real one.

Alison Drake (Ruth Chatterton) runs a major automobile company by day and has her way with compliant young men at night in the very subversive, and long-censored, pre-Code comedy, *Female* (Warner Bros./Photofest).

At a party Alison holds at her mansion soon afterward, we learn a bit more about why she's chosen this lifestyle. All the men who are interested in her are attracted to her money or want to sell her something. Frustrated, she dresses down and goes to a carnival sideshow, where she meets a man (George Brent) at a shooting gallery. They enjoy each other's company, but, when she indicates an interest in having sex with him, he refuses, saying that he never goes home with "pick-ups."

The next day, and to the astonishment of both, they meet again at her company's factory. He is Jim Thorne, a talented engineer her company has hired from a competitor. She invites him to her mansion that evening under the pretext of discussing his plans for a new automatic gearshift and tries to seduce him. She is unsuccessful, however, and he insists on a purely professional relationship. Insistent, she pursues other strategies to win his attentions and, ultimately, he succumbs. But, when he presents her with a marriage license the following day, she tells him that she'd prefer to keep things casual. Furious, he quits. His rejection only makes him more attractive to her. Eventually, she realizes that she is in love and agrees to marry him.

They reunite just as Drake Motors is in the midst of a financial crisis. Jim helps her find a solution. And she tells him that, in the future, he will run the company, while she will be his wife and have lots of children with him.

*

When *Female* was released, it was both a box-office hit and the recipient of mixed reviews. In his notice for the *New York Times*, for example, Mordaunt Hall summed up the feelings of several of his fellow critics when he wrote that, although the film "possesses its reprehensible moments, it has the saving grace of having been produced with a sense of humor."[3] As we might also suspect, the people who responded most emphatically to the film's so-called "reprehensible moments" were the film industry's censors. And when the big Production Code crackdown came in mid–1934, *Female* was placed on a list of films *never* to be re-released under any circumstances. As a result, it sat untouched in the Warner Brothers studio vault for decades.

One great irony in all of this, of course, is that what most twenty-first-century viewers might find reprehensible about *Female* is not so much the heroine's casual attitudes toward sex but her very uncharacteristic turnabout and complete surrender at film's end to the one man who stands up to her. For these modern viewers, it seems as though the film's refreshingly feminist premise is betrayed by a decidedly anti-feminist resolution.

14. Female and College Coach *(1933)*; Looking for Trouble *(1934)*

All this noted, *Female* has many strengths. The script by Markey and Scola (and whomever else may have also worked on it) is often quite sharp and witty, especially in the film's early scenes. Chatterton's performance, especially when she has good lines and situations to work with, is superb. We really believe that her Alison Drake is both as smart and tough enough to run a large automotive company and as egotistical and easily dismissive of others who get in the way of anything she wants. In addition, two other contributions to the film that deserve special mention are the bold, striking art deco set design scheme in the scenes set in Alison's mansion and her sometimes flamboyant wardrobe, both of which are quite effective in visually reinforcing Alison's bold, sometimes flamboyant personality. The sets were conceived by Jack Okey (1889–1963), an art director who worked on more than 110 films for various studios between 1920 and 1959. The costumes were designed by Orry-Kelly (1897–1964), who worked on more than 300 films between 1930 and 1963. One of the first serious fashion designers to contribute his talents to film, he is widely recognized today for helping to revolutionize the art of costume design in the cinema.

*

In several respects, it's unfortunate that Wellman didn't have the chance to be *Female*'s sole director.

First, the film's shooting would have probably gone much more smoothly with regards to Chatterton. After his rocky start with her on *Frisco Jenny*, Wellman and the temperamental star had developed a good working relationship while shooting both that film and then *Lilly Turner*. Most likely, he would not have had to face the *prima donna* behavior that Dieterle contended with during his ten uneasy days on the film.

Second, while Chatterton is quite forthright and fearless in some of *Female*'s scenes, it's fun to imagine how much better she might have been if she had worked with Wellman throughout the production. When she felt the circumstances were right and the director supportive, she could deliver very bold, engaging performances, and, when she worked with Wellman, she never seemed to have a problem going full-throttle. The director, too, had a talent for getting good actresses to bring strong, complex female characters to life on the screen in ways that relatively few of his directing contemporaries—especially those toiling away on the studio assembly lines—could do. Very likely, he would have been able to see even more facets to the intriguing Alison Drake and work with Chatterton to incorporate them into her performance.

Finally, especially by 1930s social standards, *Female* is driven by quite a subversive premise, and Wellman, a director with a decidedly subversive sensibility, would have felt right in his element refining the script and shooting this film. Who knows? Perhaps he would have even fashioned a resolution more in keeping with the film's "reprehensible" premise.

With all this in mind, Wellman's contribution to *Female* is worth noting both because it was significant and because the film is widely appreciated as one of those pre-Code "gems" today largely for its socially subversive subject matter, witty script, tight pacing, and, of course, Chatterton's stand-out performance. While not all-Wellman, it remains an excellent example of how a well-managed studio could, despite all the turmoil that swirled around the production, ultimately deliver a largely cohesive film with enduring appeal.

*

Soon after completing his work on *Female*, Wellman took on production duties for a rather odd, unsettling comedy called *College Coach*, his last during his stint at Warner Brothers and one that, in many ways, brought him back full-circle to his first, 1930's *Maybe It's Love*.

Although some amount of Wellman's cynical take on human nature is present in nearly all of his films, cynicism reigns supreme in *College Coach*, a story in which all the major characters are, to varying degrees, corrupt, and, in which everything eventually works out just fine.

Both the original story and screenplay for *College Coach* were written by studio staffers Manuel Seff and Niven Busch. Seff (1895–1969) contributed story scenarios and screenplays to about three dozen films between 1932 and 1950, perhaps the most famous being 1933's *Footlight Parade*. A journalist and novelist as well as a screenwriter, Busch (1903–1991) worked on about thirty films between 1932 and 1958, sometimes adapting his own novels, such as 1944's *Duel in the Sun* and 1948's *The Furies*, to the screen.

The cast of *College Coach* includes a quite a collection of familiar Warner Brothers performers, including Dick Powell, Pat O'Brien, Ann Dvorak, and Lyle Talbot. An intriguing aside is that it also includes two other actors in bit parts who would go on to illustrious film careers: John Wayne and Ward Bond. We've discussed Dvorak and Talbot in previous chapters. At the time he worked on *College Coach*, Powell (1904–1963) was an emerging star at Warner Brothers, mainly as a result of his work as a light comedian and singer in such musical hits as *42nd Street*, *Golddiggers of 1933*, and *Footlight Parade*, all churned out on the Warner Brothers assembly line during 1933. As an actor, he would eventually reinvent himself as a familiar face in hard-hitting films noir such as *Murder, My Sweet* (1944), *Johnny O'Clock* (1947), *and Pitfall* (1948). In addition to acting, he also achieved success as a producer, director, and studio head. O'Brien (1899–1983) was another familiar film face, racking up more than 150 film

14. Female and College Coach (1933); Looking for Trouble (1934)

and television credits between 1930 and 1982. He played both leads and supporting roles, often paired with his good friend James Cagney. Among his best-remembered films are *Angels with Dirty Faces* (with Cagney, 1938) and *Knute Rockne All American* (1940).

Production of *College Coach* took place in the fall of 1933, and, among the locations used in the filming were the Los Angeles Memorial Coliseum and Exposition Park, also in Los Angeles. The film was budgeted at an estimated $245,000.

*

College Coach opens on a meeting of the board of trustees at struggling Calvert College. To stay afloat financially, the board members decide to hire James Gore (O'Brien), an utterly ruthless, and consistently successful, football coach. This move, they calculate, will turn around the school's failing football program, attract hordes of people to games, and generate substantial new revenue streams for the institution.

Gore is soon hired, and, as he goes about building his team, he stops at nothing—from paying seasoned players to compete against young amateurs to playing dirty—to win. Along the way, much happens. Gore's wife

Pat O'Brien is Coach Gore and Ann Dvorak is Claire, his bored wife, in *College Coach* (Warner Bros./Photofest).

Claire (Dvorak), feeling neglected by her football-obsessed husband, takes up with Buck Weaver (Talbot), a womanizing football player who, when showing a former girlfriend's photo to another male character, utters the naughty—and characteristically pre–Code—line, "How'd you like to stick your finger in her coffee?" Doing his part to assure that success in football will lead to the building of a new chemistry facility on campus, chemistry teacher, Professor Trask (Donald Meek), gives failing student-athletes passing grades. And at one point, Gore's win-at-any-cost tactics result in a serious on-field injury and then death of an opposing player, a development Gore blithely shrugs off by citing that each year there are dozens of such football-related deaths. The only one, it seems, with any qualms of conscience, is student-athlete Phil Sargent (Powell), but even he ultimately compromises his principles.

Happily for everyone, Calvert wins the climatic big game and the wayward Claire Gore returns to her husband, who, although he promises to change his ways and be more attentive to her, seems more likely to remain just as he is. Curiously, she seems to be just fine with this, subtly suggesting that in the future she will resume her straying ways.

*

Opening in theaters on November 4, 1933, *College Coach* was a modest success at the box office and received mixed reviews from critics. "It is unfortunate that *College Coach* collapses into routine and inferior entertainment after an excellent start," wrote Mordaunt Hall. "Unable or unwilling to develop a hard-boiled thesis with the vigor and heartlessness that are implicit in its theme, the film goes soft and apologetic and sentimental."[4] Echoing Hall's concerns, the *New York Sun*'s critic noted that, while the film "is done with a certain down-to-earth quality," its "satirical ideas are clumsily projected."[5]

Contemporary viewers tend to be equally dismissive of *College Coach*, with online reviewers offering various appraisals from "fairly predictable" to "interestingly immoral," to "nasty."[6] Likening it to 1930's *Maybe It's Love*, in terms of both its basic plot and lack of potential, Wellman biographer Frank Thompson tactfully wrote that it did nevertheless manage to be a better-crafted film, "a fine, cynical comedy, briskly directed and well-acted [albeit] in a matter-of-fact sort of way."[7]

College Coach is obviously not one of Wellman's better pre–Code efforts, and it is an inauspicious end to his extremely productive and often brilliant period at Warner Brothers.

The film isn't without its strengths, however. Pat O'Brien is quite effective portraying the ruthless and relentless Coach Gore. A few of the supporting players—such as the always-dependable Donald Meek as the

14. Female and College Coach *(1933)*; Looking for Trouble *(1934)*

corruptible Professor Trask—do fine work. Many of the big scenes are directed with authority and style. And, as was the Warner Brothers way, the story moves along at a fast, invigorating pace.

Yet, the film also has a breezy, self-indulgent, I-really-don't-give-a-damn air about it that seems to seep into every scene. Some of the casting—notably the slight, unmuscular Dick Powell and much-too-old Lyle Talbot as star college football players—is ridiculous. So is the insertion of a scene of Powell playing the piano and singing the Sammy Fain and Irving Kahal the romantic tidbit "Lonely Lane," which has nothing to do with anything, except perhaps to give Powell a chance to show off his vocal cords instead of his upper-arm muscles. We often sense, too, that the film doesn't quite know that it wants to be: a parody of more conventional college football movies, a scathing critique of the corruption and callousness long associated with big-time college football programs, an outright farce, all of the above, or none of the above. If Wellman and the story's writers could have decided on one of the first three options and, like a disciplined football offensive back, taken the ball and run with it, the result would most likely have been a much better film.

Perhaps more than any artistic shortcoming, though, *College Coach* may have been the result of Wellman's creative frustration and, by this point, his professional exhaustion. In just three years, he had worked on nineteen feature films, eighteen of them from start to finish. True to Zanuck's initial promise, the director had received a good number of interesting and challenging projects, certainly more than the number Paramount had given him in 1928 and 1929. Still, he had little control over assignments, and still, he had to contend with the constant interference from Jack Warner and other studio executives.

It was clearly time for Wellman to make a change, time to finally take off the contractual shackles he had worn dating back to the early 1920s at Fox, Paramount, and Warner Brothers. And the logical next step, he felt, was to check in with Darryl Zanuck at his former mentor's newly formed Twentieth Century Pictures.

*

To no one's surprise, Wellman left Warner Brothers and, within a few weeks, had agreed to a much less restrictive working arrangement with Zanuck and his new enterprise: one that gave him the right of refusal on any film script offered him.

The first script Wellman accepted was called *Trouble Shooters*, a title that was later changed to *Looking for Trouble*.

The original story was by a J. Robert ("J.R.") Bren and, according to the author, had been inspired by his own experiences working as a telephone troubleshooter. After *Looking for Trouble*, which was his first writing credit for films, Bren (1903–1981) remained a screenwriter, receiving more than thirty other credits in a variety of low-budget films and a few television programs between 1934 and 1957.

The screenplay credit was shared by Leonard Praskins and Elmer Harris. Between the late 1920s and mid-1950s, Praskins (1896–1968) compiled about thirty credits mostly for low-budget theatrical releases, his last being 1956's *Gorilla at Large*. Beginning in the 1950s, he also wrote for television, most notably for such classic series as *Maverick*, *Wagon Train*, and *The Virginian*. Harris (1878–1966), who has more than fifty film credits between 1915 and 1936 (most of these during the silent era), also wrote a number of plays. Perhaps the most famous of his plays is *Johnny Belinda*, which, in 1948, was adapted into the acclaimed Academy Award-winning film of the same name.

To play the lead in *Looking for Trouble*, a wise-cracking telephone trouble shooter named Joe Graham, Zanuck arranged to obtain the services of actor Spencer Tracy, who, at the time, was under contract with Fox Films. Known for both his very natural, no-nonsense performing style and his versatility, Tracy (1900–1967) has long been regarded as one of the great acting talents of Hollywood's studio era. At the time, however, he had been struggling to connect with audiences. Although he'd appeared in about two dozen films since first signing with Fox in 1930, often giving excellent performances, none of his films had been a big commercial hit and stardom had remained elusive. In 1935, however, his fortunes changed when he signed with MGM, was given the kinds of roles that enabled him to connect better with audiences, and quickly became one of Hollywood's biggest stars. During his career, he received nine Best Actor Academy Award nominations, winning consecutive acting Oscars for his work in *Captains Courageous* (1937) and *Boys Town* (1938).

The supporting cast for *Looking for Trouble* included comic actor Jack Oakie (not to be confused with art director Jack Okey) as Tracy's sidekick and actress Constance Cummings as Tracy's love interest. Oakie (1903–1978) whose long career spanned from the early 1920s to the late 1960s, performed for the stage, radio, and television as well as film. Perhaps his best-known role today is playing a comic version of the Italian dictator Benito Mussolini in Charlie Chaplin's scathing send-up of fascism, *The Great Dictator* (1940), a turn that earned him a Best Supporting Actor Academy Award nomination. Cummings (1910–2005), worked for the stage and television as well as for films in a career that spanned sixty years, from 1926 to 1986. She never became a big star in films. But she did achieve acclaim on the stage later in life, winning Tony, Obie, and Drama Desk Awards for Best Actress for her work in playwright Arthur

Kopit's *Wings* and receiving another Drama Desk Award nomination in 1982 for her work in a revival production of the Enid Bagnold play *The Chalk Garden*.

Although Wellman was working with many people new to him on *Looking for Trouble*, one familiar face was cinematographer James Van Trees, who had previously collaborated with him on *The Star Witness*, *Lilly Turner*, *Heroes for Sale*, and *Midnight Mary*.

Shooting took place in the fall of 1933, mostly at the Samuel Goldwyn Studios in Hollywood, which Twentieth Century Pictures often used at the time. Scenes were also shot at various locations in the Los Angeles area, including the Iverson Ranch in the Chatsworth neighborhood of Los Angeles.

Although Wellman had somewhat softened his "Wild Bill" persona during his tenure at Warner Brothers, his more rambunctious side re-emerged in a big way during this production. At one point, a fistfight broke out between him and a Mike Lally, a second assistant director on *Midnight Mary* who was visiting the set. Then, at another point, the director and Spencer Tracy exchanged blows, the first of at least four altercations between the two that took place over the next few years. Reasons for the on-set fisticuffs, beyond the hotheaded personalities involved, remain unknown.[8] Needless to say, the ironic relationship between the film's title and its director's lifelong talent for finding trouble has not been lost on film historians. And, needless to say, the director and the star never worked together again.

*

The story of *Looking for Trouble* centers on Joe Graham (Tracy), a telephone repairman based in Los Angeles. One day, he is asked to work a night shift, and, when his partner, Dan Sutter (Morgan Conway), can't make it, Joe is paired with Casey (Oakie), a practical jokester, just transferred in from the nearby city of Azuza. Joe, who dislikes and distrusts Dan, later informs their boss at the phone company of Dan's disreputable behavior, and Dan is fired.

Meanwhile, Joe, who can be moody and jealous, is in the throes of an on-again-off-again relationship with Ethel Greenwood (Cummings), an operator at the phone company, and learns to his dismay that, when the two are on the outs with each other, she spends time with Dan. Soon, she leaves her job and goes to work for Dan, whose new real estate business, unknown to her, is actually a "front" for a racketeering operation that is tapping into the phone lines of the investment firm next door in order to get advance information about stock market trading.

One day, the investment company complains to the phone company

Comic actor Jack Oakie (left) and Spencer Tracy make an offbeat pair of telephone company troubleshooters in Wellman's first post–Warner Brothers and last pre–Code film, 1934's *Looking for Trouble* (United Artists/Photofest).

about its lines malfunctioning, and Joe and Casey are called in to investigate. Not only do they identify the tap, they meet Dan and a couple of henchmen as they are breaking into the investment company's vault to steal two million dollars in U.S. Treasury certificates. Joe and Casey are tied up, but they cleverly escape and notify the police who arrive in time to stop the robbery in progress. Dan, however, escapes and flees to his apartment. Joe and the police quickly follow. When they arrive, they learn that Dan has just been shot and killed. The police immediately suspect Ethel, who, still clueless about Dan's illegal activities, has agreed to meet him in the apartment before they leave together for Mexico to get married. Since overwhelming evidence points to her, Ethel is arrested both for killing Dan and for aiding his illegal activities.

Convinced that Ethel isn't guilty of either of these charges, Joe decides to look for Pearl (Arline Judge), Dan's previous girlfriend, who has suspiciously dropped out of sight. Finally, Joe finds her in nearby Long Beach, but, as they talk, a major earthquake strikes and Pearl is critically injured. Seeing that she is dying, Joe improvises a special phone connection with the Los Angele Police Department. Then, just before she dies, Pearl confesses to the murder and her motive (Dan had cheated her out of money).

Once cleared, Ethel expresses her gratitude to Joe for his efforts, apologizes for getting tangled up with Dan, and tells Joe that he is the one she's really loved all along. All these issues seemingly resolved, the two agree to marry.

*

Distributed by United Artists for Twentieth Century Pictures, *Looking for Trouble* opened in theaters on March 29, 1934, to both modest box office success and mixed critical reviews. Seeing the film as little more than a light diversion, Mordaunt Hall found it "highly entertaining" when it focused on Joe and Casey, but added that, when it focuses on Joe and Ethel, "it slumps and becomes more than slightly wearying."[9] Hall also credited Tracy in a somewhat backhanded way for doing "all that is possible to make his part believable."[10] A more favorable notice came from the *Los Angeles Times*, whose reviewer praised the film's writing, directing, and acting, noting that "Wellman's gift for trenchant direction is admirably applied."[11]

Compared with the vast majority of Wellman's pre–Code films, however, there is a scarcity of twenty-first-century perspectives on *Looking for Trouble*. Among these, film writer Mark Waltz has called it a "mild mixture of comedy and drama helped by a mix of two different personalities."[12] Another, film writer Walter Albert, has deemed it "very enjoyable," while also noting Wellman's "tight direction" and the film's "highly capable cast."[13] And online blogger Jenny P. has complimented the film on its "healthy doses of wit throughout."[14]

One reason for what seems to be a lack of interest may be *Looking for Trouble*'s relative lack of distinctly pre–Code content. What little there is in the film comes courtesy of Jack Oakie's Casey. In addition to making a few suggestively sexual comments, he also does something intriguing (and quite Wellman-esque) when he is calling down a list of phone numbers to help Joe locate Dan's old girlfriend, Pearl. One number turns out to be the number for a brothel, and, after Casey hangs up, he keeps the number to use later for what we assume are his own purposes.

More likely, though, the relative lack of attention twenty-first-century viewers have paid to *Looking for Trouble* is due to the film's dubious quality. Despite the presence of Spencer Tracy, who does everything he can to make Joe Graham appealing; some intriguing earthquake scenes reminiscent of comparable moments in *Frisco Jenny*; and a brisk pace, the film— especially for a Wellman-Zanuck joint effort—is remarkably unengaging. The script, which seems overly plotted and often pointless, could be the main culprit. Unlike Wellman's better pre–Code films, this story doesn't appear to be about anything of real importance. Yes, there is a romance between Joe and Ethel, but, as written, Ethel is an especially weak character who can't even see through the crooked, conniving Dan and, near the film's end, is even ready to elope with him to Mexico. Constance Cummings may have been a fine actress, but, as Mordaunt Hall noted in his review of the film, she'd been given, in her assignment to portray Ethel, "a thankless task."[15]

*

In addition to being Wellman's first film after his stint on the Warner Brothers assembly line, *Looking for Trouble* was the last film of his released before the Production Code was fully enforced on July 1, 1934. Although he would continue to turn out films for another quarter century—along the way making many good and several great ones—he would never enjoy the kind of freedom he'd had at Warner Brothers in the early 1930s. An exhilarating, no-holds-barred era had ended, and he was acutely aware that it had.

Afterthoughts
"It is, perhaps, the end of the beginning"

After leaving Warner Brothers and venturing forth as an independent filmmaker in late 1933, William Wellman continued his storied career, directing more than three dozen more films over the next quarter century. Thankfully, he wasn't under the gun to churn out five or six films each year; could select his own projects; and—to his great delight—could also spend more time with his beloved wife, Dottie, and a growing family that eventually included seven children and then many grandchildren. Although he now had to abide by Hollywood's Production Code, he, like many of his more imaginative directing colleagues, found clever ways to work around the Code's restrictions and essentially tell the story he'd wanted to tell. After completing what would be his last film, 1958's *Lafayette Escadrille*, he did consider a few more filmmaking opportunities but, for various reasons, didn't follow through with them.

Instead, he spent most of the last decade and a half of his life in a sort of contented retirement. During this time, he wrote two memoirs, *A Short Time for Insanity* (1974) and the unpublished *Growing Old Disgracefully*; received some overdue industry recognition, including, in 1973, a coveted Lifetime Achievement Award from the Directors Guild of America; and diligently tended the garden at his and Dottie's home in the Los Angeles neighborhood of Brentwood. In September 1975, he was diagnosed with leukemia and refused treatment, preferring to spend his final days at home. Then, just three months later, on December 9, he passed away. He was seventy-nine. Dottie, who was sixty-two at the time, never remarried and lived in their Brentwood home, staying involved with their children, grandchildren, and, eventually, great grandchildren, until she died, at the ripe age of ninety-five, in 2009.

*

Among the more than three dozen films Wellman directed after 1933, many of them—the excellent *A Star Is Born* (1937), the biting comedy

Nothing Sacred (1937), the adventure story *Beau Geste* (1939), the dark western *The Ox-Bow Incident* (1943), and the poignant war films *The Story of G.I. Joe* (1945) and *Battleground* (1949), among others—are today widely recognized as classics. Yet, while he was one of Hollywood's most respected directors, major industry honors and serious critical acclaim remained hard to come by. He was nominated three times for the Best Director Academy Award—for *A Star Is Born*, *Battleground*, and *The High and the Mighty* (1954). And he did win an Oscar (his only one) for Best Original Story for *A Star Is Born*. But, as had been the case with such superb and deserving films as *Wings*, *Beggars of Life*, *The Public Enemy*, and *Wild Boys of the Road*, his contributions were, more often than not, overlooked or under-appreciated. Later, in the 1960s and 1970s, as other leading directors of his era (such as Chaplin, Ford, Hawks, Welles, Lang, and Hitchcock) were lionized as the great film artists, the "auteurs," Wellman was still often dismissed as little more than a competent craftsman, a studio hired hand.

It has only been since the last part of the twentieth century, as Wellman's films have been reevaluated, that his artistic stock has risen appreciably. Since then, in fact, it has continued to grow steadily with each passing year, as more film historians and aficionados come to appreciate both his simple eloquence as a craftsman and his unflinchingly honest portrayals of societies and the human beings that inhabit them. While it is long overdue, Wellman is finally getting the respect he richly deserves.

*

Looking at Wellman's manic, often inspired pre–Code years within the long arc of his professional life, perhaps the best way to characterize them might be similar to what Winston Churchill once said about the victorious and decisive Battles of El Alamein in the early days of World War II. "Now this is not the end," Churchill noted. "It is not even the beginning of the end. But it is, perhaps, the end of the beginning."[16]

When he signed with Warner Brothers on March 23, 1930, William Wellman was by no means a novice. He had already been in the movie business for a little more than a decade and was no stranger to any facet of it. He had done his apprenticeship as an office messenger, a property man, and an assistant director. And, working on the assembly lines at Fox, Paramount, and other studios, he had also directed twenty feature films. By this time, he was a bona fide industry veteran.

He still, however, had much more to learn. And, while he had to manage the pressures of tight assembly-line schedules and endure the interference of Warner Brothers executives, he worked constantly, and often on projects that genuinely interested him. By late 1933, he'd not only doubled the number of films he'd directed, but he'd also grown by leaps and bounds as an artist, honing his craft and refining his perspectives on such deeply felt themes as the meaning of justice, the fragility of love, and the brutality of war that he would return to again and again in his films for the next quarter century. Then, as he ventured forth as a freshly minted independent director, he was better prepared than ever to handle the challenges that came with this new role in a tough and often unforgiving industry.

Yes, the pre–Code years were the end of the beginning for this assembly-line workhorse and budding auteur, a time of stunning professional growth and achievement when a brilliant young director truly and fully came into his own.

Chapter Notes

Introduction

1. William Wellman, Jr., *Wild Bill: Hollywood Rebel* (New York: Pantheon Books, 2015), p. 248.
2. Ibid., pp. 126–127.
3. Nickname given to Fairbanks by writer Tracey Goessel in Goessel's book *The First King of Hollywood: The Life of Douglas Fairbanks* (Chicago: Chicago Review Press, 2015). It is a riff on Fairbanks's original nickname, "the King of Hollywood." When Fairbanks's career faded in the 1930s, the regal title was popularly transferred to actor Clark Gable.
4. Wellman, Jr., p. 127.
5. Variety Staff, "You Never Know Women," *Variety*, July 28, 1926.
6. Sarah Smith, *Children, Cinema and Censorship: From Dracula to the Dead-End Kids* (Hoboken, N.J.: Wiley-Blackwell, 2005), p. 38.
7. Leonard Leff and Jerold L. Simmons, *The Dame in the Kimono: Hollywood, Censorship, and the Production Code* (Lexington: University Press of Kentucky, 2001), pp. 270–271, 286–287.
8. Mick LaSalle, as quoted by Wellman, Jr., p. 255.
9. George F. Custen, *Twentieth Century's Fox: Darryl F. Zanuck and the Culture of Hollywood* (New York: Basic Books, 1997), p. 3.
10. Charlie Barton, in interview with John Gallagher as quoted in Wellman, Jr., p. 250.

Chapter 1

1. William A. Wellman, *A Short Time for Insanity: An Autobiography* (New York: Hawthorn Books, 1974), p. 28.
2. The film was retitled *Eleven Men and a Girl* when it began airing on American television in the 1950s. This may have been to distinguish it from a 1935 film also titled *Maybe It's Love*. Today, the 1930 film is listed in different sources by one, the other, or both titles. I went with *Maybe It's Love* because it was the film's title when released and because it remains the more frequently listed title of the two.
3. Frank T. Thompson, *William A. Wellman* (Metuchen, N.J.: Scarecrow, 1983), p. 107.
4. George F. Custen, *Twentieth Century's Fox: Darryl F. Zanuck and the Culture of Hollywood* (New York: Basic Books, 1997), p. 75.
5. Poetic realism was a film movement in France in the 1930s known for blending the realism of everyday life with a sense of poetic melancholy. The films often featured working-class characters and settings, but, rather than focusing on social issues, they emphasized mood, atmosphere, and the emotional struggles of the characters.
6. Danny Reid, "*Other Men's Women*: Finding Love in The Wrong Place," *Pre-Code.com*, September 12, 2012.
7. Dan Callahan, *Barbara Stanwyck: The Miracle Woman* (Jackson: University Press of Mississippi, 2012), p. 49.
8. "Another Triangle," *New York Times*, April 20, 1931, p. 16.
9. Felicia Feaster, "*Other Men's Women*," Turner Classic Movies website, September 12, 2007.
10. Thompson, p. 108.

Chapter 2

1. Frank T. Thompson, *William A. Wellman* (Metuchen, N.J.: Scarecrow, 1983), p. 113.
2. *Ibid.*, p. 114.
3. Orson Welles, "Interview with Michael Parkinson," British Broadcasting Corporation, 1974.
4. Gangster Films, "AFI's 10 Top 10," American Film Institute website, 2008.
5. William Wellman, Jr., *Wild Bill: Hollywood Rebel* (New York: Pantheon Books, 2015), pp. 263–264.
6. Andre David Sennwald, "Two Thugs," *New York Times*, April 24, 1931, p. 27.
7. *Ibid.*
8. *Variety* Staff, "*The Public Enemy*," *Variety*, April 29, 1931.
9. Todd Robinson, *Wild Bill: Hollywood Maverick*, Turner Classic Movies, 1995 documentary, interview with Martin Scorsese.
10. "*The Public Enemy*: Reviews," *TV Guide Magazine*.
11. Glenn Erickson, "Ultimate Gangsters' Collection," *DVD Savant*, May 11, 2013.
12. John William Kellette (composer), James Kendis, James Brockman, Nat Vincent (lyricists), "I'm Forever Blowing Bubbles" (New York: Kendis, Brockman Music Company, January 4, 1919).
13. Erickson.
14. Chris Barsanti, "Review: *The Public Enemy*," *Slant Magazine*, February 11, 2005.
15. Matt Zoller Seitz, "30 Minutes on: *The Public Enemy*," rogerebert.com, January 11, 2019.
16. Kenneth Tynan, "Cagney and the Mob," *Sight and Sound Magazine*, May 1951.
17. *Ibid.*
18. *Ibid.*
19. Doug Warren, *Cagney: The Authorized Biography* (New York: St. Martin's Press, 1983), p. 203.
20. Richard Maltby, "*The Public Enemy*," *Senses of Cinema*, Issue 29, December 2003. In this article, Maltby goes into greater detail about the actual gangland personalities and events in Chicago in the 1920s that much of *The Public Enemy* is based on.
21. Robinson.

Chapter 3

1. Frank T. Thompson, *William A. Wellman* (Metuchen, N.J.: Scarecrow, 1983), p. xi.
2. David [no last name], "Review of *Night Nurse*," *Goodreads*, December 20, 2010.
3. William Wellman, Jr., *Wild Bill: Hollywood Rebel* (New York: Pantheon Books, 2015), p. 273.
4. Wheeler Winston Dixon, "*Night Nurse* (1931)," *Senses of Cinema*, Issue 78, March 2016. "Night Nurse, Original Print Information," *Turner Classic Movies* website.
5. *Schenectady Gazette*, Schenectady, New York, August 24, 1931.
6. *East Lansing Press*, East Lansing, Michigan, September 18, 1931.
7. L.N., "The Screen: Life in the Medical World," *New York Times*, July 17, 1931, p. 23.
8. *Ibid.*
9. *Variety* Staff, "Night Nurse," *Variety*, December 31, 1930 (date likely incorrect).
10. *Ibid.*
11. Jeff Stafford, "Night Nurse," *Turner Classic Movies* website, October 27, 2004.
12. Danny Reid, "*Night Nurse*: The Maternal Instinct Goes Rogue," *Pre-Code.com*, July 12, 2013.
13. Veronica Magdalene, "*Night Nurse* (1931)," *Little Miss Magdalene.com*, May 25, 2021.
14. "Mucifer," "Why this is the best film ever (especially if you are a pediatric night nurse)," *Night Nurse*, IMDb website, November 8, 1998.
15. Wellman was also one of the people who claimed credit for the invention of the boom microphone. There has, however, never been a clear consensus about *who* actually invented it.
16. Mick LaSalle, "*Baby Face* now better (and racier) than ever before," *San Francisco Chronicle*, Feb. 3, 2006.
17. Turner Classic Movies, *Leading Men: The 50 Most Unforgettable Actors of the Studio Era* (San Francisco: Chronicle Books, 2006).

Chapter 4

1. Stephanie Thames, "*The Star Witness*," *Turner Classic Movie* website, June 30, 2006.

2. William A. Wellman, *A Short Time for Insanity: An Autobiography* (New York: Hawthorn Books, 1974), p. 204.
3. *Ibid.*
4. Thames.
5. William Wellman, Jr., *Wild Bill: Hollywood Rebel* (New York: Pantheon Books, 2015), p. 275.
6. Mordaunt Hall, "The Screen: The Gangster's Nemesis," *New York Times*, August 4, 1931, p. 19.
7. Danny Reid, "*The Star Witness:* Limp Wasps," *Pre-Code.com*, July 22, 2019.
8. Glenn Erickson, "The Star Witness," trailersfromhell.com, April 6, 2019.
9. Sakana1, "*The Star Witness,*" Letterboxd.com.
10. hellohildy, "*The Star Witness,*" Letterboxd.com.
11. Doylenf6, "*The Star Witness,*" Letterboxd.com.
12. Sakana1.

Chapter 5

1. William Wellman, Jr., *Wild Bill: Hollywood Rebel* (New York: Pantheon Books, 2015), p. 281.
2. Cliff Aliperti, "*Safe in Hell* (1931): Talkie Triumph for Tough Dorothy Mackaill," *Immortal Ephemera*, November 16, 2012.
3. *Ibid.*
4. "*Safe in Hell,*" *Variety*, December 22, 1931, p. 19.
5. "*Safe in Hell,*" *Time*, December 28, 1931.
6. Mordaunt Hall, "THE SCREEN: Spatting Couples of *Private Lives* Meet with High Favor, Impressive Version of *Mississippi*, On the Gridiron, In a Crook's Retreat," *New York Times*, December 19, 1931, p. 16.
7. M.G. Conlan, "Wellman's Proto-Noir Masterpiece," *Safe in Hell*—IMDb website, June 14, 2010.
8. Hilda Crane, "Amazingly Bleak," *Safe in Hell*—IMDb website, August 21, 2005.
9. Danny Reid, "*Safe in Hell* (1931): The Tropical Inferno," *Pre-Code.com*, September 18, 2012.
10. Betsy Sherman, "Film Review: *Safe in Hell*—A Fallen Woman Picture and a Sleazy Buddy Movie," *The Arts Fuse*, November 14, 2017.

11. Frank T. Thompson, *William A. Wellman* (Metuchen, N.J.: Scarecrow, 1983), p. 119.
12. John Gallagher, DVD Commentary for *Heroes for Sale, Forbidden Hollywood Collection: Volume Three, Turner Classic Movies*, March 24, 2009.
13. Stephen Bourne, "Nina Mae McKinney," *Films in Review*, January/February 1991, p. 24.
14. I.S. Mowis, "Sidney Hickox Biography," IMDb website.

Chapter 6

1. Brian Cady, "*The Hatchet Man,*" *Turner Classic Movies* website, June 26, 2003.
2. "Character Actor J. Carrol Naish Dies," *Washington Post*, January 27, 1973.
3. Glenn Erickson, "Warners *Forbidden Hollywood Collection Volume 7,*" *DVD Savant*, May 30, 2013.
4. *Ibid.*
5. Danny Reid, "*The Hatchet Man*: Slice of Life," *Pre-Code.com*, August 25, 2014.
6. Davis and Stanwyck also appeared in cameos as themselves in the 1944 film *Hollywood Canteen*, but they did not appear in any scenes together.
7. Margarita Landazuri, "*So Big* (1932)," *Turner Classic Movies* website, April 20, 2006.
8. *Ibid.*
9. *Ibid.*
10. *Ibid.*
11. *Ibid.*
12. *Ibid.*
13. Andre David Sennwald, "An Edna Ferber Novel," *New York Times*, April 30, 1932, p. 19.
14. Patrick Nash, "*So Big* (1932)," three moviebuffs.com, June 20, 2012.
15. Melanie Novak, "*So Big* (1932): Epic of American Womanhood," melanienovak.com, February 3, 2022.
16. Fairbanks letter to John Gallagher, March 13, 1978. As quoted in William Wellman, Jr., *Wild Bill: Hollywood Rebel* (New York: Pantheon Books, 2015), pp. 276, 600.

Chapter 7

17. Jeff Stafford, "*Love Is a Racket,*" *Turner Classic Movies* website, March 24, 2006.

18. *Ibid.*
19. Dennis Schwartz, "*Love Is a Racket,*" *Dennis Schwartz Movie Reviews*, August 5, 2019.
20. Erich Kuersten, "Pre-Code Capsules VII: *LOVE IS A RACKET, HEAT LIGHTNING, THE BIG SHAKEDOWN, THE KEYHOLE, TARZAN THE FEARLESS,*" *Academic Film Journal of Film and Media*, July 24, 2011.
21. krorie, "Cynicism Draped with Roses," *Love Is a Racket* user review, IMDb, April 16, 2006.
22. 1930s Time Machine, "Like a Friend You Met on Holiday," *Love Is a Racket* user review, IMDb, September 8, 2022.
23. Bensonj31, "Just Misses Being a Pre-Code Classic," *Love Is a Racket* user review, IMDb, October 31, 2000.
24. 1930s Time Machine.
25. Scott Wilson, *Resting Places: The Burial Sites of More than 14,000 Famous Persons* (Jefferson, NC: McFarland, 2016), p. 170.
26. Danny Reid, "*Love Is a Racket* (1931) with Douglas Fairbanks, Jr.," *Pre-Code.com*, January 13, 2014.

Chapter 8

1. "Manifest destiny" is a phrase used to describe the widespread belief in the United States in the nineteenth century that American settlers were destined to expand westward across North America, and that this belief was both obvious ("manifest") and certain ("destiny").
2. Jeremy Arnold, "*The Purchase Price,*" Turner Classic Movies website, September 12, 2007.
3. Andre David Sennwald, "Life on a Ranch," *New York Times*, July 16, 1932, p. 5.
4. *Ibid.*
5. Arnold.
6. *Ibid.*
7. Glenn Erickson, "TCM Archives: The Forbidden Hollywood Collection Volume 3," *DVD Savant*, March 13, 2009.
8. David Nusair, "*The Purchase Price,*" *Reel Film Reviews*, August 20, 2023.
9. *Ibid.*
10. Pa Kettle is a character in the Ma and Pa Kettle series of films released in the late 1940s and early 1950s that depicted the comic adventures of an unrefined rural couple.
11. John Mueller, *Astaire Dancing: The Musical Films* (London: Hamish Hamilton, 1986), p. 7 (quote attributed to Selznick).
12. Scott McGee, "*The Conquerors*" Turner Classic Movies website, September 12, 2007.
13. *Variety* Staff, "*The Conquerors,*" *Variety*, November 22, 1932, p. 17.
14. *Ibid.*
15. Cliff Aliperti, "*The Conquerors* (1932) Starring Richard Dix and Ann Harding," *Immortal Ephemera*, November 18, 2010.
16. Frank T. Thompson, *William A. Wellman* (Metuchen, N.J.: Scarecrow, 1983), pp. 129–130.
17. Aliperti.
18. Thompson, p. 128.
19. Aliperti.

Chapter 9

1. Frank T. Thompson, *William A. Wellman* (Metuchen, N.J.: Scarecrow, 1983), p. 130 (story and quotes attributed to Wellman's unpublished memoir *Growing Old Disgracefully*).
2. *Ibid.*
3. *Ibid.*
4. Frank Miller, "*Frisco Jenny,*" Turner Classic Movies website, September 12, 2007.
5. "The Mizners: A Very Interesting Family," Benicia Historical Society website, May 19, 2014.
6. Alva Johnston, *The Legendary Mizners* (New York: Farrar, Straus & Young, 1953), p. 66.
7. Harold Bubil, "Architect Addison Mizner: Villain or Visionary?" *Sarasota Herald Tribune*, January 27, 2008.
8. Johnston.
9. David Thomson, *Have You Seen…?* (New York: Alfred A. Knopf, 2008), p. 751.
10. Miller.
11. *Ibid.*
12. "Frisco Jenny," *New York Herald Tribune*, January 7, 1933.
13. Stuart Galbraith IV, "Forbidden Hollywood Three (*Other Men's Women/ Purchase Price/Frisco Jenny/Midnight Mary/Heroes for Sale/Wild Boys of the Road*)," *DVD Talk*, March 24, 2009.

14. *Ibid.*
15. Marc Fusion, "*Frisco Jenny* (1932)," marcfusion.com, June 14, 2018.
16. Mordaunt Hall, "Ruth Chatterton and George Brent in a Film Version of the Play *Lilly Turner*," *New York Times*, June 15, 1933, p. 21.
17. *Ibid.*
18. Margarita Landazuri, "*Lilly Turner*," *Turner Classic Movies* website, September 12, 2007.
19. *Ibid.*
20. Danny Reid, "*Lilly Turner*: Down and Out," *Pre-Code.com*, September 7, 2018.
21. *Ibid.*
22. James Travers, "*Lilly Turner* (1933)," FrenchFilms.org, 2012.
23. *Ibid.*
24. Mick LaSalle, *Complicated Women: Sex and Power in Pre-Code Hollywood* (New York: St. Martin's Griffin, 2000), p. 80.

Chapter 10

1. Mordaunt Hall, "THE SCREEN: Warriors of the Clouds, Laughter and Love," *New York Times*, March 22, 1930.
2. James H. Farmer, *Celluloid Wings: The Impact of Movies on Aviation* (Blue Ridge Summit, PA: Tab Books, 1984), p. 71.
3. Frank T. Thompson, *William A. Wellman* (Metuchen, N.J.: Scarecrow, 1983), p. 135.
4. Stephen Pendo, *Aviation in the Cinema* (Lanham, MD: Scarecrow, 1985), p. 275.
5. Hall, "THE SCREEN: An Aviation Drama," *New York Times*, May 4, 1933.
6. William Wellman, Jr., *Wild Bill: Hollywood Rebel* (New York: Pantheon Books, 2015), p. 277.
7. Glenn Erickson, "*Central Airport*," *DVD Savant*, April 30, 2010.
8. Danny Reid, "*Central Airport*: And Brother Makes Three," *Pre-Code.com*, September 24, 2013.
9. Jeff Stafford, "*Central Airport*," *Turner Classic Movies* website, September 12, 2007.
10. G. Bill, "Melodramatic but Touching," IMDb, *Central Airport* (1933), December 12, 2018.
11. Robert Temple, "Wonderful Early Aviation Epic," IMDb, *Central Airport* (1933), November 11, 2007.
12. AlsExGal, "Daring Pre-Code in the Political as well as Sexual Category," IMDb, *Central Airport* (1933), April 10, 2010.
13. *Ibid.*

Chapter 11

1. Jay Carr, "*Heroes for Sale*," *Turner Classic Movies* website, September 12, 2007.
2. "*Heroes for Sale*," *New York World Telegram*, July 21, 1933.
3. "*Heroes for Sale*," *New York Herald Tribune*, July 22, 1933.
4. Frank Nugent, "Pity the Hero," *New York Times*, July 22, 1933, p. 14.
5. Sheila O'Malley, "*Heroes for Sale* (1933); Dr. William Wellman," *The Sheila Variations*, April 18, 2010.
6. Ben Sachs, "*Heroes for Sale*," *Chicago Reader*, May 29, 2014.
7. Sean Axmaker, "William Wellman's Forbidden Hollywood—DVDs for the Week," *Paralax View*, March 23, 2009.
8. Just Another Film Buff, "*Heroes for Sale* (1933)," *The Seventh Art*, May 23, 2020.
9. Expressionism is a style of art that aspires to express emotional experience rather than physical reality.

Chapter 12

1. John Gallagher, "Rediscovering *Midnight Mary*," *Films in Review*, March/April 1995.
2. William Wellman, Jr., *Wild Bill: Hollywood Rebel* (New York: Pantheon Books, 2015), p. 286.
3. *Ibid.*
4. Mick LaSalle, *Complicated Women: Sex and Power in Pre-Code Hollywood* (New York: St. Martin's Griffin, 2000), p. 148. Young is also on record making a similar remark to William Wellman, Jr., in 1996—Wellman, Jr., p. 287.
5. Margaret Murray, "By a 'Gunman's Moll,'" *San Francisco Examiner*, May 8, 1932, p. 80—June 5, 1932, p. 92.
6. Jeffrey Vance and Tony Maietta, DVD Commentary for *Midnight Mary*, *Forbidden Hollywood Collection: Volume*

Three, Turner Classic Movies, March 24, 2009.
7. *Ibid.*
8. Gallagher.
9. Andre David Sennwald, "Pictures Now on View Along Broadway," *New York Times*, July 15, 1933.
10. Cliff Aliperti, "*Midnight Mary* (1933) Starring Loretta Young, Ricardo Cortez, Franchot Tone," *Immortal Ephemera*, January 9, 2013.
11. Lindsey D., "*Midnight Mary* (1933)," *The Motion Pictures* (themotionpictures.net), March 31, 2013.
12. Movie Picture Gal, "Sparkling and Compelling," Midnight Mary, IMDb website, June 15, 2006.
13. Sunlilly, "Pre-Code Bliss!" Midnight Mary, IMDb website, November 20, 2005.
14. Danny Reid, "*Midnight Mary*: Staunchly Surviving," *Pre-Code.com*, August 29, 2010.
15. Jay S. Steinberg, "*Midnight Mary*," Turner Classic Movies website, September 12, 2007.
16. Vance and Maietta.
17. Robert H. Hethmon, "Days with the Group Theater: An Interview with Clifford Odets," *Michigan Quarterly Review*, Spring 2002.
18. Wellman, Jr., p. 287.

Chapter 13

1. *The Bicycle Thief* is also known by the title *Bicycle Thieves*.
2. Danny Ahearn, *How to Commit a Murder*, Goodreads.com (all newspaper quotes were taken from this online page).
3. William Wellman, Jr., Commentary for DVD of *Wild Boys of the Road*, Forbidden Hollywood Collection, Volume Three, Turner Classic Movies Archives, 2009.
4. Variety Staff, "*Wild Boys of the Road*," *Variety*, September 26, 1933, p. 20.
5. Cliff Aliperti, "*Wild Boys of the Road* (1933) Meets 'Boy and Girl Tramps of America,'" *Immortal Ephemera*, September 14, 2015 (*Screenland* review quoted in this article).
6. Frank Nugent, "America's Juvenile Hoboes," *New York Times*, September 22, 1933, p. 14.
7. *Ibid.*

8. *Ibid.*
9. Gendolyn Audrey Foster, "*Wild Boys of the Road*," National Film Registry, 2013.
10. Mick LaSalle, "*Wild Boys of the Road* takes us to the depths of American hard times," *San Francisco Chronicle*, August 17, 2020.
11. Arthur S. Ward, "Brilliant, Heart-Wrenching Depression Gem," "*Wild Boys of the Road*," IMDb, January 21, 2003.
12. The Little Songbird, "Wild Emotions on the Run," "*Wild Boys of the Road*," IMDb, March 20, 2020.
13. PTB-8, "The Roughest, Toughest, and the Best," "*Wild Boys of the Road*," IMDb, September 13, 2011.

Chapter 14

1. William Wellman, Jr., *Wild Bill: Hollywood Rebel* (New York: Pantheon Books, 2015), p. 304.
2. Brian Cady, "*Female*," Turner Classic Movies website, April 25, 2003.
3. Mordaunt Hall, "Ruth Chatterton as a Business Woman Who Delights in Emulating Catherine the Great," *New York Times*, November 4, 1933, p. 18.
4. Mordaunt Hall, "On the Gridiron," *New York Times*, November 11, 1933, p. 10.
5. "*College Coach*," *New York Sun*, November 11, 1933.
6. User Reviews, "College Coach, 1933," IMDb.
7. Frank T. Thompson, *William A. Wellman* (Metuchen, N.J.: Scarecrow, 1983), p. 140.
8. Wellman, Jr., pp. 308–309.
9. Mordaunt Hall, "Spencer Tracy, Constance Cummings, and Jack Oakie in a Melodrama of the Telephone 'Trouble Shooters,'" *New York Times*, April 12, 1934, p. 27.
10. *Ibid.*
11. "Looking for Trouble," *Los Angeles Times*, April 7, 1934.
12. Mark Waltz, "*Looking for Trouble*," *Old Movies Are Great*, March 29, 2013.
13. Walter Albert, "Movie Review by Walter Albert: *Looking for Trouble* (1934)," *Mystery File*, September 27, 2012.
14. Jenny P, "A Rarely Seen Comedy/Drama by Wellman," "*Looking for Trouble*, 1934," IMDB website, June 7, 2006.
15. Hall/"Trouble Shooters."

Afterthoughts

16. Winston Churchill, "The End of the Beginning," speech delivered at the Lord Mayor's Day Luncheon, November 10, 1942.

Bibliography

Albert, Walter. "Movie Review by Walter Albert: *Looking for Trouble* (1934)." *Mystery File,* September 27, 2012.
Aliperti, Cliff. "*Eleven Men and a Girl* (1930) starring Joan Bennett and Joe E. Brown." *Immortal Ephemera,* May 10, 2011.
_____. "*Midnight Mary* (1933) Starring Loretta Young, Ricardo Cortez, Franchot Tone." *Immortal Ephemera,* January 9, 2013.
_____. "*Safe in Hell* (1931): Talkie Triumph for Tough Dorothy Mackaill." *Immortal Ephemera,* November 16, 2012.
_____. "*Wild Boys of the Road* (1933) Meets 'Boy and Girl Tramps of America.'" *Immortal Ephemera,* September 14, 2015.
Arnold, Jeremy. "*The Purchase Price.*" Turner Classic Movies website, September 12, 2007.
Axmaker, Sean. "William Wellman's Forbidden Hollywood—DVDs for the Week." *Paralax View,* March 23, 2009.
Barsanti, Chris. "Review: *The Public Enemy.*" *Slant Magazine,* February 11, 2005.
Bourne, Stephen. "Nina Mae McKinney." *Films in Review,* January/February 1991, p. 24.
Brownlow, Kevin. *The Parade's Gone By.* Berkeley: University of California Press, 1968.
Bubil, Harold. "Architect Addison Mizner: Villain or Visionary?" *Sarasota Herald Tribune,* January 27, 2008.
Cady, Brian. "*Female.*" Turner Classic Movies website, April 25, 2003.
_____. "*The Hatchet Man.*" Turner Classic Movies website, June 26, 2003.
Carr, Jay. "*Heroes for Sale.*" Turner Classic Movies website, September 12, 2007.
"Character Actor J. Carrol Naish Dies." *Washington Post,* January 27, 1973.
"*College Coach.*" *New York Sun,* November 11, 1933.
Conlan, M.G. "Wellman's Proto-Noir Masterpiece." *Safe in Hell*—IMDb website, June 14, 2010.
Crane, Hilda. "Amazingly Bleak." *Safe in Hell*—IMDb website, August 21, 2005.
Custen, George F. *Twentieth Century's Fox: Darryl F. Zanuck and the Culture of Hollywood.* New York: Basic Books, 1997.
D., Lindsey. "*Midnight Mary* (1933)." *The Motion Pictures,* March 31, 2013.
Dixon, Wheeler Winston. "*Night Nurse* (1931)." *Senses of Cinema,* Issue 78, March 2016.
Erickson, Glenn. "*Central Airport.*" *DVD Savant,* April 30, 2010.
_____. "*Love Is a Racket.*" *DVD Savant,* November 30, 2013.
_____. "The Star Witness." trailersfromhell.com, April 6, 2019.
_____. "TCM Archives: Forbidden Hollywood Volume 2." *DVD Savant,* March 1, 2008.
_____. "Ultimate Gangsters' Collection: Classics." *DVD Savant,* May 11, 2013.
_____. "Warners *Forbidden Hollywood Collection Volume 7.*" *DVD Savant,* May 30, 2013.
Feaster, Felicia. "*Other Men's Women.*" Turner Classic Movies website, September 12, 2007.
Foster, Gendolyn Audrey. "*Wild Boys of the Road.*" National Film Registry, 2013.
Friel, Patrick. "The scrappy pre-Code years of William A. Wellman—FilmStruck's director of the week." *Chicago Reader,* August 14, 2018.
"*Frisco Jenny.*" *New York Herald Tribune,* January 7, 1933.

Fristoe, Roger. "*Safe In Hell.*" *Turner Classic Movies* website, December 7, 2006.
Fusion, Marc. *Frisco Jenny* (1932). marcfusion.com, June 14, 2018.
Galbraith, Stuart, IV. "Forbidden Hollywood Three (*Other Men's Women/Purchase Price/ Frisco Jenny/Midnight Mary/Heroes for Sale/Wild Boys of the Road*)." *DVD Talk*, March 24, 2009.
Gallagher, John. DVD Commentary for *Heroes for Sale, Forbidden Hollywood Collection: Volume Three. Turner Classic Movies,* March 24, 2009.
_____. Rediscovering *Midnight Mary.*" *Films in Review,* March/April 1995.
Gisriel, Jim. "Eleven Men and a Girl (or Maybe It's Love) 1930 Movie Review." YouTube, 2014.
Grieve, Laura. "Tonight's Movie: *Central Airport* (1933)." *Laura's Miscellaneous Musings*, July 5, 2022.
_____. "Tonight's Movie: *Love Is a Racket* (1932)." *Laura's Miscellaneous Musings*, January 26, 2008.
Hall, Mordaunt. "An Aviation Drama." *New York Times,* May 4, 1933.
_____. "The Gangster's Nemesis." *New York Times,* August 4, 1931.
_____. "On the Gridiron." *New York Times,* November 11, 1933.
_____. "Ruth Chatterton and George Brent in a Film Version of the Play *Lilly Turner.*" *New York Times,* June 15, 1933.
_____. "Ruth Chatterton as a Business Woman Who Delights in Emulating Catherine the Great." *New York Times,* November 4, 1933.
_____. "Spatting Couples of *Private Lives* Meet with High Favor, Impressive Version of *Mississippi*, on the Gridiron, in a Crook's Retreat." *New York Times,* December 19, 1931.
_____. "Spencer Tracy, Constance Cummings, and Jack Oakie in a Melodrama of the Telephone 'Trouble Shooters.'" *New York Times,* April 12, 1934.
"*Heroes for Sale.*" *New York Herald Tribune,* July 22, 1933.
"*Heroes for Sale.*" *New York World Telegram,* July 21, 1933.
Hethmon, Robert H. "Days with the Group Theater: An Interview with Clifford Odets." *Michigan Quarterly Review,* Spring 2002.
Johnston, Alva. *The Legendary Mizners.* New York: Farrar, Straus & Young, 1953.
Just Another Film Buff. "*Heroes for Sale* (1933)." *The Seventh Art,* May 23, 2020.
Kuersten, Erich. "Pre-Code Capsules VII: *LOVE IS A RACKET, HEAT LIGHTNING, THE BIG SHAKEDOWN, THE KEYHOLE, TARZAN THE FEARLESS.*" *Academic Film Journal of Film and Media,* July 24, 2011.
Landazuri, Margarita. "*Eleven Men and a Girl*" (*Maybe It's Love*). *Turner Classic Movies* website, August 26, 2003.
_____. "*Lilly Turner.*" *Turner Classic Movies* website, September 12, 2007.
_____. "*So Big* (1932)." *Turner Classic Movies* website, April 20, 2006.
LaSalle, Mick. *Complicated Women: Sex and Power in Pre-Code Hollywood.* New York: St. Martin's Griffin, 2000.
_____. "*Wild Boys of the Road* takes us to the depths of American hard times." *San Francisco Chronicle,* August 17, 2020.
Leff, Leonard, and Jerold L. Simmons. *The Dame in the Kimono: Hollywood, Censorship, and the Production Code.* Lexington: University Press of Kentucky, 2001.
"Looking for Trouble." *Los Angeles Times,* April 7, 1934.
Maltby, Richard. "*The Public Enemy.*" *Senses of Cinema,* Issue 29, December 2003.
McKinley, Will. "5 Reasons to Watch *Nigt Nurse* (1931)." willmckinley.wordpress.com, August 5, 2014.
Miller, Frank. "*Frisco Jenny.*" *Turner Classic Movies* website, September 12, 2007.
"The Mizners: A Very Interesting Family." Benicia Historical Society website, May 19, 2014.
Mowis, I.S. "Sidney Hickox Biography." IMDb website.
Murray, Margaret. "By a 'Gunman's Moll.'" *San Francisco Examiner,* May 8, 1932–June 5, 1932.
N., L. "The Screen: Life in the Medical World." *New York Times,* July 17, 1931.
Nash, Patrick. "*So Big* (1932)." threemoviebuffs.com, June 20, 2012.
Nixon, Rob. "*The Public Enemy.*" *Turner Classic Movies* website, July 28, 2003

Bibliography

Novak, Melanie. "*So Big* (1932): Epic of American Womanhood." melanienovak.com, February 3, 2022.
Nugent, Frank. "America's Juvenile Hoboes." *New York Times*, September 22, 1933.
———. "Pity the Hero." *New York Times*, July 22, 1933.
O'Malley, Sheila. "*Heroes for Sale* (1933); Dr. William Wellman." *The Sheila Variations*, April 18, 2010.
Reid, Danny. "*Central Airport*: And Brother Makes Three." *Pre-Code.com*, September 24, 2013.
———. "*Eleven Men and a Girl* (1930)." *Pre-Code.com*, November 27, 2011.
———. "*The Hatchet Man*: Slice of Life." *Pre-Code.com*, August 25, 2014.
———. "*Lilly Turner*: Down and Out." *Pre-Code.com*, September 7, 2018.
———. "*Love Is a Racket* (1931) with Douglas Fairbanks, Jr." *Pre-Code.com*, January 13, 2014.
———. "*Midnight Mary*: Staunchly Surviving." *Pre-Code.com*, August 29, 2010.
———. "*Night Nurse*: The Maternal Instinct Goes Rogue." *Pre-Code.com*, July 12, 2013.
———. "*Other Men's Women*: Finding Love in The Wrong Place." *Pre-Code.com*, September 12, 2012.
———. "*Safe in Hell* (1931): The Tropical Inferno." *Pre-Code.com*, September 18, 2012.
———. "*The Star Witness*: Limp Wasps." *Pre-Code.com*, July 22, 2019.
Robinson, Todd. *Wild Bill: Hollywood Maverick*. Turner Classic Movies, 1995 documentary.
Sachs, Ben. "*Heroes for Sale*." *Chicago Reader*, May 29, 2014.
"*Safe in Hell*." *Time*, December 28, 1931.
Sarris, Andrew. "Notes of the Auteur Theory in 1962." *Film Culture* 27, Winter 1962–1963.
Schickel, Richard. *The Men Who Made the Movies: William A. Wellman*. Turner Classic Movies, 2007 documentary.
Schwartz, Dennis. "*Central Airport*: 'The excellent aerial footage keeps this one from crashing.'" *Ozus' World Movie Reviews*, December 26, 2007.
———. "*Love Is a Racket*." *Dennis Schwartz Movie Reviews*, August 5, 2019.
Seitz, Matt Zoller. "30 Minutes on: *The Public Enemy*." rogerebert.com, January 11, 2019.
Sennwald, Andre David. "An Edna Ferber Novel." *New York Times*, April 30, 1932.
———. "Pictures Now on View Along Broadway," *New York Times*, July 15, 1933.
———. "Two Thugs." *New York Times*, April, 24, 1931.
Sherman, Betsy. "Film Review: *Safe in Hell*—A Fallen Woman Picture and a Sleazy Buddy Movie." *The Arts Fuse*, November 14, 2017.
Smith, Imogen Sara. "And if I felt half as good as you look, I'd go out and kill myself while it lasted." "*Love Is a Racket* (1932)." oldmoviesaregreat.wordpress.com, January 29, 2009.
Smith, Sarah. *Children, Cinema and Censorship: From Dracula to the Dead End Kids*. Hoboken, N.J.: Wiley-Blackwell, 2005.
Stafford, Jeff. "*Central Airport*." Turner Classic Movies website, September 12, 2007.
———. "*Love Is a Racket*." Turner Classic Movies website, March 24, 2006.
———. "*Night Nurse*." Turner Classic Movies website, October 27, 2004.
———. "*Wild Boys of the Road*." Turner Classic Movies website, March 4, 2009.
Steinberg, Jay S. "*Midnight Mary*." Turner Classic Movies website, September 12, 2007.
Thames, Stephanie. "*The Star Witness*." Turner Classic Movie website, June 30, 2006.
Thompson, Frank T. *William A. Wellman*. Metuchen, N.J.: Scarecrow, 1983.
Thomson, David. *Have You Seen…?* New York: Alfred A. Knopf, 2008.
Travers, James. "*Lilly Turner* (1933)." FrenchFilms.org, 2012.
Tynan, Kenneth. "Cagney and the Mob." *Sight and Sound Magazine*, May 1951.
Vance, Jeffrey, and Tony Maietta. DVD Commentary for *Midnight Mary*. Forbidden Hollywood Collection: Volume Three, Turner Classic Movies, March 24, 2009.
Variety Staff. "*Night Nurse*." *Variety*, December 31, 1930.
———. "*The Public Enemy*." *Variety*, April 29, 1931.
———. "*Safe in Hell*." *Variety*, December 22, 1931.
———. "*You Never Know Women*." *Variety*, July 28, 1926.
———. "*Wild Boys of the Road*." *Variety*, September 26, 1933.
Vieira, Mark A. *Forbidden Hollywood: The Pre-Code Era (1930–1934): When Sin Ruled the Movies*. Philadelphia: Running Press, 2019.

Waltz, Mark. "*Looking for Trouble.*" *Old Movies Are Great,* March 29, 2013.
Ward, Arthur S. "Brilliant, Heart-Wrenching Depression Gem." "*Wild Boys of the Road,*" IMDb, January 21, 2003.
Wellman, William A. *A Short Time for Insanity: An Autobiography.* New York: Hawthorn Books, 1974.
Wellman, William, Jr. Commentary for DVD of *Wild Boys of the Road, Forbidden Hollywood Collection, Volume Three.* Turner Classic Movies Archives, 2009.
Wellman, William, Jr. *Wild Bill: Hollywood Rebel.* New York: Pantheon Books, 2015.

Index

Abbott, George 134–135
Abdullah, Achmed 85–86
Academy Awards 9, 29, 45, 47, 57, 60, 92, 151, 174, 200, 206
Ade, George 22
Adrian 166, 176
Ahearn, Danny 179
Albert, Walter 203
Alexander, J. Grubb 86, 92
Aliperti, Cliff 119–120
American Film Institute, Lifetime Achievement Award 57; list Top 10 Gangster Films 34
Arbuckle, Roscoe "Fatty" 10
Armstrong, Louis 81
Astor, Mary 27, 29–30
aviation films (late 1920s–early 1930s) 141–142
Axmaker, Sean 159

Baldwin, Earl 179
Barrat, Robert 154, 162
Barsanti, Chris 43
Barsky, Bud 62–63
Barthelmess, Richard 142, 143, 149–150, 156, 161
Barton, Charlie 6, 18–19
Battleground 206
Beau Geste (1939) 3
Beaumont, Gerald 26
Beer and Blood 34
Beggars of Life 10, 206
Belasco, David 86
Bennett, Joan 23, 24–25
Berkeley, Busby 154
Blackwood, George 192
Blondell, Joan 30–31, 35, 49, 51, 57–58
Bond, Lilian 72
Bond, Ward 180
Branch, Houston 72
Bren, J. Robert 199–200

Brent, George 93, 110, 112, 114–115, 137, 139, 192
Bright, John 33, 34–35, 46–47
Brooks, Louise 36
Brown, Joe E. 23, 24
Brown, Johnny Mack 192
Brown, Tom 149–150
Busch, Niven 196
"By a 'Gunman's Moll'" 165

Cady, Brian 85
Cagney, James 30–31, 33, 34, 42, 43–45, 47, 50; influence on other actors 44–45
Calhern, Louis 128, 129, 133–134
Callahan, Dan 30
Capra, Frank 49
Carr, Jay 153
The Cat's Pajamas 8
Central Airport 17, 141–151; Wellman's contributions to 142, 147–149
Chatterton, Ruth 125–126, 127–128, 129, 133, 137, 139, 140, 191, 192, 193, 195
Churchill, Winston 206
Cimarron 92
Clarke, Donald Henderson 191
Clarke, Mae 46
Cohan, George M. 45
Cohn, Harry 72
Coll, Vincent "Mad Dog" 65
College Coach 17, 196–199
The College Widow 22
Columbia Pictures 49, 72
"Common Ground" 126
Conlin, M.G. 76
The Conquerors 17, 109, 115–124; Wellman's contributions to 120–122
Cook, Donald 35–36, 42, 46, 78, 82, 128, 133–134
Coonan, Dorothy 180–181, 189, 205
Cooperstown, CA 117
Cortez, Ricardo 166, 168, 174–175

221

222 Index

Cortez, Stanley 175
Crane, Hilde 76–77
Cronjager, Edward 116, 122
Cummings, Constance 200–201
Cunningham, Cecil 107
Curtiz, Michael 45, 72–73, 87, 192
Custen, George F. 15

The Daily Worker 179
Darro, Frankie 180, 188, 189
Davenport, Harry 70
Davis, Bette 93, 95
Dee, Frances 99–100, 106–107
Del Ruth, Roy 72
"Desperate Youth" 179
Devine, Andy 166, 176
Dieterle, William 192
Digges, Dudley 84, 86, 90
Dix, Richard 116, 118, 123
Dixon, Wheeler Winston 50
Dodsworth 128
Doubleday 92
Dunning, Philip 134
Dvorak, Ann 99, 101, 105–106, 196, 197

Edmonton Journal 179
Eilers, Sally 142, 149–150
Emergency Banking Act 155
Erickson, Glenn 39, 43, 66, 89–90, 113, 146
Estabrook, Howard 116

Fairbanks, Douglas, Jr. 97, 99, 101, 105
Fairbanks, Douglas, Sr. 7, 60, 105
Female 16, 191–196; Wellman's contributions to 195–196
Ferber, Edna 91–92
Film Daily 66, 72
Flynn, Rita 42
the forgotten man 153–154
Foster, Gwendolyn Audrey 185
Fox, William 8
Frisco Jenny 17, 125–134; Wellman's contributions to 131–133
Fulton, Maude 25–26, 72
Fusion, Mark 131

Gable, Clark 49, 58–60
Galbraith, Stuart IV 131
Gallagher, John 80
Galveston Daily News 119
Garrett, Oliver H.P. 49–50
Glasmon, Kubec 33, 34–35, 46–47
Gold Diggers of 1933 154
Golden Age of Indiana Literature 22
Goldwyn, Samuel 8
Graham, Betty Jane 59

Grapewin, Charley 70, 180
Gray, James 166, 170, 176
Grot, Anton 84, 86–87
Growing Old Disgracefully 205

Hall, Mordaunt 66, 76, 89, 119, 131, 137, 141, 146, 194, 198, 203, 204
Hallelujah! 81
Haller, Ernest 192
Hamilton, William 116, 122
Harding, Ann 116, 118, 123
Harlem Renaissance 82
Harlow, Jean 36, 46
Harris, Elmer 200
The Hatchet Man 17, 84, 85–91; Wellman's contributions to 90
"Hawk's Mate" 143
Hays, Will 11
Hays Office 1, 3, 11, 166
Hayward, Lillie 126
Heroes for Sale 16, 152–163; Wellman's contributions to 159–160
Hickox, Sid 72, 82–83, 84, 86, 93, 128, 132, 143, 149, 192
The High and the Mighty 151, 206
Hitchcock, Alfred 123
Holloway, Sterling 180
Hollywood in 1920s 10–12
Hollywood Reporter 169
The Honorable Mr. Wong 85
How to Commit a Murder 179
Hubbard, Lucien 9, 62–63
Huston, Walter 64, 68–69
Hymer, Warren 176

"I'm Forever Blowing Bubbles" 39–40
In Old San Francisco 132
Ince, Ralph 67

Jackson, Joseph 72
James, Rian 99, 143
The Jazz Singer 11
Jennings, Devereaux 46
Just Another Film Buff 159

Kansas City Star 112–113
Kenyon, Charles 49–50
Kibbee, Guy 116, 123, 139
The Knickerbocker Buckaroo 7
Kuersten, Erich 103

Lally, Mike 201
Lansing State Journal 179
Larkin, John Francis 126
LaSalle, Mick 13, 56, 140, 165, 185
The Legion of the Condemned 10
The Light That Failed 3

Index

Lilly Turner 17, 134–140; Wellman's contributions to 138–139
Looking for Trouble 199–204; Wellman's contributions to 203–204
Loos, Anita 166
Lord, Daniel A. 11–12
Lord, Jack 80
Lord, Robert 92, 116, 126, 153–154
Los Angeles Times 203
Love Is a Racket 17, 98–108; Wellman's contributions to 98, 104–105
Lyon, Ben 51, 59, 60

Mackaill, Dorothy 71, 73, 79–81
MacMahon, Aline 154, 156, 161–162
Magdalena, Veronica 54
Maietta, Tony 169
The Man Who Won 8
manifest destiny 109, 122
Mantz, Paul 142, 143–144
Markey, Gene 135, 166, 192, 195
Maybe It's Love (*Eleven Men and a Girl*) 22–25
McCarthy, Celia 6
McDermott, Edward 56
McGill, Barney 28, 59
McHugh, Frank 139
McKinney, Nina Mae 72, 81
Meek, Donald 198–199
Men with Wings 151
Mercer, Beryl 46
Merkle, Una 166, 176
Midnight Mary 17, 164–177; Wellman's contributions to 169–173
Miller, Frank 130
Miller, Marilyn 72
Mitchell, Grant 67–68, 180, 189
Mizner, Wilson 125, 126–127, 154
Moffitt, John C. 143
Monroe, Marilyn 60
Moore, Colleen 92
Moore, Dickie 94, 95
Morley, James 128, 132, 149
The Motion Picture Herald 103
Mowis, I.S. 82
"The Mud Lark" 110
Murray, Margaret 165
Muse, Clarence 72, 81, 82

Naish, J. Carroll 84, 86, 90
Nash, Patrick 95–96
Nebraska State Journal 179
New York Daily Mirror 95
New York Herald Tribune 131
New York Sun 198
New York Times 31, 38, 49, 53, 66, 95, 158
New York World Telegram 158

The New Yorker 95
Night Nurse 17, 48–61; Wellman's contributions to 53–56
Nothing Sacred 123, 206
Novak, Melanie 96
Nugent, Frank 158, 184
Nusair, David 113

Oakie, Jack 200, 202
O'Brien, Pat 196–197, 198
O'Connor, Robert Emmett 46
Odets, Clifford 175
Okey, Jack 195
Oliver, Edna May 116, 118, 123
O'Malley, Sheila 158–159
Orry-Kelly 195
Other Men's Women 17, 25–31; Wellman's contributions to 28–29, 31
The Ox-Bow Incident 21, 121, 206

Paramount Pictures 5, 6, 8
Paris, Michael 142
Pendo, Stephen 144
Perkins, Grace 49
Pershing, John J. 7, 8
Phillips, Edwin 180–181, 189
Pickford, Mary 105
poetic realism 29
Powell, Dick 196, 199
Praskins, Leonard 200
Pre-Code era 1–4, 12–13, 7, 85, 166, 173
Preminger, Otto 160
Production Code 1, 3–4, 11, 12–13, 76, 140, 142, 152, 153, 166, 173, 178, 194, 204, 205
Psycho 34
The Public Enemy 16, 33–47, 206; Wellman's contributions to 39–43
The Purchase Price 17, 109–115; Wellman's contributions to 113–114

Rappe, Virginia 10
Redbook Magazine 126
Reid, Danny 29, 54, 66, 77, 90, 108, 138, 146, 169
Rene, Leon 81
Rene, Otis 81
"ripped-from-the-headlines" films 15, 153
RKO Pictures 116
Robinson, Edward G. 86, 90
Rogers, Will 7
Roosevelt, Franklin 155

Sachs, Ben 159
Safe in Hell 17, 71–83; Wellman's contributions to 77–79
Sale, Charles "Chic" 63, 64, 68, 69–70
San Francisco (1936 film) 132

224　　　　　　　　　　　　　Index

San Francisco Examiner 165
Saturday Evening Post 110
Saunders, John Monk 9
Schulberg, B.P. 5–6
Schwartz, Dennis 103
Scola, Kathryn 135, 166, 192
Scorsese, Martin 38
Screenland Magazine 184
Seitz, Matt Zoller 43–44
Self, Manuel 196
Selznick, David O. 116–117, 123
Selznick, Myron 5
Sennwald, Andre David 38, 95, 112, 169
Seymour, James. 143
Sherman, Betsy 77
Shirley, Anne 115
Short Time for Insanity, A 205
So Big 17, 84, 91–97; Wellman's contribution to 96
sound revolution in film 11–12
Stafford, Jeff 53–54, 146
Stanwyck, Barbara 47, 49, 51, 56–57, 59, 72, 94, 95, 96–97, 11, 112, 114
A Star Is Born (1937) 123, 205
The Star Witness 17, 62–70; Wellman's contributions to 67–68
The Steel Highway 25
Steinberg, Jay 169
Steiner, Max 116
Stella Dallas (1937 film) 97
The Story of G.I Joe 206
Stringer, Arthur 110

"Take Me Away" 110
Talbot, Lyle 110, 196
Taylor, William Desmond 11
Terrett, Courtney (Courtenay) 99
Thalberg, Irving 58
Thames, Stephanie 63, 66
Thew, Harvey 35, 46–47
Thompson, Frank 22, 24 32, 79, 119, 120, 142, 198
Tiffin, Pamela 45
Time Magazine 76
Todd, Arthur L. 180, 190
Tone, Franchot 166, 172, 175–176
Tong Wars 87
Toomey, Regis 30
Tracy, Lee 99, 105, 106
Tracy, Spencer 200, 202

Travers, James 138
Turner Classic Movies 53, 76, 142
TV Guide Magazine 39
Twentieth Century Pictures 199
Tynan, Kenneth 44

Vance, Jeffrey 169
Van Trees, James 63, 135, 154, 162–163, 166, 176, 201
Variety 8, 31, 38, 53, 76, 95, 103, 112, 137, 146, 184
Victoria Daily Times 179
Vidor, King 81, 97
Vorkapich, Slavko 117, 122

Waagmeester, Antje Paarlberg 92
Waltz, Mark 203
Warner, Jack L. 15, 182, 183, 199
Warner Brothers 2, 3, 4, 13–16, 50, 152, 163, 177; studio assembly-line 15–16
Warner Ranch 155
Weiss, Hymie 34
Welles, Orson 34
Wellman, Arthur Gouverneur 6
Wellman, Dorothy *see* Coonan, Dorothy
Wellman, William, Jr. 50, 165, 180
Westcott, Gordon 154, 162
When Husbands Flirt 8
"When It's Sleepy Time Down South" 81
Wild Bill: Hollywood Maverick 2
Wild Boys of the Road 16, 178–190, 206; Wellman's contributions to 185–189
Wilmington News-Journal 179
Wings 5, 8–10, 206
Winninger, Charles 60
Wise, Robert 92
Withers, Grant 27, 30
Wong, Anna May 91
Woods, Edward 42
Wyman, Jane 92

Yankee Doodle Dandy 45
Yellow Sky 3
yellowface 85
You Never Know Women 8
Young, Loretta 86, 90–91, 154, 156, 162, 164, 165, 166, 168, 172, 173–174

Zanuck, Darryl F. 5, 14–15, 21–22, 58, 72, 125–126, 152, 153, 154, 178, 199